British women of the Eastern Front

MANCHESTER
1824

Manchester University Press

British women of the Eastern Front
War, writing and experience in Serbia and Russia, 1914–20

ANGELA K. SMITH

Manchester University Press

Copyright © Angela K. Smith 2016

The right of Angela K. Smith to be identified as the author of this work has been asserted by her in accordance with the Copyright, Designs and Patents Act 1988.

Published by Manchester University Press
Altrincham Street, Manchester M1 7JA
www.manchesteruniversitypress.co.uk

British Library Cataloguing-in-Publication Data
A catalogue record for this book is available from the British Library

Library of Congress Cataloging-in-Publication Data applied for

ISBN 978-0-7190-9618-1 hardback

First published 2016

The publisher has no responsibility for the persistence or accuracy of URLs for any external or third-party internet websites referred to in this book, and does not guarantee that any content on such websites is, or will remain, accurate or appropriate.

Typeset by Out of House Publishing
Printed in Great Britain by TJ International Ltd, Padstow

For Ben Sargent
and in memory of Mary Jacobs
(1954–2012)

Contents

Acknowledgements

This book has taken at least five years to write, though I have been interested in many of the women included in it for much longer than that. Its completion, to coincide with the centenary of the First World War, feels particularly timely. As so many of the familiar old stories of the war are once again in the public eye, these women of the Eastern Front offer new and different narratives to contribute to the broader picture.

Firstly, thanks must go to my patient, supportive and encouraging readers, Mary Brewer, Jane Potter, Nadia Atia, Krista Cowman and most especially Deborah Smith for correcting the whole manuscript. I am grateful for the ongoing support of friends and colleagues at Plymouth University, in particular Rachel Christofides, Kathryn Gray, Min Wild, Dafydd Moore and the School of Humanities and Performing Arts for the funded sabbatical time that enabled me to finally complete the manuscript. I am especially grateful to the late Mary Jacobs, who encouraged me to persevere and finish such a worthwhile project.

Thanks are due to other friends, colleagues and readers whose advice and support has ensured that I produce a better book: Laura Salisbury, Christine Hallett, Alison Fell, Mary Joannou, Lucy Durneen, Babs Horton, Wendy Pawsey, Marina Williamson. And many thanks to Sarah Beaman, Andrew Muggleton and Jackson and Finlay for all the hospitality that has made my research trips to London so pleasurable.

I am especially grateful to James Quinn from the School of Geography, Earth and Environmental Sciences at Plymouth University for making my maps. The staff at Plymouth University library have been continually helpful, as have the staff at the Department of Documents at the Imperial War Museum and the Glasgow City Archives at the Mitchell Library, which holds the archive of the

Scottish Women's Hospitals. Many thanks are due to the latter for permission to quote extensively from this archive. I would like to thank Eric and Ginny Stobart for allowing me to use the papers of Mabel St Clair Stobart and to quote extensively from her work. Thanks are also due to Caroline Allen-Jones for allowing me to quote from the papers of Miss F. E. Rendel and to Mr Neil C. Hunter for permission to quote from the papers of Miss Ysabel Birkbeck. Thanks also to the Studland Village Hall Committee for their kind permission to reproduce the cover image, *Lady of the Black Horse* by George James Rankin.

Short extracts from a number of papers lodged with the Department of Documents at the Imperial War Museum are reproduced here. Efforts have been made to trace the copyright holders. The author and the Imperial War Museum would be grateful for any information that might help to trace those copyright holders whose identities or addresses are not currently known.

Every effort has been made to trace all copyright holders where applicable, but if any have been omitted please contact the publisher. Apologies are offered to those whom it has proved impossible to identify.

An earlier version of Chapter 4 was published as ' "Beacons of Britishness": British Nurses and Female Doctors as Prisoners of War', in *First World War Nursing: New Perspectives*, ed. Alison S. Fell and Christine E. Hallett (London and New York: Routledge, 2013).

Most of all I would like to thank my family. My late father, John R. Smith, supported the early stages of this work and would have loved to see it in print. For support, interest and encouragement I would like to thank my brother, Simon Smith. I am grateful to my very understanding son, Ben Sargent, for whom the development of this book has been a backdrop to his childhood. Most of all I would like to thank Jim Sargent, whose ceaseless loving support can make anything possible.

Abbreviations

FANY	First Aid Nursing Yeomanry
IWM	Imperial War Museum, London
ML	Mitchell Library, Glasgow
NUWSS	National Union of Women's Suffrage Societies
POW	Prisoner of War
QAIMNSR	Queen Alexandra's Imperial Military Nursing Service Reserve
RAMC	Royal Army Medical Corps
SFWSS	Scottish Federation of Women's Suffrage Societies
SRF	Serbian Relief Fund
SWH	Scottish Women's Hospitals
TFNS	Territorial Force Nursing Service
VAD	Voluntary Aid Detachment
WAAC	Women's Army Auxiliary Corps
WSPU	Women's Social and Political Union
WSWCC	Women's Sick and Wounded Convoy Corps

Note on place names. Many of the place names in this volume are subject to variations of spelling as a result of complications in translation. I have tried to be consistent throughout, but many of the women cited use a range of different spellings. I have indicated this where appropriate.

Maps

Map 1 The Balkans in 1914

Maps

Map 2 Russia in 1914

Introduction: the road east

You will hear with me sounds, the uncanny howl of starving jackals and wolves, the 'zizz' of the mosquito, the low moan of sick men, the chattering in soft Russian accents of happy convalescent children, the great joyful choir of a thousand nightingales in the Topchidar woods, the nightly chorus of myriads of frogs, the crooning songs of Serbia, and the intoxicating rhythm of the Cossack dance. You will inhale with me the delicious fragrance of spring-time in Macedonia, the stench of a Bulgarian prison camp, and the awful odour of a ship's hold filled with Crimean sick and wounded. You will feel the furnace-like glare of the sun, the cutting blast of the Vardar wind, and the driving sleet in your face. But enough – let me begin from the beginning.[1]

Isabel Emslie Hutton was a British woman doctor who served with the Scottish Women's Hospitals in Serbia and Russia during the First World War and its aftermath. In the opening pages of her memoir, *With a Woman's Unit in Serbia, Salonika and Sebastopol* (1928), she invites her readers to go with her on a sensual journey, back through the sights, sounds and smells of an alien and exotic landscape, back to the East, to the Orient. It is a well-written and evocative document, intended to convey to the reader the complete experience of her war. In the quotation above, Hutton draws on all the senses in an attempt to articulate the range of experience that the war granted to her. Despite the presence of the sick and wounded, this is clearly not the Western Front. Like many of the women who wrote of their service, she was a part of an established and well-organised relief organisa-tion and committed to humanitarian aid, but the individuality of her voice, ten years after the Armistice, clearly defines the way in which she responded to her personal involvement in the war. Other women's voices, too, provide an equally unique record. This opening also begins to suggest why the Eastern Front was such a desirable place for British women to encounter, offering all manner of sensations that could not easily be found elsewhere.

When the First World War broke out in August 1914 the response of the British people was excited and enthusiastic. There had been talk of war for years; many preparations had been made. The Boer War a decade earlier had revealed any shortcomings in the army, leading to expansion and investment. The long queues of men outside the recruiting offices have become part of the enduring myth. No one seemed to anticipate that war could be anything but a success, such was the level of national confidence. The declaration of war on 4th August was a very good reason for a party and the general expectation was that it would all be over by Christmas, so anyone intending to do their bit needed to get involved as soon as possible. One thing that was different about this war from the outset, however, was that many women, as well as their men, believed that they could play a part in the great national adventure, despite the fact that historically war had always been a man's game. And as Isabel Emslie Hutton suggests, the part would turn out to be a diverse and intriguing one for some British women, offering rare opportunities to see, hear and taste worlds and cultures they would not have anticipated.

The war on the Western Front has been well documented, as has, to some extent, British women's share of it. But this was the first real multi-national war, complicated by the European empires, with fighting on many fronts, east as well as west. It began in the Balkans and it is the Balkans that will form a central focus here. The aim of this book is to explore the experiences and contributions of British women performing various kinds of active service across the Eastern Front in Serbia, Russia and Romania, paying particular attention to the ways in which they chose to represent that experience though a range of written records. There has been no such scholarly study before; most previous works have focused on women's work in Britain, France and Belgium. But while the British military were reluctant to accept the services of women in 1914, even those from the medical profession, other countries in Europe welcomed their expertise. Serbia and Russia were prominent among these. British women's medical teams had already built up a good relationship with Eastern European governments and armies in the First Balkan War of 1912, during which a number of independent women's hospital units had made the journey to support the nations caught up in the conflict with the Ottoman

Empire. Upon the outbreak of war in 1914, British women again came to the aid of the Balkan nations and many were decorated for their services and honoured by the Serbian government after the war, yet they have been excluded from most conventional historical narratives. Following the fall of Serbia in 1915, many of the women's units moved further east to work on the Romanian and Russian Fronts, only to be caught up in revolution. This book seeks to explore their many experiences and achievements by interpreting their own words, examining the many and varied written records that the women have left behind.

As Jane Marcus has pointed out, most of the British women's hospital units, those run by women and employing women doctors, operated not on the Western Front alongside their obvious male colleagues, but in the Balkans and Russia. She suggests that:

> The 'Balkanization' of British women doctors and nurses in Serbia and Russia may be seen as part of a larger historical repression of the Eastern Front in favor of the story of Western Europe in histories of the war. The Eastern Front is the female 'other' of World War I history.[2]

When Marcus writes 'Balkanization', she means 'marginalisation', but with a particular set of nationalist implications that will be explored in this book. As a site of conflict, there has been a tendency to marginalise the Eastern Front in historical narratives. There were also very few British men here and in general it has been through the eyes of men that the physical experience of the British war has been presented. Serbia, the forgotten ally, with its challenging terrain and weather conditions, offered women the opportunity to contribute to the war, where they faced many of the same threats and hardships as combat soldiers. The principal research question of the book explores the extent to which British women's responses to their experiences in the east were shaped by their nationality, society and culture, drawing particularly on Victorian and Edwardian ideas of gender roles. This works in conjunction with an exploration of the cultural perceptions of an alien experience of the East or the 'Orient' that provided a working environment that was completely different from that of the Western Front. As well as offering the women more opportunities for independent service, it also exposed them to cultures that were profoundly different from those that had produced them. Analysis of this juxtaposition of cultures is also a central objective of the book.

The Scottish Women's Hospitals (SWH), led by suffragist Dr Elsie Inglis, sent units to the Balkans. So did the Red Cross. Here British women found the opportunity to do their bit in support of the Serbian military. And when Serbia fell, they followed these same troops east. All these journeys represented ventures into the unknown. As Larry Wolff has argued:

> It was Western Europe that invented Eastern Europe as its complemen-tary other half in the eighteenth century, the age of Enlightenment. It was also the Enlightenment with its intellectual centers in Western Europe, that cultivated and appropriated to itself the notion of 'civilisa-tion,' an eighteenth-century neologism, and civilisation discovered its complement, within the same continent, in shadowed lands of back-wardness, even barbarism. Such was the invention of Eastern Europe.[3]

Eastern Europe, particularly Serbia, represented this antithesis of civi-lisation after centuries of Ottoman rule. It was the war that offered women the opportunity to explore these shadowed lands, places that might otherwise have been closed to them.

The First World War was to be a very new kind of war on many levels. In the decades before 1914 the shape of society had been changing. Cultural shifts that had begun in the Victorian era were developing at a fast pace with the new century. The technologies that would make this conflict the 'war to end all wars' had been tested in South Africa, but the full extent of the devastation they would cause was not yet understood. Other developing technologies such as the motor vehicle, the aeroplane and the submarine were about to come into their own as the tools of war. New methods of communication such as the telegraph and the telephone would enable the developed nations to move much more quickly than in previous conflicts. And new inventions in weaponry would change the face of the battlefield in ways not yet imagined.

The rise of the Labour Movement had led to questions being asked about the structures of society. Calls for manhood suffrage and a series of Reform Acts were beginning to break down the hierarchies of cen-turies. Against this backdrop the Women's Suffrage Movement, which had been lobbying for nearly fifty years, had exploded into the twen-tieth century with the formation of the Women's Social and Political Union (WSPU) in 1903. Although opinion remained divided with regard to the tactics employed by the WSPU, there was no ignoring them or their claims for greater opportunities for women in this newly developing society. The Women's Suffrage Movement was to have a direct impact on women's involvement in the war, particularly on the Eastern Front, providing an ideal ready-made infrastructure to co-ordinate the activities of women's hospital units.

British histories of the First World War tend to begin on 4th August 1914, when Great Britain was forced to declare war on Germany after the invasion of neutral Belgium. The British Expeditionary Force was quickly dispatched across the channel to help the French armies to repel the advancing Germans, thus beginning the four years of stalemate on the Western Front. It was here that many of the lasting impressions of the war were formed. Although the British army had been involved in a series of colonial wars, the South African War being the most significant, there had been no major European war since the Crimea in 1856, more than half a century earlier. So for Britain at least, 1914 marks a clear starting point. However, this was not the case for all protagonists. Many of those on the Eastern Front, the focus of this study, had been fighting for years. What we know as the Great War was, for them, a continuation of a nationalist struggle already underway.

It is understood that the assassination of the Archduke Franz Ferdinand, heir to the Austro-Hungarian Empire, together with his wife, in Sarajevo on 28th June 1914, triggered the outbreak of the war across Europe. The perpetrator, a student named Gavrilo Princip, was a Serbian nationalist, despite his Bosnian/Austrian background. The statement was a protest against Austrian opposition to Serbian nationalism, but the repercussions were far reaching as a result of a series of alliances that had been put in place by the Great Powers of Europe in the preceding decade. But for Princip and his fellow conspirators, rather than the action being the start of something new, it was no doubt intended as the continuation of a campaign that had been going on for decades, indeed centuries, a conflict that in many ways defined the Serbian people and engaged the sympathies of much of the rest of Europe.

The Serbia that welcomed so many British women during the course of the war had been involved in many other localised conflicts for nearly a century, but the histories that shaped the Serbian national identity of the twentieth century were hundreds of years older, dating back to the medieval kingdom that preceded Ottoman rule. Perhaps surprisingly, this legacy had a profound emotional impact on the British women who passed through the Balkans during the war and after, so it is important to examine some of the key historical events. In 1937 Rebecca West travelled across the region, drawn both by this legacy and a continuing cultural impression of exoticism and difference. In her 1942 book, *Black Lamb and Grey Falcon: A Journey through Yugoslavia*, she documents Serbian history, revealing the importance of these old stories to the modern Yugoslav state. The black lamb and the grey falcon of the title both refer directly to aspects of Serbian history that resonate into the twentieth century.

Medieval Serbia lost her independence on 28th June 1389, defeated by the Turks on the 'Field of Blackbirds', at the battle of Kosovo Polje. It is no accident that this is the same date chosen by Princip for the fatal shooting in 1914. Twenty years prior to 1389, under the Nemanja dynasty, the Serbian Empire had reached its zenith, stretching from the Danube to the Peloponnese.[4] Although this empire had begun to crumble by 1389, the mythology that surrounds the battle of Kosovo overrides this history, presenting the defeated Serbian prince, Lazar, as a martyr whose fateful decisions would determine the future of the country in perpetuity. These myths are manifest in the Serbian tradition of epic poetry that first recorded the events surrounding the battle and subsequently became a central part of the artistic foundation upon which Serbian nationalistic culture was built. The best known of these poems, 'The Downfall of the Serbian Empire', by the nineteenth-century poet Vuk Karadzic (1787–1864), which tells of Lazar's fateful choice, was still being recited by the Serbian soldiers of Mabel St Clair Stobart's flying column in 1915, and by West's Serbian guides in 1937. It tells the story that the prophet Elijah visited Lazar on the day of the battle, in the form of a grey hawk, the same grey falcon of West's title. Elijah offers Lazar a choice.

> Tsar Lazar, of honourable stock,
> Of what kind will you have your kingdom?
> Do you want a heavenly kingdom?
> Do you want an earthly kingdom?[5]

The latter would mean victory over the Ottomans at Kosovo Polje; the former, earthly defeat, but immortality in heaven. Surrounded by his own force, confronted by the amassed Turks on the other side of the plain, Lazar reasons thus:

> Dear God, where are these things, and how are they?
> What kingdom shall I choose?

Shall I choose a heavenly kingdom?
Shall I choose an earthly kingdom?
If I choose an earthly kingdom,
An earthly kingdom lasts only a little time,
But a heavenly kingdom will last for eternity and its centuries.[6]

Lazar chooses the latter and in so doing brings about the defeat of the Serbs and 500 years of servitude to the Turks, but with the tantalising promise of that heavenly kingdom just out of reach. In 1914 the Serbs were still looking for the heavenly kingdom.

The shadow of the grey falcon lingered in the twentieth century, despite the achievement of an independent Serbia in 1830. Mabel St Clair Stobart was moved by the story when she and the soldiers of her flying column had to retreat across the Field of Blackbirds in 1915.

And now, when we set foot upon that steppe, it seemed that those 500 years that had passed since the first Kossovo [*sic*] day had been expunged. For the Serbian Army, now defeated by the allies of those same Turks, was still, like a ghost from the past, fleeing across the silent plain. The panoplies had fallen from their horses, the armour from their men: it was now a skeleton army, in skeleton clothes, but it was carrying the same soul, of the same nation, to guard as a holy treasure, till the day of the Lord shall come.[7]

Stobart's imagery is stark and powerful and illustrates the power of the myth even against the backdrop of the First World War. She, like the Serbian soldiers, is hypnotised by the ghost of Lazar and his devastating choice. Later still, Rebecca West notes that Yugoslavs repeated the poem to themselves as they awaited the invasion of the Nazis, suggesting that 'The poem of the Tsar Lazar and the grey falcon tells a story which celebrates the death-wish; but its hidden meaning pulses with life.'[8]

The impact of these stories on Serbian cultural development cannot be overestimated. For nearly 500 years the country had remained part of the Ottoman Empire, along with the other Balkan states for whom independence was a myth of history. Yet these myths, fuelled by poetry and informed by the development of a counter Western civilisation, formed the basis of a growing nationalism across the Balkans in the early part of the nineteenth century. Richard C. Hall argues that 'In this regard the Balkan peoples sought to emulate the political and economic success of western Europe, especially Germany, by adopting the western European concept of nationalism as a model for their own national development.'[9] However, after centuries of Turkish rule, Serbia and her neighbours had adopted many characteristics of the East, characteristics that would not be fully shed for a long time. The Ottoman Empire ruled in the Balkans for centuries with some success, it must be said, in part because of this injection of Eastern culture and in part because of a system of government that could incorporate the significant ethnic diversity of the region. Hall explains that:

> This concept of western European nationalism displaced the old Ottoman millet system in the Balkans, which had permitted each major religious group a significant amount of self-administration. The millet system allowed Moslems, Orthodox, Catholics, and Jews to all live in proximity to each other without intruding on each other. It gave the Balkan peoples a limited degree of cultural autonomy.[10]

The long-term lack of national identity enabled the people of these lands to exist across boundaries, living within the religious-based cultural groups that suited them. As a part of a larger empire they drew their own boundaries and answered to a single government body.[11] By the nineteenth century the desire was to move away from this model, to become more like the Great Powers of Western Europe. Although this was clearly attractive, Serbia had to deal with the international cultural conviction that she was not sufficiently civilised in Western European terms. Although not as 'Oriental' as their Ottoman masters, the Serbs and other Balkan peoples were still markedly different, perhaps as a result of the multiple national, ethnic and religious influences that informed them. They also carried the historical label 'barbarian'. Mark Mazower suggests that '[F]rom the start the Balkans was more than just a geographical concept. The term, unlike its predecessors, was loaded with negative connotations – of violence, savagery, primitivism – to an extent for which it is hard to find a parallel.... Europe quickly came to associate the region with violence and bloodshed.'[12] This, added to the other differences in the Balkan people, resulted in an impression of marginality that was difficult to overcome.

Maria Todorova has explored this marginalisation of the Balkans, suggesting 'That the Balkans have been described as the "other" of Europe does not need special proof. What has been emphasised about the Balkans is that its inhabitants do not conform to the standards of behaviour devised as normative by and for the cultured world.'[13] Moreover, the Balkans had a reputation to overcome. Todorova suggests that in the eyes of the West in the early twentieth century,

'"Oriental" most often employed, stands for filth, passivity, unreliability, misogyny, propensity as for intrigue, insincerity, opportunism, laziness, superstition, lethargy, sluggishness, inefficiency, and incompetent bureaucracy. "Balkan" while overlapping with "Oriental," had additional characteristics as cruelty, boorishness, instability, and unpredictability.'[14] In order to become a successful independent state on the Western model, Serbia had a lot of issues to address. It needed to harness its own cultural identity, drawing on selective ideas from the past, but at the same time to assimilate with the Great Powers of the 'civilised' West, to convince the West that it too was civilised. Todorova investigates the means by which Serbia set about doing this, identifying a way of reading Serbia and the Balkans as a means of crossing between two worlds. Todorova argues that:

> What practically all descriptions of the Balkans offered as a central characteristic was their transitory status. The West and the Orient are usually presented as incompatible entities, antiworlds, but completed antiworlds.... The Balkans on the other hand, have always evoked the image of a bridge or crossroads.... The Balkans have been compared to a bridge between East and West, between Europe and Asia.[15]

The impermanence of national boundaries in the Balkans certainly contributed to this, and the disruptions of the First World War endorsed it. But there were other significant issues that impacted on the status of Serbia and her neighbours, issues that developed this notion of the Balkans as a bridge between East and West. One significant factor was the Orthodox Christianity at the heart of the region, coexisting with Catholicism and Islam, but still a dominant force; and one that remains bound up with the myth of Serbian history.

Because the faith-based choice made by Prince Lazar, put to him by the grey falcon, Elijah, is so pivotal in Serbian national memory, it is perhaps inevitable that the Orthodox Church should be a foundation stone of national culture. And, perhaps contrary to expectation, the Orthodox Church was able not just to survive, but also thrive under Ottoman rule. Mark Mazower suggests that 'In general, there was no Muslim analogue to the widespread Christian impulse to drive out the infidel and the heretic. On the contrary, Islamic law prescribed the toleration of Christian and Jewish communities of believers.'[16] Indeed, this was no doubt supported by the fact that the Turks were able to extract higher taxes from their Christian subjects, so had no real interest in encouraging conversion. The Orthodox Church had been under greater threat from the armies of Catholicism, but for five centuries their Ottoman rulers acted as a useful buffer against this danger. As a consequence, the subject people of the Balkans were able to retain the Christian faith that defined them in a much more significant way than the many ethnic differences in the region. And this faith in itself is interesting in terms of the way the East might be viewed by travelling British women. It contained both the familiar, in terms of its dogma, and the alien, as manifested in its elaborate rituals. It was both East and West simultaneously, a further bridge between the two cultures that could both comfort and fascinate visitors from the West.

The Ottoman Empire authorised the first small autonomous Serbian state in 1830, after a series of wars beginning in 1804, during which two separate dynasties arose competing for the crown of Serbia, the Kavageogevichs and the Obrenovics, who would alternate on the throne until the fall of the first Yugoslavia. But ideas of independence continued to grow and develop across the Balkans with other states campaigning for their own national identity. All it would take to overthrow the Turks was Balkan unity, but that is where the real problems lay. In 1876 Serbia and Montenegro launched a first attack on their Ottoman masters. In 1877–78 Russia led a more successful campaign that resulted in the formation of a Bulgarian state and gained extra territories for Serbia and Montenegro. This conflict, concluded by the Treaty of San Stefano in 1878, was, Hall argues, 'the first and only time in modern history, a Balkan people [Bulgaria] had attained all their national goals'.[17] But this success brought its own problems. Michael S. Neiberg suggests that:

> The Balkans had been a region of concern to European statesmen for decades. The region's rising nationalist tensions and dizzying ethnic diversity confounded all attempts to find lasting solutions to the seemingly endless conflicts between rival ethnic and religious groups. European diplomats understood that ethnic, economic and political connections between Balkan groups and several of the Great Powers meant that a conflict in this region could easily expand.[18]

It was this fear that inspired the Congress of Berlin in 1878, intent on imposing controls on the Balkans that would keep them in check. The Congress significantly diminished the new Bulgaria and reduced Serbia, returning power to the Ottoman sultan. It can hardly have been a surprise that this treaty added fuel to the fires of nationalism across the region.

In the Serbian state the desire for nationalism and expansion found voice in an organisation called the 'Black Hand', a conspiracy that grew out of the army. In 1904, in a decisive action that shocked the rest of Europe, this organisation murdered the Serbian king, Alexander Obrenovic, and his wife. His successor, Peter Kavageogevich, was considerably more ambitious for the future of Serbia and shared these nationalist tendencies. So did his newly appointed Prime Minister, Nicola Pastich. Both men were anti-Habsburg, looking to shed Austrian influence in the country as much as Ottoman rule. The first decade of the twentieth century saw, paradoxically, an increase in both rivalry between the Balkan states and a string of alliances. Each individual monarch wanted more territory and, ideally, domination of the region, but the only chance any stood of achieving this aim would be if they all worked together to overthrow Ottoman control once and for all. Given the tinderbox nature of this arrangement, it seems hardly surprising that the Great European Powers of the nineteenth century were happy to see Ottoman rule continue. But by the beginning of the new century the old Ottoman Empire was decaying. It had, after all, lasted for several hundred years. The internal revolution led by the Committee for Unity and Progress, known internationally as the Young Turks, in 1908, pushed the Balkan states into action. If they were to achieve the status they wanted, they could not afford for the Ottoman Empire to reform itself. In the same year, Austria-Hungary annexed Bosnia-Hercegovina, thus illustrating another significant threat to the expansion of Balkan powers, particularly Serbia.

Despite many dynastic and ethnic differences, during the course of 1912, the Balkan league was formed. Together, Serbia, Bulgaria, Greece and Montenegro had the military might to force out the remnants of Ottoman rule. They did precisely that in October 1912.

> When the Ottomans refused to consider reforms leading to autonomy in their European provinces, the Balkan alliance mobilized. Efforts by the Great Powers to prevent the outbreak of war were feeble and futile. The First Balkan War began 8 October 1912 with a Montenegrin attack on Ottoman positions.[19]

It was in this first war, which officially lasted only a few weeks, that many of the British women who were to become prominent during the First World War first saw active service. Mabel St Clair Stobart had her first taste of war here with her Women's Sick and Wounded Convoy Corps (WSWCC) working for the Queen of Bulgaria. She wrote her first serious book, *War and Women* (1913), to record her experiences and to begin to articulate her developing ideas on feminism and militarism.[20]

By the end of the first war, the Serbians had expelled the Ottomans from northern Macedonia, Kosovo and northern Albania. They then claimed all of these territories as part of Serbia. But although the Turks were gone, none of the Balkan states had really achieved their aims. And it was not long before they began to argue among themselves. By the summer of 1913, it was clear that no resolution regarding the division of territory could be reached and Bulgaria attacked Serbia. The Second Balkan War saw the Bulgarians fighting a loose configuration of Serbia, Montenegro, Rumania and the last of the Ottomans. It was hard to see how there could be an outright winner, yet Serbia seemed to come off best. Hall suggests that:

> With their victory in the Second Balkan War, the Serbs became the dominant South Slav power. The war confirmed that most Macedonians would live under direct Serbian control. By the time of the treaty of Bucharest, Montenegro had become a Serbian satellite. The victory also bestowed upon the Serbs great prestige among the South Slavs in the Dual Monarchy [Austria-Hungary]. Afterwards Belgrade competed directly with Vienna and Budapest for the loyalty of the Croats, Slovenes, and Bosnians who lived in the Empire.[21]

But the brutality of these conflicts, of atrocities committed on all sides, shocked Western Europe and reinforced the long-held notions of barbarism that accompanied their position in the East. Trotsky recorded:

> That's how all this looks when you see it close up. Meat is rotting, human flesh as well as the flesh of oxen; villages have become pillars of fire; men are exterminating 'persons not under twelve years of age'; everyone is brutalised, losing their human aspect.[22]

Tim Judah argues that:

> The Balkan Wars were to set the precedent in this century for massive waves of ethnic cleansing and the forced migrations of hundreds of thousands of people. All the worst evils that were witnessed in the former Yugoslavia between 1991 and 1995 were present in the Balkan Wars.[23]

These actions reflect that history of 'barbarism' that had long tainted the reputation of the Balkans, rendering them not quite 'civilised'.

With Russia now the only remaining Great Power to have an ally in the Balkans, the stage was set for a wider conflict. Serbia was suitably alienated from Austria-Hungary, yet remained ambitious in nationalist terms. It is easy to see how the assassination of 28th June 1914 had such devastating effects. As Hall suggests, 'for the Balkans, the Balkan wars and the First World War were inseparable'.[24] The murder of the archduke was merely the next step in an ongoing conflict, and one that had already left Serbia a little battle-weary despite its success.

It comes as no surprise then, to learn that although the assassin was from Austrian territories, the Austrians were determined to hold Serbia directly responsible for the attack. The Serbian Prime Minister, Pastich, wrote on 1st July 1914:

> The Austrian and Hungarian press are blaming Serbia more and more for the Serajevo [*sic*] outrage. Their aim is transparent, viz., to destroy that high moral reputation which Serbia now enjoys in Europe, and to take the fullest advantage politically against Serbia of the act of a young and ill-balanced fanatic.[25]

The Austrian Consular agent in Serbia, however, wrote on 6th July 1914:

> The news of the terrible crime in Serajevo, [*sic*] which had been only too successful, created here a sensation in the fullest sense of the word. There was practically no sign of consternation or indignation; the predominant mood was one of satisfaction and even joy, and this was often quite open without reserve, and even found expression in a brutal way.[26]

The former stresses Serbia's civilised role in Europe, the latter emphasises an inherent brutality. Both are certainly exaggerated but the bridge between the East and the West shakes in anticipation of further war. The Austrian government used the assassination as an excuse to open up old grievances with Serbia, demanding, for example, the return of the territory of Bosnia, which Serbia had acquired during the Balkan Wars, citing the old Treaty of Berlin as justification. Serbia, claiming innocence, was unlikely to comply. There was a growing danger of renewed military action. The British ambassador at Vienna wrote to Sir Edward Grey on 27th July 1914:

> I have had conversations with all my colleagues representing the Great Powers. The impression left on my mind is that the Austro-Hungarian

note was so drawn up as to make war inevitable; that the Austro-Hungarian Government are fully resolved to have war with Serbia; that they consider their position as a Great Power to be at stake; and that until punishment has been administered to Serbia it is unlikely that they will listen to mediation. This country has gone wild at the prospect of war with Serbia, and its postponement or prevention would undoubtedly be a great disappointment.[27]

If Austria attacked Serbia, then the latter's ally, Russia, would be obliged to come to her aid. If Russia joined the fight, in turn her allies, France and Great Britain, would also be called in. Meanwhile, Germany would be required to assist Austria. In the blink of an eye, all the Great Powers would be at war, all triggered by Serbia. And, of course, this was exactly how it happened. Over the next four years, Serbia was, indeed, punished. But so were many thousands of others as well.

The pre-war history of Russia was in many ways bound up with that of Serbia as a consequence of shared Slavic roots. But whereas Serbia had long been a dominion of the Ottoman Empire, Russia had become a formidable imperial power. Russia was geographically enormous,[28] embracing both Eastern and Western cultures, with a population in the region of 169 million in 1914, two and a half times bigger than her nearest rival, Germany.[29] Although the empire spread into Asia, the ruling Romanovs were European. But their position in the West had only really developed in the seventeenth and eighteenth centuries. It was the Russian tsar, Peter the Great, who began this 'civilising' process as he developed his country in the last years of the seventeenth century, symbolised by his construction of his capital, St Petersburg, against all the odds on the marshy banks of the Neva. Despite this, Larry Wolff has argued that Russia was very much a part of the East–West dichotomy constructed by the Enlightenment.

> The idea of Eastern Europe was invented in Western Europe in the age of Enlightenment, and Russia was included in the idea. Russia was subjected to the same process of discovery, alignment, condescension, and intellectual mastery, was located and identified by the same formulas: between Europe and Asia, between civilisation and barbarism.[30]

It was during the reign of Catherine the Great (1762–96) that Russia began to bridge the cultural gap between East and West, much as the Balkans were to do a century or so later. Wolff suggests that 'The Enlightenment would reconceive Russia in a redemptive spirit that envisioned an emergence from barbarism, an improvement of manners.'[31] This was no doubt in part inspired by Catherine's long-term correspondence with Voltaire, her engagement with ideas that foregrounded philosophy, science and the arts. It was also enhanced by the development of the Russian literatures that pervaded Western Europe in the nineteenth century, beginning with the Romanticism of Pushkin and Lermontov, developing into the highly influential works of writers such as Dostoevsky and Tolstoy. From these leanings a Russian intelligentsia emerged, producing families like the Usovs, with whom the young Florence Farmborough went to live in Moscow in 1908.

Despite this development of ideas, in 1914 the Romanov regime clung on to a level of autocracy that had long since disappeared from the rest of Europe. Around them, with the strong influence of the other Great Powers, things were beginning to change. As D. C. B. Lieven argues:

> In the half century before 1914, in Russia as elsewhere, traditional religious, patriarchal and local loyalties which had long underpinned society were increasingly dissolving under the joint impact of the ideas of the Enlightenment and French Revolution, transmitted through modern systems of mass education and communications and the great social transformation brought about by the development of industry and capitalism.[32]

Things had been much slower to change in Russia. The tsarist regime had not even abolished serfdom until 1861. But despite a slow start, the late nineteenth century had seen a significant acceleration in the rate of social change. By 1914 Russia had experienced twenty-five years of rapid economic growth, with particular developments in railways,[33] education[34] and defence spending. But political divisions in society were especially marked. Peter Gatrell states that:

> A gulf existed between plebeian social groups (workers and peasants) on the one hand, and propertied elements on the other. Such divisions were not unique to Russia, but they were especially acute in Russia because capitalism was still in its infancy and socially deprived groups did not recognise the legitimacy of private property in land or assets.[35]

Because of the slow nature of political development, Russia missed out on a lot of the political unrest that hit much of Europe in the mid-nineteenth century.[36] But as the rate of change accelerated, so

Russia became vulnerable to political upheaval on a scale unseen elsewhere.

The growing tensions came to the surface in 1905. Change was still too slow and there was a great deal of resentment of the tsarist regime. The urban workers went on strike, supported by the army and navy. In the countryside the peasants also engaged in protests against their lot. The Tsar was forced to act and was able, temporarily, to bring matters under control. He offered a number of concessions including the setting up of a parliament, the Duma, although this remained a fairly toothless organisation. There were land and franchise reforms. But at the same time, treatment of the revolutionaries was harsh, suggesting that appropriate lessons had not been learnt. It was to this environment of economic and industrial advancement, yet socially backward and lacking in political harmony, that Florence Farmborough came to take up her post as governess with the Usovs.

As the international rivalry that would eventually result in the war increased, Russia, like the other Great Powers, was forced to reassess her loyalties. Her traditional role as the 'friend of Serbia', together with mounting imperial tensions with Austria-Hungary, influenced the evolution of the alliance systems that would eventually result in the capitulation of all of Europe to war. In the period 1909–14, following Austria's annexation of Bosnia-Hercegovina, this rivalry increased, with Russia maintaining and emphasising the role of 'liberator of the Balkans' established in 1878 with the Treaty of San Stefano. It seemed inevitable that Russia would be instrumental in the declaration of a major international war.

Sean McMeekin has recently argued that Russia was more than just a player in the game that resulted in the war; that instead was a major force behind the outbreak, with very deliberate war aims that matched those of other major Powers. He argues that:

> Trenches, Verdun, and the poppies of Flanders Field may be the lasting images of the Great War in Western imagination, but it would be difficult to argue today that anything of lasting strategic importance was at stake in the Franco-German clash in Flanders. That action's lack of identifiable foreign policy goals helps explain why the carnage there seemed so senseless and so badly scarred the men who fought and bled there.[37]

Russia's aim, McMeekin argues, centred on imperial ambitions, just as Germany was conscious of her imperial weakness. He also suggests that Russia was complicit in the conspiracy that resulted in the assassinations of June 1914, and that this complicity was part of a larger Russian plot use the Balkans to force the final collapse of Turkey. Russia's main strategic aim was the conquest of the decaying Ottoman Empire, particularly the colonisation of Constantinople. Although he does acknowledge the long-standing Russian Slavic connections with Serbia, McMeekin principally argues that compelling evidence places responsibility for the First World War at the door of Russia, evidence based on her manipulating rather than supporting Serbia. And the ultimate outcome of the war was every bit as politically disastrous for Russia as it was for Germany, paving the way for revolution.

Robert Service concludes that:

> The Great War produced a situation in Russia, Austria and Germany that shattered the Romanov, Habsburg and Hohenzollern monarchies. It also made possible the Bolshevik seizure of power in October 1917. Except for the Great War, Lenin would have remained an *émigré* theorist scribbling in Swiss libraries; and even if Nicholas II had been deposed in a peacetime transfer of power, the inception of a communist order would hardly have been likely.[38]

The consequences of the revolutions for the British women working in Russia in 1917 were dramatic; whether they were long-term residents like Farmborough or Mary Britnieva, or whether they were members of hospital units such as the SWH on more recent postings, the upheaval had a profound effect on their experience.

That British women should look to play a part in the First World War was hardly surprising. The understanding of women's role in society had been subtly changing for half a century, since the earliest claims for women's suffrage. Although the conventional Victorian stereotype of woman as homemaker remained strong, the idea that women should be military nurses had become quite established. The work of Florence Nightingale and others in the Crimea had demonstrated that women could certainly bring something to the table, although concerns remained about the inappropriateness of exposing women to any real danger. But as warfare itself began to change with the outbreak of the Second Boer War, 1899–1902, so women's role in it was also forced to develop. Anne Summers suggests that 'before the [Boer] war the received wisdom on female military nurses had been that their role, if any, was in base hospitals.... But the experience of the war threw the terms "base" and "front" into question.'[39] For the first time a small group of women accompanied a private hospital unit led by Frederick Treves of the London Hospital, to become part of a mobile field hospital and thus very close indeed to the front line. Women moved with the action, served on hospital trains and recorded their experiences in letters to the press. 'The female nurses of the Boer War demonstrated that even a service "composed of ladies" could live and work and display great stamina in fairly rough conditions.'[40] These achievements 'gave substance to pre-war arguments ... [t]hat women had the right and capacity to participate with men in the defence and expansion of the Empire'.[41] There would be no let-up in these arguments and the determination of women to prove that they could serve as usefully as men would become particularly significant during the First World War.

The success of female nurses in the Boer War and the growth of the Women's Suffrage Movement led to important developments in the establishment of women as military nurses in the first decade of the twentieth century. In 1902 the Queen Alexandra's Imperial Military Nursing Service Reserve (QAIMNSR) was set up to replace the old Army Nursing Service. Following the Territorial and Reserve Forces Act of 1907, 1908 saw the establishment of the Territorial Force Nursing Service (TFNS). The year 1907 also saw the first founding of the First Aid Yeomanry Corps. Mabel St Clair Stobart records her first encounter with the organisation in her autobiography, *Miracles and Adventures*.

> We were to be nurses mounted on horseback, yeomanry nurses, and we had visions of galloping bravely on to the battlefields and snatching the wounded from under the cannons' mouths and rendering them first aid. We rode horses, wore scarlet tunics, helmets, and divided skirts, and brandished whips and were doubtless picturesque. But though it was a move in the right direction, it was all unpractical and would have led to nowhere except to derision.[42]

The organisation eventually evolved into the First Aid Nursing Yeomanry (FANY) and did much important work during the First World War in the West.[43] Stobart, however, went elsewhere for her service.

In 1909, from origins within the Red Cross, the government inaugurated the 'scheme for the organisation of voluntary aid in England and Wales'. The Voluntary Aid Detachments (VADs) as they became known, were made up of both men and women, but in the years before the war far more women than men joined up. They presented a very good way into war service for many participants, particularly those who were not motivated by political activism. Anne Summers notes that:

VADs were hardly ever mentioned in the Suffrage Press. The suffragist Mrs St Clair Stobart whose Women's Sick and Wounded Convoy Corps was a registered VAD in the County of London branch of the Red Cross, and Dr Elsie Maud Inglis, the founder of the Scottish Women's Suffrage Federation who was commandant of an Edinburgh VAD in this period were exceptional in their participation in preparations for war service.[44]

Stobart's WSWCC, her alternative to the FANY, had also been founded in 1909. And following the publication of Robert Baden-Powell's *Scouting for Boys* in 1908, it quickly became clear that there was a significant demand for an equivalent movement for girls, leading to the formation of the Girl Guides, a similar sort of training ground for empire service, in 1909. Quasi-military organisations for women were all the rage in Edwardian Britain.[45]

Summers notes that:

By 1914 few people thought of military nursing as a man's job. The TFNS had been constructed on an all-female basis, and the VAD scheme had quickly deleted its original provision for supplementary male hospital staff. At least 32,000 women served as military nurses between 1914 and 1919.[46]

The numbers speak for themselves. By 1912 the VAD numbered 26,000 women, the QAIMNSR 300 and the TFNS stood at 3,000. By 1914 the VAD had grown to a membership of 50,000. Christine Hallett's excellent 2014 study of Allied nurses during the First World War, *Veiled Warriors*, examines the activities of all these nursing organisations in detail, but with the greatest emphasis on the Western Front, as that is where most official military nurses served.[47] Yet these women were almost all deployed either in Britain or on the Western Front. None of these organisations travelled to the Eastern Front to work with the Allied armies of Serbia or Russia. To find out the origins of British women's service in the East we have to turn to the Women's Suffrage Movement, and to consider the much more ambiguous role of women doctors on active service in the First World War.

While the role of women as military nurses had grown consistently in the years following the Crimean war, the idea of women as professionally trained medical practitioners on an equal footing with men was a much harder pill to swallow. It took the Royal Army Medical Corp (RAMC) a long time to accept women doctors on the Western Front.[48] Most women doctors who wanted to participate in the war from the outset had to look elsewhere for an opportunity to serve, despite the advances made in the nineteenth century. It was the Eastern Front that provided them with their own theatre of war.

The pioneering women, who first qualified as doctors in the nineteenth century, representing the advancement of their sex, were often inevitably linked to the rise of the Women's Suffrage Movement. The first woman to qualify as a physician in England, Elizabeth Garrett Anderson, was the sister of the leading suffragist Millicent Garrett Fawcett.[49] Although Garrett Anderson was less of a suffrage activist than her sister, her own feminism was of profound importance to the long-term development of women in medicine. But Elizabeth Garrett Anderson's path to a medical career was not an easy one. She had to complete much of her study through private tuition and was continually vetoed by men, both qualified physicians and other students, as she tried to gain hospital experience. She finally became the first British woman doctor in 1865, but the battles were far from over. No hospital would employ her so she set up her own private practice. Her principal interest, perhaps unsurprisingly, was women's medicine and so she set up the St Mary's Dispensary for Women and Children in 1866. She was a success against the odds. In 1873 she became a member of the British Medical Association: as it turned out, the first and last woman member for nineteen years as the organisation voted against the admittance of further women. But in 1874 she co-founded the London School of Medicine for Women with another pioneer, Sophia Jex-Blake, which included the New Hospital for Women, enabling other women to qualify and work as doctors.

The career of Dr Elsie Inglis, a prominent figure in this book, can be seen as a direct response to the achievements of Garrett Anderson.[50] Inglis was born in 1864, a year before Garrett Anderson qualified. In 1886 she became a beneficiary of a split between Sophia Jex-Blake and the London Medical School, when Jex-Blake moved north to set up the Edinburgh School of Medicine for Women. This enabled Inglis to follow her dream of becoming a doctor without having to leave her widowed father, to whom she was devoted. Twenty years on, not much had changed with regard to prejudice against medical women and Inglis had to face similar opposition to mixed classes when she moved to Glasgow to complete her clinical training. She qualified in 1892 and took up a post as resident medical officer at Garret Anderson's New Hospital for Women in London. Inglis too was continually struck by the lack of proper facilities for women and chose to specialise in women's medical care. Her association with Garrett Anderson had led her to Millicent Fawcett, now the President of the National Union of Women's Suffrage Societies (NUWSS), and inspired her towards her own activism.

Inglis returned to Edinburgh to set up her own practice in 1894. Her success as a women's physician and as a suffrage campaigner went hand in hand during this period. In 1904 she opened a women's hospital called the Hospice in Edinburgh, specialising in surgery, gynaecology and midwifery. Already Honorary Secretary of the Edinburgh National Society for Women's Suffrage, in 1909 with the formation of the Scottish Federation of Women's Suffrage Societies (SFWSS) she also became Honorary Secretary to this organisation. This was to prove of vital importance when the First World War broke out.

The connection between the First World War and the Women's Suffrage Movement is stronger than usually understood. As previously mentioned, the WSPU had become a prominent organisation in the decade before the outbreak of the war. The Pankhurst women brought something quite new to the campaign with their emphasis on agitation and militant action rather than the peaceful lobbying of the NUWSS. Although this new development won the women as many enemies as it did friends, they were very difficult to ignore or overlook. They represented a significant political voice by 1914, and the issue of the vote was established on the political agendas of all parties, whether or not they supported it. When war broke out almost all the societies formally dropped their campaigning and offered their services in various ways to the war effort.[51] I have argued in detail elsewhere that the idea that the campaign actually ceased during the war years is quite inaccurate, that in fact, all suffragists continued to fight for the vote, adapting their methods in line with the war situation.[52] For the purposes of this study, it is the direct involvement of the suffrage societies in the funding and equipping of hospital units for the various fronts that is of most significance.

It is worth noting that many of the women who served on the Eastern Front had been involved with the Women's Suffrage

Movement in some way before the war. This is probably not surprising. The link between activism and doing one's bit for the war effort in a society that traditionally confined women to the domestic sphere is probably self-explanatory. The mechanisms of the Women's Suffrage Movement were well established by 1914, providing an ideal institutional infrastructure for the hospital units and other war effort organisations. Elsie Inglis was a seasoned campaigner by 1914. The Scottish Women's Hospitals for Foreign Service was one of the most successful women's organisations of the war, funded and supported by the SFWSS, driven by Inglis. They worked on the Western Front as well as the Eastern. Of primary importance, they enabled women doctors to get to the heart of the action and save lives. In 1951, former SWH orderly E. M. Butler published a novel recalling the activities of her unit, *Daylight in a Dream*. Butler's novel paints a heroic and inspiring portrait of their leader.

> Dr Everet [read Dr Inglis], slight and taut, as light as a leaf and as gallant as a guardsman, was there to keep an eye on her 'girls', as she liked to call them, and to see that they behaved. There was a driving-power in her fragile body which would have put a Rolls-Royce to shame, a genius for getting miracles to happen, and administrative gifts hardly distinguishable from statesmanship; for she refused to recognise impossibilities, and the hearts of her subordinates often sank like lead when she issued orders which must be obeyed and yet seemed impossible to fulfil. But leaden hearts grew light when their owners, as nearly always happened, suddenly saw a way.[53]

Such a description might also have suited Mabel St Clair Stobart, who was also a determined supporter of the Suffrage Movement through action, reflecting the WSPU motto of 'deeds not words' despite her discomfort with militant activism. Her WSWCC also took women doctors to the front line for the first time. And there were many others who will also be considered here.

It is this 'female other' of the First World War who takes centre stage in this book. Many of the women involved were part of efficiently run institutions, such as the SWH. Although this was the biggest institutional presence in the East, with hospital units in the Balkans, Russia and Romania, it was not the only one. The Serbian Relief Fund (SRF) was the brainchild of Mabel Groutich, the American wife of the Serbian Secretary of State for Foreign affairs, who had come to England at the start of the war in order to appeal for medical supplies and personnel for her adopted country. Serbia had lost many of its doctors and nurses during the Balkan Wars and was poorly equipped to embark on another conflict. Groutich took her first party of eight medical personnel back to Serbia in August 1914, including Flora Sandes, who would go on to have a most unusual wartime career. Then working with the SWH, Groutich set up the SRF with a view to sending out medical units made up of both men and women. The first of these, under the leadership of Lady Leila Paget, travelled to the Balkans in November 1914 and established a 600-bed hospital at Skopje, Macedonia (SRF1). Paget was also a veteran of the Balkan Wars, so ideally placed to lead and organise this first hospital. Mabel St Clair Stobart, also very experienced, led the Third Serbian Relief Fund Unit (SRF3) out in April 1915. The Red Cross too sent units, to the Balkans and to Russia, in conjunction with the International Red Cross operating in those countries. There were also other privately funded organisations such as the two British Farmers' Hospitals for Serbians, so called because they were financed from a fund raised entirely from British farmers and landowners. The need for these units was identified as a result of newspaper reports of the sufferings of the Serbians during the typhus winter of 1914–15.[54] Such was the concentration of British institutional relief units of various sorts in Serbia in 1915 that the Foreign Office appointed Sir Ralf Paget as the British Commissioner for the co-ordination of relief work, to oversee the British contribution. It represented a subtle official recognition. A great many of the staff of these units were women.

Even within the relief organisations and hospital units, the women took on many roles depending on what was happening in the war. For example, Serbia was very quiet in the summer of 1915, enabling the women to focus on the health needs of the local population rather than the welfare of soldiers. With most of the men away in the army, these populations were almost entirely made up of women and children. Sickness was rife, as Serbia's medical care system was in tatters after years of war. With the invasion of the opposing armies in September of that year, the treatment of wounded soldiers took priority for all the units; the defeat and subsequent retreat that followed again expanded the range of people needing medical support as soldiers, civilians and relief workers alike fled for their lives. As the Serbian army returned to retake the country in 1918, much of their work was built around bringing relief to a population that had lived under enemy rule for three years, dealing now with lack of food, medicine and other basic resources. After the war many women stayed on in the country to work with the numerous orphans who survived the fighting. But not all the women considered here were connected to established relief institutions. Even in Serbia, which saw the greatest number of organised units, there were some lone women who found their way into other spheres of the war. The most notable of these is surely Flora Sandes, the only British woman to see active service as a soldier in the First World War. But she was not the only lone adventurer. Dr Caroline Twigge Matthews offered her medical services to the Serbian military quite independently, and travelled the Balkans alone, resulting in a very different and rather less positive war experience.

Although some organisations such as the Red Cross and the SWH were active in Russia 1914–17, some of the British women considered here were not part of any such institution. Mary Britnieva and Florence Farmborough, fluent Russian speakers who had lived in the country for years, joined the Russian Red Cross. Although supported by a formal institution, their voices do tend to sound more isolated, as foreign women, particularly as society begins to crumble around them. Although Farmborough was completely accepted as a 'sister' by the Russian women with whom she worked, the reactions of the soldiers, particularly in the face of revolution, could be more problematic. Their work tended to be built much more closely around the needs of the army. The military mechanisms in Russia allocated Red Cross 'flying columns' to particular regiments, so women like Farmborough followed the soldiers along the line as they fought.

This book explores the long-overlooked contributions to the conflict of all these women, using their own words, through the diaries, letters, memoirs and documents that they left behind, in order to illustrate the importance of their overall contribution to the Allied war effort in the East as well as the West. Many of the women – Stobart, Inglis and others – will recur throughout the pages as their stories interlink. Although they followed different paths through the war, these paths crossed from time to time, allowing their narratives to interweave to produce a coherent picture of the overall experience of British women. Their stories and their geographies overlap. The vast majority of these women came from the middle and the upper classes of British society. This was inevitable as they were much more likely to have the resources or the professional training to enable them to travel. They were also much more likely to leave written records of their experiences. Nonetheless, a wide a range of women's voices will form the breadth of this study, reinforcing the importance of both their role and their legacy in the Balkans and the East. Chapter 1, 'Travel writers and romantics?', introduces some of those key women's voices and examines how their writings may be read as literary texts as well as historical documents. For many British women, the exoticism and difference of the East proved to be a powerful draw. The 'otherness' of their experiences in Serbia and Russia inspired them to adopt a range of different styles in their writing. Almost all memoirs engage with the journeys of the women as individuals across unfamiliar, at times even alien landscapes, as well as dealing with the harsh reality of war experience. Their literary heritage is often apparent in their language. This chapter examines some of the key primary texts through the genre of travel writing in particular and explores the alternative literary strategies employed by the women to tell their stories. It provides a context for women's travel writing at the beginning of the twentieth century, looking back to its development in the nineteenth. It draws upon the most literary works written by women who worked across the region of study, to establish their literary credentials and explore how their writing develops as a response to the experience of the war and their understanding of the histories behind it.

Chapter 2, 'Early days: the typhus colony and other stories', examines the early work of British women in the east. The SRF1 travelled to the Balkans in the autumn 1914, led by Lady Paget, wife of Sir Ralf. Lady Paget set up her hospital in Skopje in mid-November 1914, in time to provide medical care during the typhus epidemic that raged across Serbia during the winter of 1914–15. Paget's unit, unlike some of the later ones, was constructed of men and women volunteers, the men taking the senior positions, but ultimately answering to a woman. The first SWH unit also arrived in late 1914 and faced the same epidemic crisis, while in Russia, British women were among the first recruits in the Russian Red Cross. The chapter places this early work in the context of the immediate histories of Serbia and Russia and their relationships with Britain and the other Allies at this early stage of the war. The impact of the Balkan Wars had a profound effect on Serbia in 1914 and 1915. The subsequent uncontainable epidemics brought about the first deaths of British women on active service in the region, delivering a significant cultural shock. In earlier wars, women did not tend to die in military service.

In Russia there were a number of British initiatives from women expatriates living there, such as the British Colony Hospital for

Wounded Russian Soldiers, set up by Lady Georgina Buchanan, the wife of the British ambassador, and Lady Muriel Paget's Anglo-Russian Base Hospital. Independent British women such as Florence Farmborough and Mary Britnieva, working for the Russian Red Cross, began keeping records that enable us to see the war from the point of view of the voiceless Russian peasant soldier. By allowing the soldiers to speak through their pages these women offer a new perspective excluded from previous histories of the region. This also enables us to understand how the women related to their patients and vice versa. The chapter seeks to contextualise the early work within the historical framework of women as military nurses in foreign countries with very different cultures.

Chapter 3, 'Role call? The female body and gender identity on the Eastern Front', explores the 'female other' of the First World War. The Eastern Front, and in particular Serbia, provided British women with unique opportunities for involvement. Serbia enabled women to experience the war at close range, often facing many of the same threats as combat soldiers. Here female bodies were put to the test in ways not previously imagined and some women explored gender roles in unexpected ways. This chapter sets out the conventional expectations of Edwardian femininity and then juxtaposes them with the actual physical and emotional experience of life on the Eastern Front. It examines the ways in which this stark new experience pushed societal understandings of gender boundaries through the experience of two very different women, Mabel Dearmer, a hospital orderly who worked and died in Serbia in 1915, and Flora Sandes, a nurse-turned-soldier whose experience questions accepted understandings of gendered war experience. The chapter considers various elements that might shape or alter gender expectations, such as dress, uniform, performance and behaviour patterns. Together these women illustrate the importance of Serbia as a battleground for sexual politics during the First World War.

Chapter 4, 'Waiting for the Allies: prisoners of war', continues the focus on the Balkans. When the Bulgarian, Austrian and German armies invaded Serbia in late 1915, most of the British women working there were immediately evacuated. A few, however, refused to leave their hospitals and their patients, even in the face of the enemy. These included Lady Paget at Skopje and Dr Elsie Inglis of the SWH at Krushevatz, Elsie Corbett and Ellen Davies at Vrinjatcha Bania and independent doctor Caroline Twigge Matthews, who came in for some very harsh treatment. These women, with the assistance of select members of their teams, continued to nurse the wounded in the occupied country, as enemy aliens and as prisoners of war. All documented the experience. Here we really see the importance of institutional support for the women. This chapter explores life for British women in captivity, the hardships they endured and their relationships with their captors, along with their achievements in the face of extraordinary danger. Both social class and gender are very important to this discussion, as both have a significant impact on the women's behaviour. It explores the definitions of their national identity, the extent of their 'Britishness', making particular use of their relationship to the legacy of empire. The chapter explores the roles adopted by these women in captivity, their attitudes towards both their captors and their patients, arguing that their imperial background, their 'Britishness', had a significant impact on their behaviour patterns and the consequences of their actions.

In Chapter 5, 'Domestic survival strategies: the Serbian retreat, 1915', the focus remains on Serbia to examine the experience of the great retreat of 1915. Those women who did not remain behind with the wounded were forced to flee along with the defeated Serbian armies and thousands of Serbian refugees. Their path took them across the mountains of Serbia, Montenegro and Albania just as the winter set in, with the noise of the guns always close behind them. This was an extraordinary journey and some fascinating accounts of it survive. This chapter explores the experience of the retreat from a gendered perspective, with a particular focus on the ways in which the women involved used their 'femininity' to survive and to help others to get through. It examines the everyday, the ordinary, the domestic and the ways in which women used these aspects of life, these everyday responsibilities of womanhood, as a survival mechanism peculiar to their own gendered experience. It focuses on the charismatic leader, Mabel St Clair Stobart, drawing on her autobiographical writings, *The Flaming Sword in Serbia and Elsewhere* (1916) and *Miracles and Adventures* (1935), analyzing her conscious self-presentation and the ways in which she chose to perform the roles of commandant, major, lady and mother simultaneously. It also builds on the ideas in Chapter 3 and considers the significance of gender in the way women chose to deal with the experience of the retreat.

Chapter 6, 'The road to revolution: Russia, 1916–17', returns to Russia, the primary focus for British women in the East once Serbia had fallen. In Serbia the British women had faced invasion, flight and captivity. In Russia they had to confront revolution and its impact on the war experience. The combination of centuries of autocratic rule with rapid social, cultural and industrial advancement ignited with terrifying results for many of those embroiled in fighting the First World War. Florence Farmborough watched it from the inside, recording in her diary the effects of both revolutions on the battle-weary soldiers, watching the society that she knew so well collapse into chaotic civil war. She was in a position to see the personal responses of ordinary people in Russia and was thus able to provide a unique document of the unrest and suffering caused by the various stages of the revolution. Women of the SWH witnessed the revolutions from various standpoints, some of them fraught with danger. Some of these women had to travel through Moscow when the revolution was in full swing and encountered unexpected dangers. This chapter explores the direct impact and the political implications of the revolutions on the many British women caught up in them, using a range of written sources. It also examines the responses of the British women to the politics of the revolution, which reflect their own social, cultural and class-related bias.

The final chapter traces the closing days of the war and explores the longer legacy of the British women. By 1918 the once-defeated Serbian army was fighting back. Some of the British women who had experienced that defeat remained with them as they regained their homeland; some, like Elsie Corbett, revisited the places where they had once been held captive. For other British women, the end of the war brought the need for escape, as Florence Farmborough embarked on an epic journey on the Trans-Siberian Railway to Vladivostok, the only way home after the revolutions. Communist Russia then closed its doors. But after the Armistice in 1918, many British women who had been involved in the plight of Serbia for four years took the decision not to go home. The SWH stayed on, engaged in continuing relief work in a broken country, running roadside dispensaries and canteens, opening hospitals and orphanages, committing themselves to Serbia more permanently. The SWH committee also worked hard to set up an Elsie Inglis Memorial Hospital in Belgrade. The chapter also considers Isabel Emslie Hutton's post-war humanitarian work in the Crimea, a last outpost of Russia, torn apart by civil war.

The rise of the USSR in the inter-war years had a significant impact on the structure of Europe as a whole, particularly the

Balkan states. In 1937, Rebecca West travelled across the Balkans, the new Yugoslavia, documenting what she saw and placing it in the context of its recent history. This chapter develops that history in the context of West's responses. *Black Lamb and Grey Falcon* (1942) is a book about travel and politics that helps to consolidate the work of many of the women considered in this book. An analysis of West's writing will act as a framing device for this conclusion, read alongside Tim Judah's arguments concerning the impact of war and history on the more recent conflicts in the Balkans. West is concerned with the Second World War, Judah with the conflicts of the 1990s. Both anticipate a turbulent future in a region that had captured the hearts and minds of British women earlier in the century, a turbulent future that promises echoes of the past, from the First World War and beyond.

Notes

1 Isabel Emslie Hutton, *With a Woman's Unit in Serbia, Salonika and Sebastopol* (London: Williams and Northgate, 1928), pp. 15–16.

2 Jane Marcus, 'Corpus/Corps/Corpse: Writing the Body in/at War', in Helen Margaret Cooper, Adrienne Munich and Susan Merrill Squier (eds), *Arms and the Woman: War, Gender and Literary Representation* (Chapel Hill and London: University of North Carolina Press, 1989), p. 135.

3 Larry Wolff, *Inventing Eastern Europe: The Map of Civilization on the Mind of the Enlightenment* (Stanford, CA: Stanford University Press, 1994), p. 4.

4 See Tim Judah, *The Serbs: History, Myth and the Destruction of Yugoslavia* (New Haven and London: Yale University Press, 1997), p. 25.

5 Quoted in Rebecca West, *Black Lamb and Grey Falcon: A Journey through Yugoslavia* (Edinburgh: Canongate, 2006 [1942]), p. 1120.

6 *Ibid.*

7 Mabel St Clair Stobart, *The Flaming Sword in Serbia and Elsewhere* (London: Hodder and Stoughton, 1917), pp. 211–12.

8 West, *Black Lamb*, p. 1145.

9 Richard C. Hall, *The Balkan Wars 1912–13: Prelude to the First World War* (London and New York: Routledge, 2000), p. 1.

10 *Ibid.*, p. 2.

11 It is worth noting that for one particular ethnic group, the Armenians, this relationship was much more complex, leading eventually to accusations of genocide during the First World War, following Turkish massacres of Armenians. For more information see Vahakn N. Dadrian, 'The Armenian Question and the Wartime Fate of the Armenians as Documented by the Officials of the Ottoman Empire's World War

I Allies: Germany and Austria Hungary', *International Journal of Middle East Studies* 34:1 (2002), 59–85.

12 Mark Mazower, *The Balkans: From the End of Byzantium to the Present Day* (London: Phoenix Press, 2001), p. 4.

13 Maria Todorova, *Imagining the Balkans* (Oxford: Oxford University Press, 2009), p. 3.

14 *Ibid.*, p. 119.

15 *Ibid.*, pp. 15–16.

16 Mazower, *The Balkans*, p. 58.

17 Hall, *The Balkan Wars*, p. 2.

18 Michael S. Neiberg (ed.), *The World War I Reader* (New York and London: New York University Press, 2007), p. 5.

19 Hall, *The Balkan Wars*, p. 15.

20 Mabel St Clair Stobart, *War and Women: From Experience in the Balkans and Elsewhere* (London: G. Bell & Sons, 1913).

21 Hall, *The Balkan Wars*, p. 129.

22 Quoted in Mazower, *The Balkans*, p. 14.

23 Judah, *The Serbs*, p. 84.

24 Hall, *The Balkan Wars*, p. 132.

25 M. N. Pastich, quoted in *War 1914: Punishing the Serbs* (London: The Stationery Office, 1999), pp. 10–11.

26 Herr Hoflehner to Count Berchtold, 6th July 1914, *ibid.*, p. 9.

27 Sir M. de Bunsen, British ambassador at Vienna, to Sir Edward Grey, *ibid.*, p. 74.

28 The Russian Empire covered a sixth of the world's earth surface. Robert Service, *A History of Modern Russia: From Tsarism to the Twenty-First Century* (Cambridge, MA: Harvard University Press, 2009), p. 3.

29 Peter Gatrell, *Russia's First World War: A Social and Economic History* (London: Pearson Education, 2005), p. 3.

30 Wolff, *Inventing Eastern Europe*, p. 15.

31 *Ibid.*, p. 11.

32 D. C. B. Liven, *Russia and the Origins of the First World War* (London: Macmillan, 1983), p. 14.

33 Train tracks increased by a third in the period 1900–13, although railway stock was old. Gatrell, *Russia's First World War*, p. 5.

34 By 1912, 57 per cent of the school-age population was in education, but literacy rates among the whole population stood at around 30 per cent, the lowest in Europe. Lieven, *Russia and the Origins of the First World War*, p. 9.

35 Gatrell, *Russia's First World War*, p. 10.

36 In December 1825 Russian army officers led 3,000 soldiers in revolt against the succession of Tsar Nicholas I in what became known as the Decembrist Revolt. It was quickly suppressed by the Tsar, but did indicate that even Russia was not immune to the social unrest that was rife across Europe in the nineteenth century. For more information see

Lionel Kochan and Richard Abraham (eds), *The Making of Modern Russia* (London: Penguin Books, 1990), pp. 155–60.

37 Sean McMeekin, *The Russian Origins of the First World War* (Cambridge, MA and London: The Belknap Press of Harvard University Press, 2011), p. 4.

38 Service, *A History of Modern Russia*, p. 26.

39 Anne Summers, *Angels and Citizens: British Women as Military Nurses 1854–1914* (London and New York: Routledge & Kegan Paul, 1988), p. 211.

40 *Ibid.*, p. 215.

41 *Ibid.*, p. 212.

42 Mabel St Clair Stobart, *Miracles and Adventures* (London: Rider & Co., 1935), p. 84.

43 For more information on the FANY see Janet Lee, 'Sisterhood at the Front: Friendship, Comradeship, and the Feminine Appropriation of Military Heroism among World War I First Aid Nursing Yeomanry (FANY)', *Women's Studies International Forum* 31:1 (January–February 2008), 16–29.

44 Summers, *Angels and Citizens*, p. 74.

45 For further information on all these organisations see Lucy Noakes, *Women in the British Army: War and the Gentle Sex, 1907–1948* (London and New York: Routledge, 2006), chs. 3–4.

46 Summers, *Angels and Citizens*, p. 269.

47 Christine E. Hallett, *Veiled Warriors: Allied Nurses of the First World War* (Oxford: Oxford University Press, 2014).

48 The first women doctors to achieve this were Louisa Garrett Anderson and Flora Murray, both suffragists, who formed the Women's Hospital Corps in September 1914 with RAMC approval. By 1915 their success had convinced the War Office to give them responsibility for a large military hospital in London. See Angela K. Smith, *Suffrage Discourse in Britain during the First World War* (Aldershot: Ashgate, 2005), ch. 5.

49 Elizabeth Garrett Anderson was also the mother of Louisa Garrett Anderson.

50 For a detailed account of the early life of Elsie Inglis, see Leah Leneman, *Elsie Inglis* (Edinburgh: NMS Publishing, 1998).

51 Sylvia Pankhurst was a notable exception to this, embracing pacifism instead of militarism.

52 See Smith, *Suffrage Discourse in Britain*.

53 E. M. Butler, *Daylight in a Dream* (London: Hogarth Press, 1951), p. 38.

54 The fund was the idea of a Mr Herbert Brown, who worked to raise money for the Red Cross from the outbreak of the war onwards. He targeted farmers and landowners, his own profession, with great success. The fund not only staffed the units but also paid for all their medical equipment. See *The Times* (28th January 1915), p. 11.

1

Travel writers and romantics?

From 1914 onwards, British women, determined to do their bit for king and country, travelled East. They were quick to realise that it was in the Balkans that their greatest opportunities lay; quick to understand how the traditional reserve of their fathers, brothers and sons would prove a significant obstacle to their involvement in the war effort on the Western Front. While on the one hand it is clear that the same ethos of duty and patriotism that caused men to enlist, also inspired many women to look for these opportunities, at the same time the war seemed to offer them something more, something rather different. For many women, the war represented a chance to escape from the restricted lives of the Edwardian world, and for some a chance to travel. And just as the notion of victory on the foreign battlefield held glamour and excitement for so many young men, so the ideas of a high romanticism, a glory of war, proved equally attractive to their sisters. In Britain and France military leaders were slow to comprehend the services women could offer, particularly in the field of medicine. But the Allies in the East were more open to the suggestion of women's participation in the war effort: recent experience in the Balkan Wars had shown the commitment and the potential of British women's medical units. Word of this interest spread quickly among the women at home in Britain, many of whom were impatient to sign up to do some practical war work.

But the East held something more. Many of the young women who were keen to play an active part in the war were from upper- or middle-class backgrounds. They were often self-supporting – they had to be, to get their places in the various hospital units if they were not trained nurses. For many, the landscapes of the Western Front were reasonably familiar. Travel in France and Germany had become much more widespread and the cultural identities of these European neigh-bours shared many traits with Britain, not least because of the close blood links of the various royal families. The East, however, suggested a different world. Other women were trained nurses, often from very different social backgrounds, for whom the need to earn a living was an imperative and the idea of foreign travel an impossible dream. All of a sudden that dream was impossible no longer. And the potential glamour and excitement was increased because the kingdoms of the East represented something else, something different and something other. Serbia, as we have seen, the first of these countries to welcome the assistance of the communities of British women, was just far enough away to be viewed differently. In 1914 it was, as John Keegan puts it, 'an aggressive, backward and domestically violent Christian kingdom'.[1] It had only fairly recently won its independence from the Ottoman Turks and the legacy of centuries of Muslim rule remained strong. It was also a country of remarkable ethnic diversity, in part as a consequence of this Ottoman heritage, but also as a result of close relations with both Austria and Russia, and the tribal structures of Balkan communities. It was a place of potential adventure: it offered a range of British women the chance to see aspects of the world that would have been unthinkable in the years before the war. And as luck would have it, many of these women were inspired to record what they saw and experienced. As Christine Hallett has suggested:

> The personal writings of nurses who were posted to hospitals far from their homes resonate with a sense of adventure and a feeling of excite-ment. The opportunity to journey to places they regarded as 'strange and exotic' meant a great deal to upper-working-class and middle-class trained nurses who lacked the means to travel. Wealthier VADs also valued the opportunities that overseas postings could present. Even women from wealthy backgrounds were expected to remain at home, listen to the stories and admire the exploits of their brothers in the army or on foreign Imperial service. Becoming a nurse meant that a woman could make adventures of her own.[2]

As these women ventured to the new landscapes of the East, they wrote about it, in diaries, in letters home, and later some of them wrote memoirs or autobiographies. As this book contests, these writ-ings have significant value to scholarship, in historical and in femi-nist terms. They help us to write new histories of women's experience, to rethink our ideas of the First World War in alternative ways. But equally, many of the written testimonies have important literary value. Although few of the women who served in the East chose to reinterpret their experiences through fiction, we can examine their works through other literary genres, and in so doing, identify this literary as well as historic importance. In this chapter, I will argue that these testimonies are influenced by and can be read through two connected literary forms. Most of the writing addressed here is life writing, as all the women are writing about profound life experiences. Equally pertinent, however, is travel writing, a genre that had become increasingly popular throughout the nineteenth century, with a particular emphasis on the 'lady' traveller.

Although many of the sources used in this book can be categorised as 'life writing', few of them represent conventional autobiography, which Philippe Lejeune described as 'A retrospective prose narrative produced by a real person concerning his own existence, focusing on his individual life, in particular on the development of his personality.'[3] The writing of these women, although constructed around their own experience, is as likely to be focused on the external world, that which they have entered as foreigners. Their own responses are usually of secondary concern. Their interest is less in self-analysis than in making sense of the impact of the war experience on all those involved. Even where the texts considered are presented as conventional autobiographies, for example in the case of Flora Sandes, they do not necessarily conform to critical expectations. As Liz Stanley suggests:

> The autobiographical archetype is the *Bildungsroman*, the tale of the progressive travelling of a life from troubled or stifled beginnings; in which obstacles are overcome and the true self actualised or revealed; and then the tale may, prototypically, end, or it may go on to document yet further troubles turned to triumphs.[4]

Sandes' two volumes of autobiography, *An English Woman-Sergeant in the Serbian Army* (1916) and *The Autobiography of a Woman Soldier* (1927), are concerned almost entirely with her wartime experience, but with the emphasis on the collective experience of the soldiers with whom she served. And although the Serbian army was ultimately on the winning side of the war, the overall sense of triumph is tempered by Sandes' representations of the hardships suffered by the Serbian people and by her own emptiness when she was finally demobbed and forced to return to her old life. As Shari Benstock argues, 'the self that would reside at the center of the text is de-centered – and often is absent altogether – in women's autobiographical texts'.[5] While Sandes is never absent from her text – indeed as the only British woman soldier in the Serbian army she must play a significant role – she uses that position to publicise the plight of her comrades. That she is accepted as one of them, a part of a larger whole, is central to the books.

Much of the life writing considered here falls into more ambiguous categories than conventional autobiography. Many of the texts are memoirs, based on diaries, published immediately after the actual experiences that they relate, often long before the end of the war. The published diaries of women such as Caroline Twigge Matthews and Ellen Chivers Davies were published so quickly that it is impossible to imagine that much editing has taken place, unlike that of Elsie Corbett, published in 1964, in which it is sometimes hard to tell what is original text and what is retrospective reflection. Some of the texts are even less easy to categorise. Trev Lynn Broughton and Linda Anderson suggest that 'many varieties of women's life-writing are not recognized as autobiography, but that some are not legible as "texts" at all'.[6] This is particularly true of some of the manuscript diaries and letters featured. For example Mabel St Clair Stobart's dairy of the Serbian retreat measures five inches by three, is pencil-scrawled in note form and barely legible. Rebecca Hogan has argued that 'immersion in the horizontal, non-hierarchical flow of events and details – in other words, radical parataxis – seems to be one of the striking features of the diary as a form'.[7] Nowhere is this disruption of form and syntax more apparent than in this diary. Yet it is still possible to read a great deal about both the woman and the broader experience in its pages.

As interest in women's autobiographical practice grew and developed from the 1980s onwards, so scholarly interest in diaries as a form of life writing has also developed. Suzanne L. Bunkers and Cynthia Hoff have argued that:

> The diary's flexibility and adaptability enhance its uses in our lives and academic disciplines. Its form, simultaneously elastic and tight, borrows from and at the same time contributes to other narrative structures. Its content is wide-ranging yet patterned, and what is excluded is as important as what is included. Because the form and content of the diary are so adaptable and flexible, the study of diaries brings into play issues of historical, social, and self-construction; exchanges between reader and text; and connections between, and differing effects of, published and manuscript diaries.[8]

The diary, as a form of life writing, becomes a vital textual source for studies such as this one, offering experiences of war previously marginalised or excluded altogether. But how reliable are they as subjective personal records, whether intended for publication or not? Liz Stanley suggests that 'Both biography and autobiography lay claim to facticity, yet both are by nature artful enterprises which select, shape and produce a very unnatural product, for no life is lived quite so much under a single spotlight as the conventional form of written auto/biographies suggests.'[9] This may also be true of diaries and letters. It is impossible to identify absolute fact and truth in these writings because they are shaped by the subjective influences of the writers. Social class, nationality, politics, gender and upbringing will all impact on the biases of the works. But for my purposes it is here that the spotlight is most useful. It is precisely the ways in which all these influences impact upon the experience of the individual that most interest me here. What these life writings convey is the way these British women understood their experience, that is, experience inevitably coloured by who they were. Nowhere is this more apparent than in the way they responded to the often harsh and sometimes exotic geographical surroundings of the East. For these reasons it is useful to examine some of the writings through one specific aspect of life writing, reading them through the tropes of travel writing.

Paul Fussell has described travel writing as 'a sub-species of memoir in which the autobiographical narrative arises from the speaker's encounter with distant or unfamiliar data and in which the narrative – unlike that of a novel or a romance – claims literal validity by constant reference to actuality'.[10] Although Fussell is principally concerned with travel writing between the wars, and pays very little attention to women travel writers of the period, his summary is appropriate in reading back through the developments of the nineteenth century. The evolution of travel writing in this period can be closely linked with the spirit of Empire that dominated British culture. As independent travellers and explorers navigated the Dominions and beyond, their writings tapped into the notions of adventure, conquest and glory at the heart of British expansion. Their successes represented not just an individual glory, as conveyed in the records of their travels which highlighted their achievements, but also a collective glory, a glory in British success as the conquests and the empire steadily grew.

Simultaneous with the growth of the British Empire, the development of Romanticism across Europe influenced the ways in which travellers reflected their experience. Carl Thompson suggests that 'from the late eighteenth century ... [t]ravel writing starts to look inwards as well as outwards',[11] reflecting a wider cultural shift in the perception and interpretation of the self. He goes on to argue that:

> With Romanticism, moreover, there came an increasing valorisation of travel, as a key means by which such *epiphanic* insights into the self might be achieved, and with them the greater degree of authenticity, autonomy and self-realisation that is usually assumed to follow from such self-knowledge....
>
> Travel writing in this mode presents the journeys being taken as an important rite of passage and as a process of self-realisation. Often indeed, they are figured as some sort of pilgrimage or quest, since these are traditionally two types of travel that bring about significant reinvention or renewal of the self.[12]

So these women's war narratives may be read as travel writings that both explore the external world and interrogate the internal. As well as learning about the war, we can study the landscapes through which they travel and understand the significant cultural implications of their various journeys, in physical, colonial and spiritual terms. But equally we can see the impact of experience on their sense of self, of identity, with the added factor of gender thrown into the mix.

Victorian travel writing was predominantly male in the first instance. Mary Louise Pratt identifies three primary facets of the 'Victorian discovery rhetoric' of these men, 'three conventional means which create qualitative and quantitative value for the explorer's achievement'.[13] Firstly the landscape is aestheticised, drawing upon the influences of both literary Romanticism and the Romanticism of landscape painting. Secondly, the landscape itself is represented in a language rich in adjectives suggesting a 'density of meaning in each passage'. And finally, Pratt suggests, there is 'the relation of mastery predicated between the seer and the seen'.[14]

This interpretation of male Victorian travel writing blends both the external and the internal; the aesthetic linguistic colonisation of the landscape provides the reflexive tools for the writers to look inward to their own journeys; the success is manifested in both physical conquest and self-discovery. But, as I shall argue elsewhere, this confidence and sense of superiority, engendered by Empire, is not unique to male experience. While it is true to say that women explorers were a much more unusual breed in the nineteenth century, some prospered nonetheless. And even if their own understanding of selfhood differed from that of their male counterparts, it had the same sense of British superiority at its roots. As Ruth Y. Jenkins suggests, 'This superiority, supporting and supported by Empire, contributed significantly to women's definitions of self, whether through complicity with Imperial ideals or through the opportunities found in distant spaces that such policies appropriated for British subjects.'[15] Women's Imperial subjectivity may have been substantially shaped by their subordinate status in society, but British society as a whole occupied a moral high ground that influenced both the men and women in its ranks.

A good example of this can be found in one of the best-known Victorian women travellers, Mary Kingsley. Kingsley spent most of her early life conforming to the role of the dutiful daughter. She cared for her ailing parents, as any self-respecting young woman might, until they died within six weeks of each other in 1892. Kingsley was then thirty, perhaps a little old for marriage. So she went travelling instead. She made two lengthy trips to Africa in 1893 and 1894, ostensibly to work gathering anthropological samples. Kingsley's adventures coincide with the 'scramble for Africa', when the European imperial powers, keen to expand their empires in a relatively untapped landmass, jostled for territories on the huge continent. The British Empire was the largest, and Mary Kingsley created a role for herself as an envoy. Determinedly British in every aspect of her selfhood, Kingsley even dressed as every inch the British woman, however inappropriate. Jane Robinson locates her thus:

> Her particular uniform was as much of anthropological interest as any garb she was likely to encounter on her travels. True to her type she presented, wherever she went, a neat trim figure in stiff, stayed black silk, black button boots and a perky black astrakhan hat. Even though blessed with a lusty sense of the ridiculous, and quite aware of how eccentric her position was as a clever and respectable Cambridge spinster conducting a search in the midst of Cameroon ... for 'fish and fetish' ... she played her part as a daughter of Empire and ambassador, should anyone be interested, for her sex.[16]

Kingsley wrote three books on her travels in West Africa, including one for Horace Marshall's 'Story of Empire' series, thus locating herself clearly within this discourse. These were extremely successful commercially, giving a new status to the idea of the woman traveller. Her writing fits well into two of Pratt's facets of 'Victorian discovery rhetoric' in terms of her language and representation of the landscapes she passes through. For example:

> I must say the forest scenery here was superbly lovely. Along this mountain side cliff to the mangrove swamp the sun could reach the soil, owing to the steepness and abruptness and the changes of curves of the ground; while the soft steamy air which came up from the swamp swathed everything, and although unpleasantly strong in smell to us, was yet evidently highly agreeable to the vegetation. Lovely wine palms and raffia palms, looking as if they had been grown under glass, so deliciously profuse was their feather-like foliage, intermingled with giant red woods, and lovely dark glossy green lianes, blooming in wreaths and festoons of white and mauve flowers, which gave a glorious wealth of beauty and colour to the scene.[17]

In this extract Kingsley emphasises the aesthetic qualities of the mangrove swamp, drawing out every sensual detail. She dwells on colour and shape and smell, enabling her reader to become immersed in the detail of the forest. This landscape is aestheticised and very visual. This fits in extremely well with another literary technique that Kingsley adopts elsewhere in her narrative: a second-person voice that directly addresses her reader. 'Knowing you don't like my going into details on such matters, I will confine my statement regarding leeches, to the fact that it was for the best that we had some trade salt with us.'[18] This is part of a similarly detailed discussion of leeches, so in fact Kingsley spares us nothing, but the direct address invites us to share her narrative in a surprisingly intimate way. Yet, unlike the works of some male Victorian travel writers, there is no particular sense here of a feeling of mastery. Kingsley claims no ownership of this land. As Pratt argues, 'far from taking possession of what she sees, she *steals* past'.[19] Indeed, quite contrary to notions of ownership, she is conscious of her own displacement. The mangrove swamp, 'unpleasantly strong in smell to us', is an alien landscape for the lady traveller: she is no more than an observer passing through and recording what she sees. As a lady traveller, it is the otherness of this African interior that fascinates her, rather than its value as a colonised territory.

Mary Kingsley was the same age as Mabel St Clair Stobart. Had Kingsley lived, it is not unreasonable to assume that she would have played an active part in the First World War with one of the many ladies' organisations. Indeed, Kingsley volunteered as a nurse in the Boer War, travelling out to South Africa in 1900. Unfortunately she died there within three months of her arrival. She would, no doubt, have had a great deal in common with Stobart, who was also a product of this Victorian Imperial culture. Like Kingsley, she was born in 1862. But Stobart was the fourth child of Samuel Bagster Boulton, a successful civil engineer and industrial pioneer in the timber and tar trade, who was later made a baronet. Like so many other girls of her class and generation, Stobart never went to school and was educated at home with her sisters, by governesses, while her brothers were sent away to Harrow and Oxford. And like many others, she educated herself through books, reading everything she could in her father's library and setting herself 'wide horizons'.[20] While her father was helping to build the railways that would underpin the empire, she was taking inspiration from the Romantic writers who had helped to shape the thinking of the day. The 'wide horizons' of which she speaks in her autobiography took shape four decades later as she became firstly a farmer in South Africa, and secondly a prominent figure in the development of women's hospital support in warfare. After the sudden, unexpected death of her first husband on his return from Africa, Stobart developed an interest in the Women's Suffrage Movement. Her absence from the country in the first years of the twentieth century meant she came to it a little late. She was not a supporter of the militant campaign, but instead believed that the best way forward was to demonstrate how useful women could be in times of war. She set up the WSWCC intent on showing the country that women had an important role to play in time of war. The WSWCC, a mobile hospital unit run and staffed by women, saw active service in the Balkan War of 1912. This led, inevitably, to her involvement in the First World War, during which, in Serbia, she became the first woman to lead a hospital unit to the front line.

Although notions of the sublime derived from her early reading may have had little impact on Stobart in her youth, they seem to have been foregrounded as she began to travel in her later life. Her Serbian writings, most prominently her 1916 book *The Flaming Sword in Serbia and Elsewhere*, effectively illustrate the influence of both Romanticism and the 'Victorian discovery rhetoric' so popular in her formative years. Stobart's record of her time in Serbia is almost as much a travelogue as it is a history. She seems to immerse herself in the landscapes and develops a fascination for the people. For much of the book she sets herself the task of describing the local population and their customs, in much the way that the imperial explorers of the nineteenth century might have done. However, her purpose is not colonisation, but to evoke sympathy in the reader to a political cause: Serbian relief. Some of her descriptions of landscape seem to resemble those of Kingsley.

> The road lay alongside the wide Morava, and we faced, all the time the forested Ovcharska mountains, 3,000 feet in height, a surprise of beauty even in this beautiful country. But when we turned the last corner, and found ourselves in the Ovcharska valley, I could scarcely contain my joy. A narrow and thickly-wooded valley, between high mountains, also densely forested; on the left of the wood, the adventurous Morava was rushing over boulders, and tumbling down steep rocks in quest of its looked-for Nirvana, in the sea, and on the right of the road, which wound in and out amongst the trees of a thick wood, were again high mountains.[21]

As with all the British women who worked in the Balkans, the beauty of the landscape overwhelms Stobart. Rugged, dramatic and *uncivilised*, it represents a world very different from the relative containment of England, although some of the Scottish women do see echoes of their homeland in the Balkan mountain ranges. Stobart's joy at the sight of the valley recalls the influence of the Romantic sublime. She personifies the river in order to reflect her own responses to what she sees. The Morava is 'adventurous', 'rushing' and 'tumbling', seeking Nirvana. Can this be how Stobart sees herself? She does not want to possess this landscape, but instead to use it to find something for herself, of herself, her own Nirvana. In this passage we get an inkling of how Stobart's narrative will come to represent that 'sub-species of memoir', one which uses the journey to explore herself and her beliefs.

Like other travellers, Stobart is also fascinated by the alien cultures of the local populations. Early in the narrative these are relatively untouched by war. Like other women writers she describes their dress, their diet, their religious practices and their family relationships, always contrasting them with her own. However, following the invasion of Serbia, the plight of the people becomes her primary concern. Here she describes soldiers and civilian refugees in retreat.

> I looked behind me, and saw, only darkness and sorrow, columns and confusion. Thousands of unoffending people were suffering heartache, separation, desolation; and as the guns reminded me, thousands of brave men were, a couple of miles away from us, facing at this moment,

a murderous death. How could I help asking myself where, in all this hell, is God?[22]

Stobart immediately answers her own question in a manner that directly illustrates the influence of both Romanticism and travel writing, by offering us an aestheticised landscape, filled with an emotion to temper the despair of the preceding paragraph.

> And immediately the answer came. As if in purposeful response, the mountains in the east threw off the blackness of the night, and showed rich purple against the lightening sky. Over the mountains rose clouds of gold, and pink, and aerial blue, and as the rays of sunlight shot triumphantly into the sky, white mists, thick and soft, that had lain hidden, became, for a moment of pure joy, bathed in all the rainbow colours; and one daring cloud of brilliant gold spread itself in the shape of a great dragon across the dark sky. Glories and beauties everywhere if we could only catch the meaning.[23]

Stobart's narratives are full of moments like this, moments of 'pure joy' in which she identifies closely with the landscape. There are a lot of adjectives in this passage. She endows the landscape with a power that seems able to overcome the desperate material circumstances that surround her. Sarah Mills argues that 'the representation of the sublime is crucial to a discussion of women's relation to landscape since the sublime subject is one who locates himself or herself in a particular spatial and power framework'.[24] Like women travel writers of the nineteenth century, Stobart locates herself in the landscape even though she is not of it. It should be empowering. For Kingsley it is. She writes, 'I luxuriated in the exquisite beauty of that valley, little thinking or knowing what there was in it besides beauty.'[25] But for Stobart, the sublime experience is tainted by the war. The need to articulate the landscape is overwhelmed by a more pressing purpose, both political and spiritual.

> But while I was wondering at it all, the glories vanished; the time for understanding had not yet come; the hills became commonplace, the prosaic light of the day was with us, and I saw once more the nightmare picture of the drab-dressed, mud-stained soldiers, splashing with their sandalled feet in the sloppy mud; sometimes stumbling, then rising, smothered with mud, without a word; weren't there worse troubles than that?[26]

Stobart borrows the techniques of travel writing, and it is clear that she wants her reader to experience the country. The writing is very sensual, drawing the reader into the dismal mud-filled scene as readily as it involves us in the aesthetic beauties of the sunrise. It is important that we understand Serbia, landscapes and identity. However, because this is also war writing, produced in mid-war, she has other agendas. Most significantly, it is political writing intended to alert contemporary readers to the plight of the Serbian people. It is also part of an exploration of self for Stobart, her spiritual self, as she tries to understand her own relationship with her religious faith.[27] While this appears to have the hallmarks of 'epiphanic insight' it does not yet achieve it.

Violetta Thurstan also adopts a language of sensuality to describe the travelogue aspect of her journey east. Thurstan was a trained nurse who worked for the Russian Red Cross in the early part of the war. Jane Potter has argued of *Field Hospital and Flying Column* (1915) the 'the narrative is propelled forward by the journeys'.[28] Following a number of adventures in Belgium at the beginning of the war, she travelled east to the Russian front through Scandinavia, before being posted to Warsaw. Thurstan was excited by the detour as it offered her the opportunity to gain a range of new experiences. Like Stobart, her instinct is to describe the inhabitants of the strange lands around the Arctic Circle.

> We went in the meantime to the little wooden inn and ate largely of strange dishes, dried reindeer flesh, smoked strips of salmon, lax, I think it is called, served with a curious sweet sauce, and drank many glasses of tea.... It seemed absolutely absurd to see a motor-car up there on the edge of the Arctic Circle, where there was not even a proper road. There were several reindeer sleighs about, and I felt that one of those would have been much more in keeping. The drivers look most attractive; they wear very gay reindeer leggings, big sheep-skin coats and wild-looking wolf-skin caps.[29]

Thurstan betrays a fascination with the 'otherness' of the Northern community, the different kinds of food, clothing and transport. There is no war in this account; Thurstan gives it over to the sensual in an entirely different way to Stobart. She wants to experience the pleasure of difference, and perhaps to colonise it. The exotic sleighs and drivers have a much greater appeal than the more mundane motor car. She continues:

> The frozen track was so uneven that we rocked from side to side, and were thrown violently about in the car, like little kernels in a very large nut. But it was a wonderful night all the same, the air was thin and

intoxicating like champagne, and the stars up in these northern lati-
tudes more dazzlingly brilliant than anything I have seen before.[30]

Although Thurstan's language is more prosaic than Stobart's, she is
interested in the sensuality of the experience nonetheless. The wonderful night, 'intoxicating like champagne', tips over into the sublime,
despite the preceding image of the nurses as nut kernels. Thurstan,
a trained nurse, will have been a product of a very different social
background from Stobart's. However, Christine Hallett has argued,
'Romanticism as a cultural form survived throughout the Victorian
era, and remained a strong element of the emotional lives of the
young people of Western Europe – both male and female – who participated in the war.'[31] Thurstan would certainly have been educated in
this cultural form and it may go some way to explaining what Hallett
terms her fusion of 'Russian exoticism with Western Romanticism'.[32]
What Thurstan seems to be seeking in the above extract is what Carl
Thompson terms 'a confrontation with alterity'. He writes that 'all travel
requires us to negotiate a complex and sometimes unsettling interplay
between alterity *and* identity, difference *and* similarity'.[33] Although the
primary purposes of the journeys undertaken by these women are not
the journey itself, the desire for this confrontation is unavoidable. It is a
part of the pioneering spirit that inspired the women to take up foreign
service in this war, service that would inevitably take them away from
the comfortable and familiar and into new territories. Writing in 1964,
former Red Cross nurse and SWH ambulance driver Elsie Corbett wrote
of herself and her lifelong companion whom she met in the service,
'Presumably we were the kind of people who wanted that kind of experience, and we got it.'[34] In undertaking this kind of war service, they all
become explorers, just like their nineteenth-century predecessors. And
this, to some extent, may explain the need to write down their experiences. Thompson continues:

> It is most obviously, of course, a report on the wider world, an account
> of an unfamiliar people or place. Yet it is also revelatory to a greater or
> lesser degree of the traveller who has produced that report, and of his
> or her values, preoccupations and assumptions. And by extension, it
> also reveals something of the culture from which that writer emerged,
> and/or the culture for which their text is intended.[35]

Hence Thurstan equates impulses generated by the starry sky with
the effects of champagne and is disappointed by the ordinary motor
car, and Stobart uses the contrast between the aestheticism of the

sunrise and the reality of the march to explore her own spiritual heritage. The women are all products of their social background, their class, their imperial upbringing, and this resonates through all the writing.

This confrontation with alterity, with difference, and the ways in which these women respond to it in writing can be very revealing. Few of the narratives contain much background information about the individual women; this is not their primary purpose. But their attitudes to the foreign landscapes and people help us to construct a bigger picture. As Casey Blanton suggests, 'what travel books are "about" is the interplay between observer and observed, between a traveller's own philosophical biases and preconceptions and the tests these ideas and prejudices endure as a result of the journey'.[36] Yvonne Fitzroy, a member of SWH, illustrates this effectively. Travelling through Russia she kept an extensive record of what she saw in her diary.

> *September 19th* [1916] In the Train.
>   We stopped at a most fascinating little wooden village for luncheon, though the filth was indescribable. It consisted of just one street, which was packed with open booths, peasants, beggars, and Jews. These last are far the best-looking members of the community – great sad-looking men in gaberdines, as different as possible from the horrid type of little town Jew. The glimpses one gets into the conditions of the peasant's life are appalling.[37]

Fitzroy's responses may make uncomfortable reading for the contemporary reader. At first glance the village is 'fascinating', implying a positive reaction on her part. However, as the diary entry progresses it becomes clear that it is anything but. The occupants of the village seem tarnished by the 'indescribable filth'. The most attractive occupants are the Jews, but as she completes her sentence it feels as though she is damning with faint praise – 'the horrid type of little town Jew' – injecting an undercurrent of anti-Semitism which can be found at various points in the narrative. Overall, the village, its conditions and its occupants shock Fitzroy. For her, the confrontation with alterity is a difficult one. Her attitudes may not have been unusual, but articulation of such ideas is fairly uncommon in these narratives. Fitzroy's discomfort with travel is apparent elsewhere in her diary, but is tempered by a sense of awe when her surroundings inspire her. Her response to Moscow and the Kremlin is quite different.

September 16th [1916] In the Train.

It's amazing. It's like walking into the Arabian Nights, into a great big fairy tale. A fairy palace over a fairy city and a fairy river.

Inside the little dim Cathedrals there is an unending chant, long-haired priests are officiating, and soldiers, peasants, or Red Cross Sisters, looking like medieval nuns, wander to and fro. They are all in the picture; the place is never marred by the unromantic pew, and the soft-footed dimness is alive to colour.... Outside the evening light is a miracle. The city below seems all gold crosses and painted domes, the red brick outer walls of the Citadel are glowing. It is beautiful this centre of Holy Russia – and mysterious – and – well, try travelling in a crowd for a week or two on ugly boats and trains, in ugly clothes, with a familiar and prosaic world behind you and, perhaps a rather terrible one to come, and then imagine what it feels like to be dropped suddenly for a short, short time into this strange Eastern City.[38]

This passage suggests that the act of travelling did not hold the same excitement for Fitzroy as it did for Violetta Thurstan or Mabel St Clair Stobart. There is no adventure in an uncomfortable train ride sandwiched between the 'prosaic' normal life of an Edwardian lady and the 'terrible' prospect of war service. But there is something innately spiritual in her reaction to the religious spaces of the Kremlin and the orthodoxy found there, that does seem to inspire that sense of the sublime once again. Indeed the beautiful centre of Holy Russia triggers for Fitzroy a kind of *epiphanic* insight, of the type that Stobart seeks. An understanding of the difference between this kind of religious observance and her own enables her explore her own feelings of spirituality in a way that she does not anticipate. She goes on to explore this in the same diary entry.

We Westerners seem, as it were, to have taken to ourselves all the credit of Christianity. We have born it away from this East, and have said, 'It is ours.' In England particularly, with our talent for common-sense, we have robbed it of so much that is beautiful. As if we could get on without it! And why should religion not appeal to the imagination? Here, no doubt, it walks hand-in-hand with ignorance, but what hope is there in the future if we cannot look forward to a union between imagination and scientific knowledge.[39]

The attraction of the East is dominant here, with religion as its centrepiece. The strange Eastern city with its unfamiliar ways of addressing the familiar inspires Fitzroy. It is precisely the *difference*, the *alterity*, of the encounter with Russian Orthodoxy that begins to liberate her own understanding of her spiritual self. It also helps her to examine cultural differences in a more sympathetic light as the beauty overpowers the ugliness of her journeying. Fitzroy does not revisit these sentiments in her diary; the experience of war nursing does not seem to assist her in this spiritual endeavour. But just for a moment, the journey offers her the possibility of a profound insight into both culture and self.

Ellen Chivers Davies, a member of the Second British Farmers' Unit in Serbia, published her extensive diary upon her return to Britain in 1916. Although Davies provides no background to the unit or indeed herself in her published diary, it gives a very comprehensive account of her war work. It is also a detailed travelogue that clearly embraces notions of alterity. In July 1915 she writes of the Serbian town of Posharevatz, seemingly untouched by the war.

> The shops in the town are very fascinating – there are rows of cobblers' shops with soft brown sandals, such as the peasants wear, hanging out-side on long strings, streets of coppersmiths where the workmen sit beating the metal into all kinds of delightful goods, and every draper's shop is gay with the bright handkerchiefs which women tie over their hair. They may be made in Manchester, probably they are, but I don't care and shall buy lots to take home.
>
> On Sunday and fete days – of which there are many – the peasants are particularly attractive and I am told that this is one of the three best districts in Serbia in which to see the typical dress of the country.[40]

Davies' narrative is one of the most effective at enabling the reader to engage with the culture and customs of the local communities. Like Kingsley, she layers her text with humour, 'they may be made in Manchester', here marking herself out as a traveller, even a tourist, an eager consumer of the new and strange products.[41] Not only is Davies interested in alterity, but she is also most attracted by difference. She wants the handkerchiefs to be unlike those made in Manchester, and the other goods produced in the town to represent this other, alternate world. Like all the British women, she seeks out the fetes and festivals, marvelling at traditional costumes that actually represent the 'everyday' for the Balkan people. The 'Slava'-day festival is a particular favourite. Mabel Stobart wrote, 'One day Major Protitch invited me and our treasurer to his Slava feast. Slava is the anniversary of the day on which the ancestors of the family were converted to Christianity.'[42] Most of the women who write about their time in Serbia recall being invited to Slava festivals, many of which were celebrated around them. Davies, in a new world, is excited by all the sights and sounds that surround her and has to share these with her readers. This taps into an established tradition with women travel writers. Here is Edith Durham with a detail from *Through the Lands of the Serb*.

> Ivanitza was so kind to me, and so beautiful, that in spite of its primitive accommodation I stayed on. As long as the food is good, one can stand rough surroundings well enough. The long street of picturesque, tumbledown wooden shops straggles along the valley; the West Morava tears through a wooded deep-cut gorge, and the cloud-capped mountains tower around. It was a lonely and lovely spot, and one that I shall never forget.
>
> On Sunday afternoon there was a little festival, and we sallied forth to a meadow about a mile and a half away. An ox-cart or two brought chairs, tables, beer, bread and cherries – all that Ivanitza required for a happy afternoon.[43]

Durham's description of the Morava resembles Stobart's. Her festival mirrors those in the writings of many of the women discussed here. She is enveloped by the landscape and absorbed into the culture, even as she emphasises its difference. Many areas of war-torn Serbia still share the characteristics of this idyllic festival picnic. However, Mark Mazower argues, 'Looking at the peasants dressed in their picturesque costumes, foreign visitors were struck by the persistence of what they regarded as an antiquated life form.'[44] There does seem to be an element of this in most accounts – the appeal of the Orient coming to the surface.

But Ellen Davies uses her travel writing in a different, more personal way, later in her diary. Like many British women in Serbia, she was posted to the spa town of Vrinjatcha Bania. She notes that 'there are so many English now that the Serbs have christened this place an "English town"'.[45] And it was here, in November 1915, that the invading Austrians and Germans took Davies prisoner, along with many other resident British women. During her period of captivity, which lasted until February 1916, Davies focused on the travel writing side of her diary. It is filled with lengthy passages about the landscape and the people of the town and surrounding mountains. But there is always the discomforting shadow of the war that colours these accounts. For example, her account of another Slava festival concludes thus:

> Usually these fete days are very gay, but this year there has been an undercurrent of sadness beneath the brave attempt at keeping the feast.

No one can forget that Serbia is not free, no one in Vrntse [*sic*] but has a brother or husband or son in the army, and of whose fate nothing as yet is known.[46]

Davies appears to develop this kind writing as a sort of therapy. Without her hospital work she becomes more involved with the local communities and her vivid descriptions of these relationships seem to offer a distraction from the reality of her captivity. She embeds herself in the beauty of the landscape and sharing it has the effect of escapism. Here is one such landscape, enjoyed in December 1915.

Under snow this mountain country is more beautiful, I think, even than Switzerland, for the sky has never that hardness, nor the light that sharp clarity which there silhouettes outlines into such intensity. Here there is mother-o'-pearl over everything, and from the snow peaks to the blue mist rising from the valley all is bathed in that wonderful light. In warmer days one lies on the short turf or in the oak forests and watches the life of the peasants in the villages beneath, while overhead is a soft blue sky and behind the clear Morava the hills are ever changing – a miracle in warm reds and browns, austere in dim purple or flushed with rosy pink as the late sun falls upon their slopes.[47]

This passage contains many of the tropes of travel writing. It conveys the sense of awe that might accompany a sublime experience. It is highly sensual, filled with colour and light. Davies uses many adjectives to present the landscape, which is both familiar, resembling Switzerland, and different, as the light casts it. It also represents an escape from the much more prosaic position, that of prisoner of war, in which she finds herself. Lying by the Morava, Davies can pretend that she is no more than a passing traveller enjoying the landscape. But the passage does something more. It seems to explore Davies' sense of herself, to reflect her emotional responses both to Serbia and to her situation. Sarah Mills suggests that 'women tend to see landscape in more relational ways; rather than seeking to subdue landscape, in their writings, they tend to represent and see landscapes in relation to their domestic spaces and networks of interaction'.[48] So for Davies the 'mother-o'-pearl' light cast over the mountains is almost opaque, allowing her not to see clearly, that is, enabling her to avoid seeing the realities of the war-torn landscape. The ever-changing hills beyond the Morava seem to offer choices depending on the colour they adopt, belying the lack of choice for the contemplating prisoner. They may be distant and inviting when warm, exciting when flushed or austere as the light fades, any of which could provide an escape. She watches the peasants, but is separate from them. This is almost voyeuristic, observing that which is 'other'. But she is no more connected to the sky or the river. The passage exudes a sense of the solitary; it is almost a transcendental experience. Davies' mountains and hills inspire a similar spiritual response to the one experienced by Yvonne Fitzroy in Moscow. Perhaps this is travel at its most satisfying despite the spectre of captivity.

When the Farmers' Unit learn that they are to leave Vrinjatcha Bania, they surreptitiously pass on all their belongings to the local population. They are astonished by the response that they get, illustrating the level of their engagement with the town's people.

> But I had not known the people would mind our going so much.... It spread like wild-fire all over the town, and we have spent most of our time making farewell visits. It is dreadful when the people actually break down as they try to say 'goodbye'.... Indeed, in spite of the wonderful good news for us, one cannot help feeling that these last days are bitter-sweet since one has learnt that one's presence matters in some odd inexplicable way, far more to the people in the town than ever one had the faintest idea of.[49]

While the country and the people have supported Davies through her period of captivity, so she has supported them as conquered peoples. The interest in community and custom recorded in her diary that has enabled her to cope with captivity has been reciprocal; an important cultural interface that can be found at the heart of many of the British women's narratives. Davies and her fellow unit members also have an important symbolic value to the local Serbs. Although they are all captives together, living under the occupation of the invading armies, the British women represent the Allies. In 1915 there was still hope that the armies of Britain and France would launch a counter attack to help the Serbs regain their territory. Although this was not immediately forthcoming, the presence of the British women, the human face of the Allies, went some way to bridging the gap in terms of morale, if nothing else.

It is clear then that many of these British women's narratives engage with an established tradition of travel writing, even where the text itself represents a more conventional autobiographical form. Carl Thompson suggests that there 'is a more general critical assumption that travel writing is usually and properly, a highly autobiographical form and a genre that is typically just as concerned to explore and present the subjectivity of the traveller-narrator as it is to explore and report the world'.[50] I do not believe that this is necessarily the case for all the British women who wrote testimonies of their experience on the Eastern Front during the First World War. Even those who dabbled with the genre of conventional autobiography had ulterior motives. Flora Sandes' first volume of autobiography, *An English Woman-Sergeant in the Serbian Army*, published in 1916, followed the fall of Serbia, with the primary objective of raising funds for and the profile of the defeated Serbs. It is a definite account of her transition from a nurse to a soldier, but it gives none of the back story one might expect from a conventional autobiography and its political and propagandist purpose strongly influences the style in which it is written. It does, however, draw on the characteristics of travel writing as a means of fulfilling this purpose. Sandes' descriptions of the Serbian landscape and sympathetic portrait of the Serbian people resemble those of the other women writers discussed, with a view to presenting a picture of a country that is worth saving. Sandes' second book, *The Autobiography of a Woman Soldier: A Brief Record of Adventures with the Serbian Army 1916–1919* (1927), is a more complete record of her wartime years. It is a much more down-to-earth book that more resembles the soldier memoirs that were becoming more popular in the late 1920s.

Paul Fussell has argued that these memoirs, too, have much in common with travel writing.

> The memorable war memoirs of the late 20s and early 30s, by Graves and Blunden and Sassoon, are very like travel books and would doubtless show different characteristics if they'd not been written in the travel context of the period between the wars. They are ironic or parodic or nightmare travels, to France and Belgium, with the channel ferries and forty-and-eights replacing the liners and chic trains of real travel, with dugouts standing for hotel-rooms and lobbies and other ranks serving the travel-book function of 'native' porters and servants.[51]

All this can also be said of the British women's memoirs, except their journeys are through Serbia, Russia and Rumania, territories even more alien than the Western Front. Elsie Corbett first travelled out to Salonika in May 1915 on a luxury steam yacht. She was working for the Red Cross, but her aristocratic background may have influenced the mode of travel. She returned to Serbia in August 1916, no doubt somewhat altered by the experience of having lived through invasion and imprisonment. This time she travelled on a hospital ship with the SWH, and found the experience much more appropriate. Instead of dugouts, the women slept in billets and tents, experiences that influenced their memoirs and accounts. Mabel Dearmer, a member of the Stobart SRF3, wrote, 'I have learned how to strike and pitch my own tent – (the clothing tent is a kind of Marquee!) – and also I am much stronger in the arms than I thought I was, and can hammer in my own tent pegs and lift packing-cases that a month ago I shouldn't have dreamt of touching.'[52] For the women, it is their Serbian orderlies or the Austrian prisoners of war who do the heavy work in their hospitals, taking on the roles Fussell denotes as 'native'. All the elements to connect life writing and travel writing can be found.

Carl Thompson goes on to argue that:

> Travel writing has frequently provided a medium in which writers can conduct an autobiographical project, exploring questions of identity and selfhood whilst simultaneously presenting to others a self-authored and as it were 'authorised' account of themselves. Moreover the generic requirement to include an element of personal detail ensures that travelogues will often offer interesting insights into what is sometimes termed an individual's *subject position*, even when travel writers have not deliberately set out to write in such a reflective fashion.[53]

One frustrating aspect of many of the British women's narratives is the lack of personal details means that it becomes difficult to ascertain with any degree of certainty who they were before they travelled east. Elsie Corbett published her account in 1964, based on her diaries of the time. She includes a Foreword explaining her upper-class background and offers snippets of information about how she has spent the intervening years. Yet her reworking of the diaries rather distracts from the authentic formation of a *subject position*. We get the memoir through the lens of an elderly woman, distilled by almost fifty years of life. She begins her account with a sort of disclaimer that has a profound impact on how we read the following pages.

> Having had brothers, cousins and friends in two World Wars I know very well how sheltered we in Serbia were from the dangers, discomforts and frustrating boredom that alternated for the men in the fighting forces. Scores of women mountaineers and explorers have endured far more hardships, for fun; and women ambulance drivers during the blitz on London in 1940 were in far greater danger than we ever were.

We were seldom short of food, or lacking some kind of shelter for the night, even if it was only an ill-pitched tent; and our surroundings were always supremely beautiful as well as extremely interesting.[54]

Much of what follows belies this assertion. Corbett drove ambulances under fire, spent long hours working in hospitals and had colleagues blown to pieces by shells. And she might have felt differently and remembered differently had she taken part in the great retreat of the winter of 1915. In her narrative it is always unclear whether she is quoting from her diary or paraphrasing it. She thus controls the impression of self that we receive, endowing it with a hindsight missing from the other accounts. That said, this is very much an 'authorised' account of the self. And it is also a self who stands the strongest comparison with 'women mountaineers and explorers', which speaks volumes about how she sees her role in Serbia. While she may not recall the danger, she does remember it as an adventure.

Conversely, Ellen Davies puts very few personal details into her account. We are told nothing of her former life, although we might infer an agricultural connection from her membership of the Second Farmers' Unit. However, Davies never explains her unit, nor gives any information about its genesis. As her account was published immediately after her return from Serbia in 1916, there is no indication of how she spent the rest of her life or how her wartime experiences might have impacted on it. However, as we have already seen, Davies' text, a probable reproduction of her diaries, in fact builds an interesting, and no doubt unconscious, *subject position* when read through the various tropes of both travel and life writing. She tells us very little about herself, but she shows us a great deal through her self-reflexive prose. Davies' is one of the most detailed and fully rounded accounts of life in Serbia. The reader gets a very strong sense of place and environment. And the immediacy of the account ensures that the full horror of the enveloping war is represented, cutting into the landscapes and their inhabitants.

It is no accident that most of the British women's accounts of their experiences in the East are based on private diaries. And although many were published shortly after composition, they quickly fell out of print and out of the public eye. Their accounts were always subordinated to those of men. Women's experience was always, as Virginia Woolf puts it, 'locked in old diaries, stuffed away in old drawers, half obliterated in the memories of the aged'.[55]

Rebecca Hogan has argued that the diary was a particularly appropriate form of life writing for women, as it is located principally in the domestic sphere. 'The diary's valorisation of the detail, its perspective of immersion, its mixing of genres, its principle of inclusiveness, and its expression of intimacy and mutuality all seem to qualify it as a form congenial to women life/writers.'[56] Although the women in Serbia and Russia were distinctly removed from the domestic sphere, they did, to some extent, take it with them. And the characteristics of diary writing that Hogan identifies can be found across the spectrum in these Eastern war narratives and relate equally well to characteristics of women's travel writing explored here. Casey Blanton suggests that:

> Women's voices contrive to tell stories about foreign places, despite the fact that their texts have been less well received than those of their male counterparts. One reason for this is that the genesis of women's authorship was typically found in the private: in diaries, letters, and photo albums – texts that remained close to the home and the family. Paradoxically perhaps, travel writing's close connection to these kinds of texts, especially the memoir, allowed women entry into the travel genre, even though respect for their books would be delayed.[57]

Diaries, letters and photographs[58] form the basis for almost all the texts considered here. And they tend to reinforce Carl Thompson's suggestion that 'there is a greater tendency for women travellers to concern themselves with the minutiae of everyday living arrangements such as food preparation, childcare and the laundering of clothes'.[59] Elsie Corbett spent much of her time in Vrinjatcha Bania working in a children's ward treating the range of infectious diseases that afflicted the local community. Later as an ambulance driver on the move with the Serbian army, she was always looking for someone to wash the unit's clothes. The way in which many of these women incorporated the experiences and value systems of the domestic sphere into their war work will be considered in a later chapter. But the ways in which they choose to write their lives and their journeys draw heavily on the experiences of their earlier lives, their places in Edwardian society and the modes of writing most commonly associated with women writers of the nineteenth century. All these factors taken together, it is clear that the study of these narratives will lead to the painting of a much bigger picture. And the enticing, alien setting of the East provides the perfect backdrop.

Notes

1 John Keegan, *The First World War* (London: Hutchinson, 1998), p. 55.
2 Christine E. Hallett, *Containing Trauma: Nursing Work in the First World War* (Manchester and New York: Manchester University Press, 2009), pp. 148–9.
3 Philippe Lejeune, cited in Linda Anderson, *Autobiography* (London: Routledge, 2001), p. 2.
4 Liz Stanley, *The Autobiographical I: The Theory and Practice of Feminist Auto/Biography* (Manchester: Manchester University Press, 1992), p. 11.
5 Shari Benstock, *The Private Self: Theory and Practice of Women's Autobiographical Writings* (Chapel Hill and London: University of North Carolina Press, 1988), p. 20.
6 Trev Lynn Broughton and Linda Anderson (eds), *Women's Lives/Women's Times: New Essays in Auto/Biography* (Albany: State University of New York Press, 1997), p. 5.
7 Rebecca Hogan 'Engendered Autobiographies: The Diary as a Feminine Form', *Prose Studies* 14:2 (1991), p. 102.
8 Suzanne L. Bunkers and Cynthia A. Hoff (eds), *Inscribing the Daily: Critical Essays on Women's Diaries* (Amherst: University of Massachusetts Press, 1996), p. 1.
9 Stanley, *The Autobiographical I*, pp. 3–4.
10 Paul Fussell, *Abroad: British Literary Travelling between the Wars* (Oxford and New York: Oxford University Press, 1982), p. 203.
11 Carl Thompson, *Travel Writing* (London and New York: Routledge, 2011), p. 111.
12 *Ibid.*, p. 115.
13 Mary Louise Pratt, *Imperial Eyes: Travel Writing and Transculture* (London and New York: Routledge, 1992), p. 204.
14 *Ibid.*, p. 204.
15 Ruth Y. Jenkins, 'The Gaze of the Victorian Woman Traveller: Spectacles and Phenomena', in Kristi Siegel (ed.), *Gender, Genre and Identity in Women's Travel Writing* (Oxford and New York: Peter Lang, 2004), p. 15.
16 Jane Robinson (ed.), *Unsuitable for Ladies: An Anthology of Women Travellers* (Oxford and New York: Oxford University Press, 1994), p. 189.
17 Mary H. Kingsley, from *Travels in West Africa: Congo Français, Corisco and Cameroons* (London: Macmillan, 1897), quoted in Mary Morris (ed.), with Larry O'Connor, *The Virago Book of Women Travellers* (London: Virago, 1996), p. 65.
18 *Ibid.*, p. 68.
19 Pratt, *Imperial Eyes*, p. 214.
20 Mabel St Clair Stobart, *Miracles and Adventures* (London: Rider & Co., 1935), p. 14.
21 Mabel St Clair Stobart, *The Flaming Sword in Serbia and Elsewhere* (London, New York and Toronto: Hodder and Stoughton, 1917), p. 104.

22 *Ibid.*, p. 176.

23 *Ibid.*

24 Sarah Mills, *Gender and Colonial Space* (Manchester and New York: Manchester University Press, 2005), p. 84.

25 Kingsley, in Morris, *The Virago Book of Women Travellers*, p. 66.

26 Stobart, *The Flaming Sword*, pp. 176–7.

27 For a detailed discussion of this issue see Angela K. Smith, 'The Mists Which Shroud These Questions: Mabel St Clair Stobart, the First World War and Faith', *Literature and History*, 3rd series, 20:2 (2011), 1–15.

28 Jane Potter, *Boys in Khaki, Girls in Print: Women's Literary Responses to the Great War 1914–1918* (Oxford: Clarendon Press, 2005), p. 171.

29 Violetta Thurstan, *Field Hospital and Flying Column: Being the Journal of an English Nursing Sister in Belgium and Russia* (New York: G. P. Putnam's Sons, 1915, p. 105.

30 *Ibid.*, pp. 105–6.

31 Christine E. Hallett, 'Russian Romances: Emotionalism and Spirituality in the Writings of "Eastern Front" Nurses, 1914–1918', *Nursing History Review* 17:1 (2009), p. 108.

32 *Ibid.*, p. 107.

33 Thompson, *Travel Writing*, p. 9.

34 Elsie Corbett, *Red Cross in Serbia 1915–1919* (Banbury: Cheney & Sons, 1964), p. 140.

35 Thompson, *Travel Writing*, p. 9.

36 Casey Blanton, *Travel Writing: The Self and the World* (London and New York: Routledge, 2002), p. 5.

37 Yvonne Fitzroy, *With the Scottish Nurses in Roumania* (London: John Murray, 1918), p. 20.

38 *Ibid.*, pp. 17–18.

39 *Ibid.*, pp. 18–19.

40 Ellen Chivers Davies, *A Farmer in Serbia* (London: Methuen & Co., 1916), p. 42.

41 For a discussion of the difference between 'travel writing' and 'tourist writing' see James Buzard, *The Beaten Track: European Tourism, Literature, and the Ways to Culture 1800–1918* (Oxford: Clarendon Press, 1993).

42 Stobart, *The Flaming Sword*, p. 31. Stobart goes on to describe this ceremony in some detail. Davies describes a similar ceremony in her account, *A Farmer in Serbia*, pp. 199–200.

43 Edith Durham, *Through the Lands of the Serb* (London: Edward Arnold, 1904), quoted in Robinson, *Unsuitable for Ladies*, p. 103. For more information on Edith Durham (1863–1944), political missionary, see Jane Robinson, *Wayward Women: A Guide to Women Travellers* (Oxford: Oxford University Press, 1990), pp. 260–1.

44 Mark Mazower, *The Balkans: From the End of Byzantium to the Present Day* (London: Phoenix Press, 2001), p. 29.

45 Davies, *A Farmer in Serbia*, p. 154.

46 *Ibid.*, pp. 200–1.

47 *Ibid.*, pp. 180–1.

48 Mills, *Gender and Colonial Space*, p. 76.

49 Davies, *A Farmer in Serbia*, p. 223.

50 Thompson, *Travel Writing*, p. 97.

51 Fussell, *Abroad*, p. 206.

52 Mabel Dearmer, *Letters from a Field Hospital* (London: Macmillan and Co., 1916), p. 121.

53 Thompson, *Travel Writing*, p. 99.

54 Corbett, *Red Cross in Serbia 1915–1919*, p. vii.

55 Virginia Woolf, 'Women and Fiction', in *Collected Essays* (London: Hogarth Press, 1966), vol. 2, p. 141.

56 Rebecca Hogan, 'Engendered Autobiographies: The Diary as Feminine Form', *Prose Studies* 14:2 (1991), p. 105.

57 Blanton, *Travel Writing*, p. 57.

58 Almost all the books contain photographs taken by the women, many of which illustrate their experiences as travellers more comprehensively than their war work. Florence Farmborough in particular compiled a comprehensive visual record, *Russian Album 1908–1918* (Salisbury: Michael Russell, 1979).

59 Thompson, *Travel Writing*, p. 186.

2

Early days: the typhus colony and other stories

Camp life suits us all. Many of us have camp beds and sleep out in the open, and feel very much 'shut in' on wet nights when we have to sleep under canvas. I don't know how we shall ever return to civilised life.[1]

There are days I feel I cannot go on with this load of responsibility, and there is no one here who can really take the lead.... [I]t is the general administration, the healing of our own sick people, and so on that is so distracting and wears one out, and living in a crowd like we do.[2]

The first British women to go east had a very tough time, but not necessarily in the ways they had expected. Inevitably, some coped better than others, embracing the freedoms of their new lives. On arrival, the first women's units had to deal with all the horrors of war as the Serbian army repelled the first invasion of Austrian troops. But despite the war-weary condition of the Serbs, they won a great victory in the first few months of the war and the beginning of 1915 saw the arrival of up to 90,000 Austrian prisoners of war. However, the lack of facilities for so many prisoners led to a new crisis. The Austrians brought with them an even greater enemy: typhus.

It was Serbia's grievance with Austria that had triggered the outbreak of war and it was not surprising that Austria's anger had presented Serbia as a nation with the major military threat of 1914. John Keegan suggests that 'Austria's principal emotional, if not rational, war aim, however, remained the punishment of Serbia, which had precipitated the July crisis by its involvement in the Sarajevo assassinations.'[3] Austria invaded Serbia on 12th August 1914, no doubt assuming that the armies would find an enemy already exhausted by war. Keegan goes on to argue that the attack 'revealed how little the Austrians understood the Serb's military qualities. In Vienna they were thought of as backward semi-barbarians.'[4] However, the Serbian military response was very effective and the Austrians were soon driven back. They invaded again in September, and at first appeared to have much more success. The Serbian army had run very short of ammunition and was awaiting fresh supplies. However, once these arrived from France, the Serbs rebuffed the Austrian invasion, again with much success. Lady Paget's and Mabel Groutich's SRF units, first on the scene, would have encountered the wounded of these early battles, but by December 1915, the Austrian army had been driven out of the country again, leaving behind the tens of thousands of prisoners of war.[5] The many wounded lingered in the hospitals, however, as these were gravely understaffed and unable to care for them properly. Most importantly, sanitary conditions were appalling as a consequence of lack of staff, supplies and understanding.

The British women arriving in Serbia in the autumn of 1914 found this inevitable backlog of wounded from the early fighting, but in the months that followed, Serbia entered a kind of 'phoney war'. After the withdrawal of Austrian troops, no further attack was made on Serbia until after Bulgaria entered the war in September 1915, leading to a much more significant invasion by three armies (Austrian, Bulgarian and German) in October 1915. But the intervening months presented a very different kind of enemy, and one that tested the depleted Serbian medical forces every bit as much as the battlefield: infectious disease. In the winter of 1914–15, Serbia became the victim of a devastating typhus epidemic, exacerbated by the shocking sanitary conditions across the country, particularly in hospitals. Leah Leneman notes:

> Typhus is a cold weather disease, carried by human body lice. It thrives in crowded, dirty conditions.... The disease was carried into Germany and Austria by Russian prisoners who infected the troops; Austrians captured by Serbs then infected the Serbian population. Estimates of the numbers who died in the epidemic ranged from 100,000 to 130,000. Of the country's 450 doctors at least 360 were infected and more than 120 died.[6]

The British medical units could not have arrived at a more opportune moment. Despite bringing with them inoculation, sanitation, valuable understanding of infectious disease and medical expertise, their first work of the war was a serious challenge. They set about caring for and curing the many Serbian soldiers who were filling the inadequate hospitals. However, they could not do this quickly enough to prevent the spread of infection. By January 1915 things were beginning to look grim.

The first SWH unit to arrive in Serbia in late 1914, led by Dr Eleanor Soltau, quickly became a fever hospital. They were posted to Kragujevatz, a key military point for the Serbian army. Eventually there were a number of hospitals here. Leneman notes that one tenth of all the typhus cases in the country occurred in this town.[7] As Eva Shaw McLaren notes in her *The History of the Scottish Women's Hospitals* (1919), 'the atmosphere was terrible – fit breeding ground for the plague which was about to descend on this already sorely stricken people'.[8] McLaren goes on:

> Towards the end of January the grim horrors of typhus darkened the land. On 23rd January Dr Soltau telegraphed and wrote to the Committee in Edinburgh. The telegraph ran as follows: 'Dire necessity for fever nurses. Can you send me ten or more overland? Equipment, mattresses, covers, blankets, linen, milk, typhol, carbolic, tow, caster oil.'[9]

McLaren's language is rather typical of the period. She adopts a kind of biblical melodrama to emphasise the desperate nature of the situation. This is a 'plague' descending on a 'sorely stricken' people. She echoes the much more abrupt telegraphic language of Soltau's 'dire necessity'. Monica Krippner argues that Soltau's use of the word 'dire' was strategic, intended to get past the Serbian censor.[10] The Serbian authorities were attempting to suppress news of the typhus epidemic, not wanting to publicise their vulnerability. But help was sent. McLaren worked for the SWH in Edinburgh rather than on the front line. However, when she wrote her history after the war, it must have seemed important to valorise the activities of the women, to ensure that the reading public understood precisely what their countrywomen had faced. McLaren was also Elsie Inglis' sister, so would have had her own personal reasons, no doubt, for ensuring that the women were understood and appropriately commemorated.

That said, it would be wrong to suggest that this valorisation is inappropriate. Nursing typhus was extremely dangerous. By late January, Soltau was already under severe stress. Lady Paget at Skopje was faced not only with many sick Serbs but was also surrounded by thousands of Austrian prisoners of war, all susceptible to the disease. While the Serbians themselves were reluctant to nurse their enemies, Paget was not and arranged with the government for a specialised fever hospital for the Austrians, called the pavilions, based in a barracks in the mountains above the town. The matron, Flora Scott, wrote a newspaper account of the project upon her return to England.

> Needless to say the barracks were in a filthy condition. They took a lot of getting ready. While this was being done the doctors sought out the patients. It was a ghastly business. In the basement of the barracks about 2000 Austrians were found. Many of them were dead, only 40 were able to stand, and they had been without food, water or light for five days.[11]

Scott's fact-based report gives an indication of the kind of conditions with which the women were confronted. There does not seem to have been much ill feeling towards the Austrian prisoners, many of whom were of Serbian origin. Indeed they provided valuable service for all the women's hospitals as orderlies throughout 1915. But their welfare was still the lowest priority, so they became even more susceptible to the 'plague'. And nursing such an infectious disease is no easy matter.

> Lady Paget, three doctors, two sisters, and one nurse went up [to the POW hospital]. No one was asked to go typhus being so dangerous. It was voluntary work. Lady Paget caught typhus almost the third day. This meant one of us nursing her. The other sister went, leaving nurse and me in the pavilions. Within the next ten days two of the doctors and a nurse took it. Oh, what a terrible time that was. It left only one doctor and myself. We tried to get help but could not, and I managed for about nine or ten days.[12]

Although the hospital units took with them considerable knowledge of how to prevent the spread of infectious disease, the isolation of this prisoners' hospital and the difficulty finding staff presented severe problems. British surgeon James Johnston Abraham was also working in the barrack hospital. He had travelled to Serbia with the First British Red Cross Serbian Mission, having been turned down by the War Office just as Elsie Inglis had been rejected. Her crime was being a woman; his was his age. Abraham was considered too old to be of use to the British army. He was thirty-eight.[13] Abraham encountered the same difficulty in staffing his fever hospital. He lost seven of his twelve orderlies and was forced to borrow one of Paget's nurses, Sister Fry, to complete his personnel. They were the only ones who came through without infection.[14] Back in Kragujevatz, the SWH coped better. One sister at the fever hospital wrote, 'The Hospital was quite half a mile from our home, lying as it did on the outskirts of the town, but we were generally glad of the walk and attributed partly to it that the health of the nurses remained good.'[15] The fresh air seemed to make all the difference. Scott, confined and over-worked, also appeared to lack some of the facilities for precaution adopted by the SWH, as McLaren recalls.

> Instead of the usual uniform and apron, we wore a white cotton combination garment with the ends tucked into high leather riding-boots. Over this, for the sake of appearance, an overall was worn, and our hair was entirely covered with a tight fitting cap. Round neck and arms we wore bandages soaked in camphor oil, and our boots were smeared with some, so that no encouragement was given to the little insect by which typhus is spread.[16]

Abraham recorded that 'We used to smear our bodies with a mixture of "Vaseline" and paraffin oil to keep the lice off us; and to this I attribute the fact that we both came through unscathed. For, though we did not know it then, the disease was carried by lice.'[17] The units who arrived in Serbia later in the year echoed these precautions, as well as ensuring that all staff had as many inoculations as possible before they arrived. Finally pulled away from the Western Front, Mabel St Clair Stobart arrived in April 1915. She was determined to house her hospital in tents in order to prevent the spread of typhus. It was decided that this hospital, the SRF3, unlike its predecessor, should not deal with typhus patients. This made it even more important to keep the disease out. Stobart notes:

> [A]ll wore a quaint-looking combination garment made of white batiste, which fastened tightly round the neck, the trouser feet, and wrists. Long boots, rubber gloves, and an oilskin bathing cap completed the fancy dress. This anti-lice armour, together with other methods, successfully kept at bay the lice which carry typhus infection.[18]

Stobart's unit arrived after the worst of the epidemic was over, which may account for some of the flippancy of the tone. Typically, also, she is less concerned with appearance. But for Flora Scott, caught up with the very worst of the devastation, there was no such easy respite.

> It was terrible. At times I felt so helpless I did not know where to go and what to do first, and I began to wonder whether it was really worth going on. We were short of clothes, water, food and fires. It was too awful to see these poor creatures suffering and in want, yet helpless to

do or give. The cold was intense, and there were deep snows, yet I could only give each man one army blanket. Many had not even shirts. Often I felt I must give in. Yet on going round their faces would light up, and they were so grateful for the slightest attention it repaid one for all one's work.[19]

Scott's despair echoes that of Soltau in the opening letter. Things gradually improved for Scott as more British medical staff arrived and convalescent Austrians began to act as orderlies. By the time she left Serbia in the last week of May 1915, the epidemic was more or less over. Abraham, too, left in May 1915. During his period of service in Serbia his weight had dropped from 12 stones to 8 stones 4 pounds, physical evidence of the hardships he had endured.[20] The experience had clearly marked Flora Scott deeply, too. Although she did not return to Serbia, she did continue to nurse the wounded in England and she was decorated with the Serbian Cross, Order of St Sava by the Serbian army for her contribution. Scott continued to write a regular column for the *Leicester Daily Post*, 'Letters from Miss Scott', for the duration of the war. Its popularity lay in the blend of the public and the private found in her writing, as demonstrated here. Much of the narrative is reportage, facts and figures that the reader may trust. Then there is a sudden injection of the personal, 'it was terrible ... at times I felt so helpless', allowing the woman to slip through. This is an effective combination, offering the reader both information and empathy. Indeed it is a common characteristic of much of the writing of the British women in Serbia.

British support during this period of dangerous infection seems to have been vital to the Serbian authorities. Their own medical provision was so depleted that they simply would not have coped. In April 1915 the SWH lent the Serbians two of their doctors to run a typhus hospital in Belgrade. Adeline Campbell and Katherine MacPhail recorded the difficulties they faced in a letter to SWH headquarters.

We find here a great scarcity of doctors – one doctor attempting to deal with 800 typhus cases in the military hospital. The Authorities are very anxious that we should work here but we are finding it difficult to get conditions as we would have them both for the patients and ourselves but we hope after a few days delay to take one or two isolation blocks in the military hospital.

In Serbia at present it is impossible to stand aside from this epidemic – and to have remained with the Unit at Kraguievatz would have been a wasted opportunity. It seems a type of work that can only be effectively tackled by British people in this country. Previously there have been no English people doing medical work in Belgrade and the American Mission which is the only foreign unit, is not undertaking typhus.[21]

Here the doctors were not only concerned with their humanitarian role, but also had an understanding of the importance of their nationality when it came to war service. As British women, from a more medically advanced country, they were able to offer the kind of support that was most needed and otherwise unavailable.

The dangers presented by typhus, identified by Scott and others, did represent a real threat to the British women. Lady Paget recovered from her typhus, but some women working through this 'phoney war' were not so lucky. Dr Elizabeth Ross was one of the few lone women working in Serbia in 1915. She had a particular specialism in tropical medicine and was an ideal addition to the staff of one of the fever hospitals at Kragujevatz. Although independent, she valued the companionship of the Scottish women also based in the town. When she fell ill with the disease in February 1915, they went up to the fever hospital to nurse her, but to no end, and she died on 14th February. In March the SWH suffered a high-profile casualty. Before the war Madge Neill Fraser had been a professional golfer, the captain of the Scottish Women's International team. In 1915 she was multitasking, working as a nurse, a dresser and a chauffeur with Elsie Inglis. Her death from typhus came as a great shock. Inglis' lengthy account of her funeral is worth recording as it gives a good indication of the impact of Fraser's death on all those around her.

> The funeral which took place on Wednesday March 10th, of Madge Neill Fraser, was very impressive. It was conducted according to the rites of the Greek Church, and with military honours. Between one and two hundred people were present – the Scottish Unit of course, in full force – then there was the representative of the Crown Prince; the leading Serbian medical and military attaches; members of the R.A.M.C. (English) commission just come out; members of the Russian Medical Unit working in Serbia; and besides a large number of civilians ...
>
> It was nearly five o'clock, and whereas all the afternoon the sky had been perfectly overcast, just as the cemetery was approached, a ray of light appeared all around the horizon, as if Nature herself could not allow that the giving of any life for others should be a matter of only gloom and tragedy. The regret and distress expressed on all hands was genuine and touching in the extreme: one little Serbian lady was

overwhelmed. She kept murmuring in her foreign accent during all the procession: 'It is so noble – so noble. To give one's life for La Patrie is fine, but to give it for the country of another, that is incredible.'[22]

This account demonstrates a number of things. The Greek Orthodox Service and the full military honours indicate the degree to which these women have been absorbed into both the civilian and military communities. The impressive range of attendees reinforces this, illustrating how far this esteem is carried. Even Serbian royalty is represented. The British military and the international community pay their respects. But Inglis' inclusion of the emotional tribute paid by the single 'little Serbian lady' grounds the ceremony in the personal, despite the presence of so many major institutions. And the invocation of 'Nature herself' gives the whole event a kind of mystical quality. All these things combine in an attempt by Inglis to justify the loss of Fraser, but have the effect of emphasising the shock. A memorial fund for Fraser was set up to raise money for the SWH for the rest of the war, drawing on her celebrity status, and a hospital unit was named after her.

Another celebrated British woman, Mabel Dearmer, died in Serbia in 1915, not from typhus at all, but from typhoid, despite the fact that all staff had been vaccinated against the disease before travelling east.[23] The Stobart camp may have been successful at keeping typhus out but they did suffer an outbreak of typhoid in July 1915. One of the first victims was Stobart herself, but with typical bravado, she makes light of her own illness. The camp experienced their first air raid while she lay ill. 'Typhoid or no typhoid, I jumped out of bed to see what had happened', she writes, watching the bombs fall and the planes sail away. 'I then went back to bed to go on with my typhoid. I ought to have died, but I don't do things that I ought.'[24] Here Stobart chooses to show the reader something of herself, her own refusal to be beaten by anything. But she also uses the typhoid of others to explore aspects of herself and her belief systems. *The Flaming Sword*, while on the one hand a political and feminist treatise, is also an exploration of the spiritual that reflects Stobart's own deliberations with faith during the war years.[25]

The SRF3 camp saw two deaths from typhoid in July 1915. The first was a nurse, Lorna Ferriss. The second was Dearmer, an artist and dramatist, who had been working as the orderly in charge of linen, and whose husband was the chaplain.[26] She became ill in early June but appeared to be making a full recovery when the camp was distracted by the death of Ferriss. Following this funeral, however, Dearmer unexpectedly took a turn for the worse and died several days later. Stobart kept a nightly vigil at Dearmer's bedside, giving herself the time to contemplate the meaning of life and death in a world where life appears increasingly cheap.

> I sat a little apart from the other watchers, and prayed – not now that she should live – life seemed too small a thing to pray for, but that our souls should be illumined to see the meaning of death. Another flash of lightning, and I saw that there is no such thing as death. Death is a misunderstanding of the mind. The body does not die, for the body has never lived; the body is matter and inert. Life is a force, forces do not die. The body is the habitation of the life-force, but the quitting of the life-force of the body, is not death. Nothing has died since nothing has ceased to live. The life-force cannot die – it has never lived; yes, yes – death is a misnomer.... Why then talk of death as though it were an ending? It is a transference of life-force from the seen to the unseen. As soon as matter begins to disintegrate, the life-force passes on – that's all. I understood.[27]

At Mabel Dearmer's death-bed Stobart experienced a startling epiphany, the beginning of a new spiritual creed. Stylistically, this passage is typical of *The Flaming Sword*. It takes the form of a dialogue with herself, a serious of short phrases connected by repetitions that trace her journey from the lightning bolt to the revelation. Each step is calculated and illustrated; each question answered. The trajectory suggests that answering this greatest of questions, what happens to the soul after death, follows a logical, almost scientific path to an inevitable conclusion. No doubt exhaustion, trauma, a feeling of responsibility, guilt and despair all played a part in the reaching of this understanding. But in trying to comprehend this death, so close to home, so much closer than the deaths of the peasants and soldiers to which she had become accustomed, Stobart looks for something more than conventional Christian faith can offer her. It rather echoes Inglis' calling upon 'Nature herself' as witness. A benevolent God would not allow this death, all these deaths, if it were simply the end: 'In the early morning, as a gust of wind swept through the tent – her tent – the life-force passed.... But I knew that the life-force had carried with it all that was real; it had taken to the Beyond Land the idea, the logos, the norm, the soul, of which the body that was left, was only a graven image.'[28] As with much of Stobart's writing, there is an eye to dramatic effect here, fortified by her use of biblical imagery, the graven image powerfully juxtaposed against the soul. But her conclusions are not biblical. *The Flaming Sword*, already built around important political messages, was not the place to elaborate on her developing Spiritualist ideas, but they are apparent nonetheless. This, and later epiphanies in Serbia, shake Stobart's religious faith to its core, but in 1916 she was not yet ready to abandon it. However, she does go on to question a god who allows this and so many other tragedies, as her journey through the book continues.

Elisabeth Ross, Lorna Ferriss and Mabel Dearmer were all given military funerals like Madge Neill Fraser and are all buried together in the cemetery at Kragujevatz. An annual commemoration ceremony still takes place every February at the graveside, an indication of the heroic status the women acquired among the Serbs. But for some of the British women in Serbia, the summer of 1915 was a relatively uneventful time. Some, like Gertrude Pares in the letter quoted at the start of this chapter, even enjoyed themselves. The fighting had temporarily stopped, so the main reason for their presence had, in effect, been removed as those wounded earlier had recovered. The typhus epidemic had proved that they were needed, but as that receded with the good weather, many were left with little work. On 27th July 1915, Ralf Paget invited all the British units in Serbia to a conference at Kragujevatz. The intention was to decide whether the units should stay on in the absence of fighting. It was agreed that they would stay for a little longer. The British presence was very important to Serbian morale.

An independent traveller, Dr Caroline Twigge Matthews, funded herself and all her equipment when she travelled out in May 1915, determined to work with the Serbian armies on the front line. Upon her arrival this proved more difficult than she expected as the military authorities in situ refused to honour the promises made to her in London. Her solitary status may not have helped her, but the fact that there wasn't much of a front line in the summer of 1915 was probably just as important. Matthews' diaries for this period read very much like travel literature as she moves around the country observing Serbian cultures and customs.[29] Things only changed for her when the Bulgarian army invaded and she was sent to the front with the 1st regiment of the Morava division. Elsie Corbett, stationed in Vrinjatcha Bania with the Red Cross, spent the summer working in the children's ward, dealing with all the ailments to which Serbian peasant children succumbed. Ellen Chivers Davies, also at Vrinjatcha with the Farmers'

Unit, had a similarly quiet summer: 'people here grumble a good deal about the lack of work, and really it does *no* good'.[30] That is, until she was sent out to be a part of a camp hospital with an outpatient dispensary in early July.

> Things here are much as they were except that a flourishing out-patient tent was started some time ago which seems immensely popular in the neighbourhood. We cannot take in-patients until our camp is ready, but one does feel that this dispensary work meets a real need.[31]

Mabel Stobart also believed that the best way for the women to be useful during the long quiet summer was to help out with the medical needs of the local population. The acute shortage of doctors and medical supplies brought about by the war and exacerbated by the typhus epidemic had a devastating effect on the medical care of the ordinary people of Serbia. In effect there was nothing left for them. Stobart was proved right, as a steady stream of peasants began to present themselves at the various hospitals set up by the women's units. While they all rose to the occasion, Stobart turned it into a sort of mini-crusade.

> We immediately pitched a bell tent at the outer edge of the hospital encampment, on the roadside, improvised a notice board from an old packing case, and, with the help of an interpreter, wrote, in Serbian, words to the effect, that if folks would bring their own bottles, medicine and medical advice would be given gratis. A doctor, a nurse, and an interpreter took charge of the tent dispensary, and we waited with eager curiosity to see what happened. The result was that within a few weeks 12000 people, men, women, and children, came to this roadside dispensary, either in ox-wagons or walking from distances of fifty, sixty, even seventy miles – ill with typhus, diphtheria, typhoid, smallpox, tuberculosis, and every conceivable and inconceivable form of disease.[32]

The dispensary was so successful that Stobart determined to set up a whole string of them across the country during the lull in the fighting. She argued that the local people, who usually had a great fear of all hospitals, regarded the women's work differently, 'because of the tents, and also because the doctors were women, the nurses were devoted, and the atmosphere was homely'.[33] She cabled the SRF requesting 'material, equipment, and personnel for additional dispensaries. "I should like twelve," I said, "but I must have six."'[34] And six she had, setting them up in carefully chosen locations as satellites around the original hospital.

There can be no doubt that this work played an enormous part in endearing the British women to the Serbian people, as they were more than happy to welcome everyone. Ellen Davies records:

> Our doctors perform small operations every day and the dispenser is really enjoying life. Certainly they have saved a great many children's lives this summer, and personally I don't think that is useless work. The mothers are touchingly grateful – we have hosts of babies coming up for treatment – and bring the quaintest offerings as appreciation....
>
> There is one charming baby, who had to have an eye removed, which is the pet of the whole place, and they all adore being photographed, which event occurs fairly frequently. We have many gipsies [*sic*] for patients, as the other hospitals don't care for them, and they are delightfully picturesque.
>
> Some soldiers who come up are sadly crippled, and look at one so pathetically with their big brown eyes just like the beautiful eyes of a dog, as if begging one to help them, and most of them are cases that ought to have done quite well if they had had proper treatment from the first.[35]

This extract gives an indication of the range of work undertaken by the dispensaries, the many different kinds of patients who sought help and the egalitarian approach taken by the dispensary staff. They have difficulty persuading the people that they do not have to pay for treatment. The idea of free medical care for all is revolutionary and inspiring. Two of the most striking things about Davies' narrative are firstly its pathos – her sympathy for the various different types of patient is very convincing – and secondly its enjoyment. There is clear sense here of the pleasure it gives the women to be able to offer this help. On the one hand this is part and parcel of the humanitarian mission on which they embarked when they left England. On the other hand it is also deeply reflective of the powerful relationship that grew between the women and the Serbians. It is a relationship that outlasted the war by many decades, but also one that would be severely tested, as we shall see later, before the Armistice was finally signed.

In Russia the war began less well despite some early optimism. After the initial invasions Russia agreed to attack Germany through Poland, then a Russian territory and a salient, in order to take the pressure off France. Germany and Austria assumed that it would take Russia much longer to mobilise its armies, owing to the size of the country and the limitations of the railways, without allowing for the fact that a significant number of Russian troops were already stationed in Poland. But a large proportion of the Russian army was consisted of cavalry, which was difficult to transport. The bulk of the infantry was made up of peasants, most illiterate, which could have represented a potential disadvantage. Yet despite superior numbers, the Russians suffered a bad early defeat at the battle of Tannenberg at the end of August 1914. Keegan states that 'The Germans counted 92,000 Russian prisoners, beside 50,000 enemy killed and wounded.... Tannenberg was the beginning of the long agony of the Tsar's armies which would culminate in their collapse in 1917.'[36] Although Russia did consolidate her position in the following months, this defeat was followed by another the next spring, at Gorlice-Tarnow. By 1915, Russia had a severe lack of munitions, particularly rifles. The German and Austrian attacks from late April onwards had dramatic effect. 'By 4 May the German Eleventh Army had reached open country and was pressing forward while 140,000 Russian prisoners marched in long columns to the rear', writes Keegan.[37] By September this number had risen to 325,000 and 3,000 guns had also been lost along with all the Polish territories. It was this landscape of defeat and retreat that greeted the few British women who worked Russia during the early days of the war.

The Russian armies would have welcomed Allied support from the start, but the British and the French had their work cut out on the Western Front. However, the relatively small British population in Russia in 1914 wanted to do something to help. Lady Georgina Buchanan, the wife of the British ambassador. was responsible for a number of initiatives in Petrograd (St Petersburg). She distributed aid to the many refugees that were already making their way to the capital and in September 1914 she was the driving force behind the opening of the British Colony Hospital for Wounded Russian Soldiers, or the King George V Hospital. It was initially intended as a convalescent hospital and operated until June 1917.[38] Anthony Cross suggests that 'the patients marveled at the chintz curtains, bright bedspreads, and crisp white linen and a degree of English comfort not to be found in other hospitals'.[39] Although this did good work, it was effectively superseded by the Anglo-Russian Base Hospital, which was up and running in 1916. But in the early stages of the war, there were relatively few British women involved in hospital work in Russia, and fewer still on the front line.

Unlike most of the women working on the Eastern Front, Violetta Thurstan was a professionally trained nurse. She worked for the Russian Red Cross, having been sent to Belgium at the beginning of the war. When the Germans invaded Belgium, Thurstan found herself a prisoner. Most women captives were shipped straight back to England, but Thurstan was sent on a different route, via Cologne, which resulted in her finding her way to Denmark. Further from England than ever, she decided to offer her services to Russia, which involved a further journey across Sweden and Finland, and an opportunity to engage with all sorts of different cultural experiences.[40] Thurstan joined a Russian Red Cross flying column or 'letuchka', special units developed to deal with the geographical difficulties of the Russian front line. Christine Hallett tells us that:

> Instead of casualty clearing stations, the Russian military medical services had much more mobile units: 'letuchka' or flying columns, which followed the advancing armies (or joined their retreats). Once they had stabilized their patient's conditions, medical officers and nurses in these units applied occlusive dressings containing salt pack or iodine swabs, which would remain in place during the long train journey back to base.[41]

This operational method was not without its problems, but Thurstan's time with the flying column was relatively brief as she had to return to Britain because of ill health in 1915 and perhaps because of this, her narrative, *Field Hospital and Flying Column*, published in 1915, reads as rather less gritty than many later records. Thurstan never loses the sense of war as a glorious enterprise, and some of her descriptions and conclusions sit uncomfortably beside other accounts.

> War would be the most glorious game in the world if it were not for the killing and wounding. In it one tastes the joy of comradeship to the full, the taking and giving, and helping and being helped in a way that would be impossible to conceive in the ordinary world. At Radzivilow, too, one could see the poetry of war, the zest of the frosty mornings, and the delight of the camp-fire at night, the warm, clean smell of the horses tethered everywhere, the keen hunger, the rough food sweetened by the sauce of danger. Even the returning wounded in the evening did not seem altogether such a bad thing out there. One has to die some time, and the Russian peasants esteem it a high honour to die for their 'little Mother' as they call their country. The vision of the High Adventure is not often vouchsafed to one, but it is a good thing to have had it – it carries one through many a night at the shambles.[42]

Although during her time at the front, Thurstan had seen her fair share of the horrors of war, and she does articulate them elsewhere in her memoir, this is her conclusion. Her writing retains that sense of travelogue throughout and here draws on clichéd impressions of war that feel a little out of place in 1915. Jane Potter suggests that 'The multiplicity of places she sees and people with whom she interacts are the focus of the narrative.'[43] But for all that, she doesn't get too close. The Russians whom she treats always remain rather alien and 'other', like the 'natives' of travel writing. She does not develop them or contemplate the wider experiences of the war, as other women seem to. Here it remains the landscape together with the alien cultures that are keys to her narrative; the physical senses are used to support the overall endorsement of the experience. 'The zest of the frosty mornings', 'the rough food sweetened by the sauce of danger' are phrases that would seem more appropriate in a *Boy's Own* adventure than in the diary of a professional nurse. Potter argues that Thurstan's writing displays 'that stiff upper-lip and control characterized as uniquely British',[44] and she is by no means alone in representing war this way; other women produced narratives that were oblique when addressing the actuality of experience. Other women allowed their 'Britishness' to colour their accounts as well as their actions, as will be discussed in Chapter 4. But this memoir does appear to be particularly romanticised in places.

E. Agnes Greg, also a trained nurse, was most probably with Thurstan when she arrived in Russia in 1915. But unlike Thurstan, who returned home quite soon, Greg stayed in the East throughout the war. She was already a seasoned veteran, having been with Mabel St Clair Stobart's WSWCC in the Balkans in 1912. One of Greg's letters home captures elements of both the horror and the romance of the war through a description of an airborne battle that took place above her camp in July 1915. The new technology of the aircraft, used for warfare for the first time in this war, continued to amaze witnesses and it seemed to be impossible to describe their dogfights without recourse to the conventional tropes of romance language.

> I saw one of the most terrible and thrilling sights I have yet seen, the day before we left the Jew's house. We were all sitting among the nettles and dock leaves having tea when we heard the sound of an aeroplane, then shots, and then 2 machines came into view, over the trees, flying very high. There were more shots, and we realized it was an air battle, and we recognized our friend an ... aeroplane, worked by one of the Russians we know. It was terrible. The Russian overtook the Austrian, and got above him, and they seemed over our heads. There were more shots, and the Austrian tried to run into the Russian. Then we saw she

was injured. She looked like a winged bird and slowly, slowly began to come down. I seized my emergency R.X. box and fled. But I had had time to cross 3 fields and wade the river before she went out of sight turning slowly like a withered leaf. When I got to the hillside, I saw the flame and smoke coming from her, and knew my R.X. Box would not be needed. It was a terrible thing nothing was left, and lying like black marble statues, the two brave men were burnt.[45]

Here Greg describes how tea in the tranquil, pastoral setting was disturbed by the invasion of modernity. The novelty is both 'terrible and thrilling'. The newness of the technology is emphasised by her stating that the aeroplane is 'worked' by a Russian who is known to them; she does not yet have the appropriate language to describe flying. The actual plane can only be described through metaphor and is automatically gendered female. It is a 'winged bird' and a 'withered leaf', both rather euphemistic terms for a killing machine. Similarly, the corpses of the pilots are like 'black marble statues', endowing them with a dignity and an authority that seems to elevate them above the more commonplace war dead. This is reinforced by the fact that the Russian pilots appear to take no pleasure in their victory. 'They said there was such a fellow feeling among flying men that it was awful to have killed two. They saluted each other before firing, and they had hoped they would give up the fight, seeing they were outmatched.'[46] The flyers seem to adopt an outmoded chivalric code that taps into the romance and nostalgia of the past, an anachronism in 1915, but one that Greg completely accepts. She writes with gratification that the Austrian pilots received a funeral with full military honours.

John Keegan argues that:

> The nature of these titanic battles on the Eastern Front is difficult to represent at a human or individual level. The Russian army, 80 per cent peasant when a majority of Russian peasants were still illiterate, left no literature to compare with that of the Western Front. 'Personal reminiscences are very rare. Nobody collected them'; without amanuenses, the voice of the Russian peasant soldier could not speak to posterity.[47]

While Keegan is clearly right about the lack of a literature comparable to that of the Western Front, he is not quite right to suggest that the Russian soldiers had no amanuenses. Two of the most notable British women to serve in Russia from the beginning of the war took on the recording of Russian experience as an important part of their narratives. For Mary Britnieva and Florence Farmborough, the need to

give the Russian soldiers a voice is paramount, together with the need
to show the rest of the world how much these men suffered. Mary
Britnieva was an Anglo-Russian, with a British father (her brother
was in the British army) living in St Petersburg before the war. As soon
as war broke out she trained as a Red Cross nurse and left for the front
with her hospital unit in late September 1914, putting her right at the
heart of the action following that first major defeat. Christine Hallett
points out that:

> The Russians experienced a Great War that was very different from any
> other. Theirs was a mobile war that ranged over thousands of miles,
> with massive, rapid advances, and precipitous retreats.... Much of the
> immediate and urgent medical and nursing care was undertaken by
> staff attached to *letuchka*, or 'flying columns': mobile hospitals housed
> in makeshift accommodation or tents, carried on cumbersome wooden
> horsedrawn wagons, but often moving almost as rapidly as an army.[48]

Britnieva's account, *One Woman's Story*, details both her wartime experiences and her post-war life. She arrived at the front very quickly and
the early chapters explore her first experiences as a nurse, with relatively little training, with passing, cryptic references to the head doctor,
who we later learn was to become her husband. But at the same time
the text is punctuated with soldiers' voices, as they pass, wounded,
through her hospital. These voices often feel as though they may be
representative of the many rather than those of particular individuals, but they are soldiers' voices nonetheless. Her first patient, ironi-
cally, was a German prisoner of war with peritonitis. In many nursing narratives, patients are identified by their rank or number or by
their wound. But Britnieva names hers. 'Koppe was hardly expected to
live, his condition being almost hopeless, but thanks to his wonderful
patience and amazing stoicism, he pulled through.... "Danke bestens,
Schwesterchen," he would say, looking at me gratefully with his serious brown eyes.'[49] Her second patient, Chadlidze, was 'a swarthy
Caucasian with flashing black eyes and magnificent teeth'.[50]

> He was very badly wounded in the leg and had just had a 'high amputa-
> tion'. He used to moan and groan so piteously complaining of the pain
> in the toes of his amputated leg.... Then, as he grew better, he began to
> talk more, often chattering so much that I had to stop him – he used to
> grow so excited, waving his arms about and nearly jumping out of bed.
> 'Ah, little Sister,' he would say with his funny eastern accent, 'if you
> only knew what a dancer I was!'[51]

But when Chadlidze discovers Koppe in the neighboring bed, he forgets his need to dance again, and rediscovers his belligerent spirit, 'Why didn't you tell me he was a German? If I had known there was one in my room I'd have stabbed him long ago! Give me my bayonet at once.' The Russian soldier speaks out in anger until Britnieva manages to pacify him and explain that both are conscripts. Her third patient is more seriously ill; Vassili is wounded in both legs and has septic poisoning. He gives voice to another familiar plea.

> 'Oh how I want to live, Sestritza,' he kept saying. 'I have a young wife and three small children, you know, oh, if only the Lord would spare me! Please do your best, dear Sister, and ask the doctors to save me. I agree to everything, they can do whatever they like only let them save me.'[52]

The soldiers' voices that Britnieva reproduces echo those found in nurses' narratives throughout the First World War, from all countries. When she allows the soldiers to speak they become part of a universal voice, all victims of the same conflict. Although these individual voices do not seem particularly singular, because the words that Britnieva gives them articulate universal messages of suffering, it does suggest that the Russian soldiers may not have been so different from their contemporaries in other countries, despite their lack of education. When Vassili dies, Britnieva finds it very difficult to cope, an important statement of her own humanity, which will in time be blunted by the horrors she has yet to see. But we have to be drawn into the first outpouring of grief so that we, as readers, do not forget that Vassili is one of many individuals, mourned by his own, unique family.

But not all soldiers' voices are quite as formulaic as these first ones. Britnieva likes to tell stories. While stationed at Teresino, she encounters Ivanoff, a young officer expected to die. He is accompanied by his orderly, Driomin, who refuses to leave his side, sleeping on the floor beside his hospital bed, demonstrating the absolute loyalty upon which their bond is formed (and another common story in Eastern Front narratives). Ivanoff does not die.

> He looked so pathetically young, and soon became a great favourite with all of us. He was of Tartar origin and had a very dark complexion. We used to tease him by telling him that lying amidst all the white sheets and pillows, with just his head showing, he looked exactly like a small fly in a large jug of milk.[53]

The image is an effective one. It shrinks him. The domesticity of the image enables the reader to imagine the soldier as youthful and vulnerable; out of place in the world of war. But Britnieva uses Ivanoff to illustrate other aspects of the war, too – resilience, survival, unexpected heroism – so his story does not end here. When well enough to move, Ivanoff is transferred to Warsaw and she assumes that will be the end of it. She later hears that he has been wounded in the civil war following the Bolshevik revolution and has died in hospital. But this proves unfounded. In 1929, while nursing in Paris, Britnieva received a letter from Ivanoff, and in 1930, they met again, developing their friendship. In fact he had been decorated for his bravery, a figure at odds with the boy she first meets in 1914. The story has a conclusion.

Britnieva develops her interest in stories when she records the experience of one particular soldier, reported to her by a fellow nurse, who had been imprisoned by the Germans. This is the longest individual tale that she records and it gives 'Petruha' a real individual voice. The story is too long to quote in full, but culminates in a self-inflicted wound. Concerned about his mutilated hand, Sister Vera invites him to tell her his story. He was captured by the Germans in East Prussia and set to work in a munitions factory as a stoker. 'I was unaccustomed to the work and my back and arms ached, but after a few days, when I got more used to things, my mind began to work again and I suddenly realized that I was doing wrong: "Oh God" – I thought in terror – "here am I actually helping to make shells and bullets for the enemy!"'[54] As a consequence, he refuses to work and is tortured by his captors. When he recovers he is sent back to the factory.

> Once again they put me down to stoke the boilers and again I refused to work, it was the only way in which I could save myself from being a foul traitor, for now I realized more clearly than ever that every shovelful of coal put on by me helped to make that which meant death, yes, Sestritza, *death*, to my brothers. And I could not kill my own blood and flesh.[55]

Again the soldier is tortured, but for longer and it takes him three months to recover before being faced with the same dilemma as before. But this time, as he is marched into the factory he notes the glinting of an axe in the sunshine in the middle of the yard. Suddenly inspired, he rushes to the axe and chops off his fingers, disabling himself for further work. Here Britnieva performs the task of amanuensis to great effect. She gives space in the narrative for Petruha to tell the story in his own words, offering no comment or judgment. That said, of course, the story itself offers a narrative of heroism and implies that that it is innate within the Russian peasant soldiers. Although it is impossible to tell how much truth there is in the story, it is certainly presented here as an actual event, and that at least must offer some insight into the way the soldiers were perceived or may have chosen to represent themselves.

If Britnieva likes to tell stories, Florence Farmborough's account is much more like a social history when it comes to her representing the voices of the soldiers. Many similar stories unfold in her narrative, nonetheless. When the First World War broke out in August 1914, Florence Farmborough was already well established in Russia. She had moved there in 1908 at the age of twenty-one and had been living in Moscow, working as an English tutor for the family of a Russian surgeon since 1910. By 1914 she had been virtually adopted by the Usov family, so she entered the war representing two worlds, that of Imperial Russia and that of Imperial Britain. Throughout the war, Farmborough kept extensive diaries. Farmborough's diary, originally 400,000 words in length, records her life and experiences during the war years in extraordinary detail. It operates as an effective historical document, illustrating the daily life of a Red Cross *letuchka* and the soldiers they encounter. We learn of Farmborough's hospital work during a long and bitter retreat on the Galician Front in 1915–16, and later on the Romanian Front, where the Russian armies enjoy more success in 1916–17. And then we hear about the political and social upheavals of the 1917 revolutions as they happened, tracking the impact on the ordinary people of Russia. Farmborough's very personal and very human reactions to all of these events provide the central focus of the memoir; we learn a great deal about her as an individual through her confidences and through her wider responses to a period of great change.

Farmborough was clearly very committed to her adopted country: her diary incorporates many representative voices. In many ways it is a much more self-aware text that Britnieva's, adopting a range of literary techniques and styles to articulate the complexity of her experience. For example, like Britnieva, she records her first experience with death, coincidentally another Vasiliy, but her response to it is quite different.

> I wanted to see him. I wanted to see Death. I opened the door quietly
> and shut it behind me. This was my first meeting with Death. It was not

so frightening as I had thought it would be; only the silence awed me. He was lying wrapped in a sheet on a stretcher, so small and thin and wizened that he looked more like a child than a grown man. His set face was grey-white, never had I seen that strange colour on a face before, and his cheeks had sunken into hollows. On each eyelid was – I looked more closely – yes, a lump of sugar! The stillness of the room, the immobility of the statuelike figure began to disturb me. Death is so terribly still, so silent, so remote.[56]

In this passage, Vasiliy has departed. In his place, embodied by the 'statuelike figure', a personified Death becomes a tangible presence in the room. This literary trope is one that is often adopted by other nurse-writers of the war. For example, Mary Borden incorporates it into her sketch ' Moonlight' (*The Forbidden Zone*, 1929), in which she personifies elements of the hospital experience, 'Three in particular, a lascivious monster, a sick bad-tempered animal, and an angel; Pain, Life and Death.'[57] Farmborough uses sensuality in an unusual way in this passage. What is immediately noticeable is the lack of sensory perception. Although she can see the dead man, what she actually sees is not Vasiliy. The image of the man has no colour or substance, he is reduced, as if to stone. And other senses are absent. There is no sound at all; death is absolutely silent. It does not inspire fear, but a disturbing undercurrent is encoded in the silence. This is a very different response from the uncontrollable tears to which Britnieva confesses, lasting several days. This is a much more mature and intellectual response, indicative of the way in which Farmborough analyses and interprets all of her war experiences.

Like Britnieva, Farmborough allows the soldiers to speak from her pages. And often, too, the voices can sound representative rather than individual. Stepan Grigoriyerich, a wounded officer, is used to demonstrate the devastating effects of war experience on the men. As she dresses his wounded arm, he takes her by surprise: ' "*Spasibo, Sestritsa.* You do not recognize me?" "No, I don't," I answered, looking at him with curiosity. He mentioned his name and added: "I played the guitar at the Georgiyevski fete in your Unit; I told you that I should come to see you and I have kept my word." '[58] Farmborough is horrified by her recognition of this man: 'then I remembered, but this man was older by many years, with haggard face and lines round his eyes, and more than a month's growth of dusky hair on his chin. The other ... had been little more than a boy.'[59] In fact only a matter of months had passed, but such had been the suffering of the Russian troops in retreat that the physical change is remarkable. This physical change is then used to reflect the spiritual change that the man has undergone, as Farmborough allows him to give voice to his own disillusion.

> 'Sleep,' he cried, 'I have forgotten how to sleep. Can one sleep when the world around is in chaos?' The engine started, the car glided out of the yard. I could not keep myself from thinking of that young soldier who had presented such a strange figure as he stood there with tears in his eyes; I had been at a loss as to how to speak to him. He was so different: an Englishman would never have stood in a yard full of people and, with tears in his eyes, spoken with sorrow of the loss of his soul.[60]

Nothing in her past life has prepared Farmborough for this level of emotional engagement. It is not 'English', yet he speaks with the desolation of a nation in retreat. Unlike Britnieva, who tends to represent the soldiers in an uncomplicatedly heroic way, Farmborough is able to allow for the real impact of defeat on the fighting men, offering us as readers a convincing picture of the life of the retreat.

Farmborough, too, comes across soldiers suffering from self-inflicted wounds. Her portrayal, while sympathetic, is far from heroic. At first she does not know what to make of the hand wound she finds in the early days of the retreat. 'One boyish hand had a fearful wound on the back of it; jagged and notched was the flesh and the knuckles were splintered and rent. On the palm was but one small hole, but, around it, the skin was covered with a thick black coating resembling a heavy contusion.'[61] A divisional doctor soon explains it to her, while admonishing the boy with cries of 'coward' although he seems more concerned with the potential permanent damage than the motivation. But Farmborough herself takes a much more measured view. This is, after all an army in retreat.

> A man with a self-inflicted wound is a difficult person to deal with; one could not hastily condemn him, for so many conflicting influences would first have to be taken into consideration and we became sensitive to the signs from which we could detect those cases which were the outcome of cowardice. On the other hand, it was not difficult to distinguish the soldiers whose excitable nature and raw-edged nerves could induce them, in a weak, desperate moment, to seek this outlet as a definite means of deliverance from the scene of their physical suffering and mental anguish.[62]

Farmborough demonstrates modern sensibilities in this passage. Cowardice is almost impossible to identify, and indeed to define.

However, the kind of trauma that would be called shell shock by her generation, or post-traumatic stress disorder later on, is much easier to identify in the men. By thinking about why they may have chosen to wound themselves, rather than overtly judging them, Farmborough begins to represent how they might be feeling. It is this sense of empathy, apparent throughout the memoir, which increases its value as a record of social history.

Because of the structures of hospital provision in the Russian military, both women have the opportunity to see the battlefield at first hand in these relatively early days of the war. Curiously the impressions of the trenches are quite different. Farmborough is perhaps more fortunate as she seems to be offered a view of some rather sanitised forts and trenches occupied by friendly soldiers. She offers a detailed record of layout and construction, 'strangely-shaped earthworks; long dark lines of iron-clad balustrades; mysterious passages winding in and out of streamlined trenches; a connected series of well-formed rabbit borrows, or the front-doors to the underground homes of a community of troglodytes'.[63] These fortifications are mysterious and perhaps inappropriately inviting. They are streamlined, which implies efficiency. The image of the rabbit burrow suggests that they are in compliance with nature, well formed. Strikingly, they are 'homes', the dwelling place of a community, all of which indicates a sense of comfort and security that seems at odds with their real purpose. The perception, no doubt, owes a lot to the fact that the trenches are occupied and the war is quiet.

The trenches that Britnieva visits are also quiet, but for very different reasons. Here the battle is over; the armies have only recently moved on. The expedition seems to take the form of a social outing, 'Our party set out gaily in two military carts for the eight-mile drive.'[64] The nurses have been assured that they will see 'no gruesome sights' as everything will have been cleared away. The reality of the trenches is, perhaps inevitably, quite different.

> There were five frozen bodies, they lay in their trench-coats, but the boots had been stolen by marauders. They were all in different crouching positions and it looked as if they had all crawled to one place. They were terrible to behold. Field-mice had made a nest in the head of one and they scuttled away under our feet. One of the bodies was intact. It was frozen to stone. As we bent over it we saw a paper lying beside the body, and, on looking closer, found it was a postcard. One of our nurses

picked it up and we discovered that it was addressed to an officer of the N. regiment and it was from his wife in Moscow. With tears streaming from our eyes we read the message.[65]

This image of the trenches is perhaps a more familiar one, with the frozen figures caught in their final awkward positions; the lost boots, always the most valuable part of a soldier's kit;[66] the nesting mice representing the unstoppable progress of the natural world adapting and surviving amid the carnage created by mankind. The experience is completed by the ever-powerful image of the postcard, that final communication from a loved one who may never know the final fate of the dead man. This is another popular image in war literature. Henri Barbusse used it in his powerful 1917 novel *Under Fire*, which Britnieva would probably have been familiar with by the time she published her memoir in 1934.

Around the dead flutter letters that have escaped from pockets or cartridge pouches while they were being placed on the ground. Over one of these bits of white paper, whose wings still beat though the mud ensnares them, I stoop slightly and read a sentence – 'My dear Henry, what a fine day it is for your birthday!'[67]

In Barbusse's novel the letter almost seems alive, as the dead soldier still lives for the writer. Rather more bitterly, the writer of Britnieva's postcard articulates a sense of foreboding because she has not heard from her husband for many weeks. The scene encapsulates many of the most iconic images of tragedy from the war. The weeping nurses complete the picture.

In the spring of 1916 Mary Britnieva was sent home on leave. She had been away at the front for eighteen months and was able to announce her engagement. She was subsequently taken ill so could not return immediately, as planned. Her narrative then omits any discussion of 1917, moving straight to her marriage in early 1918. Florence Farmborough had a month's leave in Moscow at the end of 1915 to recuperate after the hardships of the retreat. She was back with her unit in January 1916, but the Russian army was then advancing, so for a while at least there is a more positive tone to her narrative. But as 1916 progresses there is a detectable undercurrent of unease in her writing. She begins to note changes in the atmosphere, rumours and suggestions, the beginnings of the revolution that would change the war and her life in the coming months.

Notes

1 Mitchell Library, Glasgow (hereafter ML), SWH Archive, Large Trunk, Undated letter, probably summer 1915, from Gertrude Pares, SWH administrator, to Miss Morris.

2 ML, SWH Archive, Large Trunk, Letter dated 5th April 1915, from Dr Eleanor Soltau to Dr Elsie Inglis.

3 John Keegan, *The First World War* (London: Hutchinson, 1998), p. 165.

4 *Ibid.*

5 Monica Krippner, *The Quality of Mercy: Women at War, Serbia 1915–18* (London and Newton Abbot: David & Charles, 1980), p. 34. Krippner states there were 70,000 Austrian POWs; however, the accuracy of Krippner's figures is unclear as she cites no sources. A figure of 90,000 is cited by James Johnston Abraham, a British surgeon working with the Red Cross in Serbia in late 1914. See extracts from his autobiography, *A Surgeon's Journey*, available at www.vlib.us/medical/serbia.htm, p. 4 (accessed 9th November 2015).

6 Leah Leneman, *In the Service of Life* (Edinburgh: Mercat Press, 1994), p. 18.

7 *Ibid.*, p. 18.

8 Eva Shaw McLaren, *The History of the Scottish Women's Hospitals* (London: Hodder and Stoughton, 1919), p. 86.

9 *Ibid.*, pp. 90–1.

10 Krippner, *The Quality of Mercy*, p. 35.

11 Imperial War Museum, London (hereafter IWM), 6977, Unidentified newspaper cutting in the papers of Miss Flora Scott, Matron of the Sixth Reserve Military Hospital, Skopje. Probably the *Leicester Daily Post* as Scott went on to write a regular column for it. No date.

12 *Ibid.*

13 In 1914 Inglis initially approached the Royal Army Medical Corps and offered her services there. The response she received has become famous: 'My good lady, go home and sit still', quoted in Leneman, *In the Service of Life*, p. 2.

14 Abraham, *Surgeon's Journey*, p. 6.

15 Quoted in McLaren, *The History of the Scottish Women's Hospitals*, p. 94.

16 Quoted *ibid.*, p. 95.

17 Abraham, *Surgeon's Journey*, p. 7.

18 Mabel St Clair Stobart, *The Flaming Sword in Serbia and Elsewhere* (London, New York and Toronto: Hodder and Stoughton, 1917), p. 49.

19 IWM, 6977, Unidentified newspaper cutting in the papers of Miss Flora Scott.

20 Abraham, *Surgeon's Journey*, p. 8.

21 ML, SWH Archive, Large Trunk, Letter dated 6th April 1915, from Adeline Campbell and Katherine MacPhail to SWH.

22 ML, SWH Archive, Large Trunk, Undated letter, probably from Elsie Inglis.

23 Typhus (prison fever) is an infectious disease caused by the *Rickettsia* bacteria, transmitted by fleas, lice or mites. High fever, severe headache, red rashes and delirium characterise it. Typhoid (enteric fever) is caused by the *Salmonella typhi* bacteria and spread through contaminated water, food or human contact. Symptoms include fever, abdominal pain, constipation and headaches.

24 Stobart, *The Flaming Sword*, p. 45.

25 For a full discussion of Stobart's spiritual journey see Angela K. Smith, 'The Mists Which Shroud these Questions: Mabel St Clair Stobart, the First World War and Faith', *Literature and History*, 3rd series, 20:2 (2011), 1–15.

26 Mabel Dearmer's service will be considered in detail in Chapter 3.

27 Stobart, *The Flaming Sword*, p. 60.

28 *Ibid.*, p. 61.

29 Caroline Twigge Matthews, *Experiences of a Woman Doctor in Serbia* (London: Mills & Boon, 1916).

30 Ellen Chivers Davies, *A Farmer in Serbia* (London: Methuen, 1916), p. 46.

31 *Ibid.*, pp. 46–7.

32 Stobart, *The Flaming Sword*, pp. 67–8.

33 *Ibid.*, p. 71.

34 *Ibid.*, p. 76.

35 Davies, *A Farmer in Serbia*, pp. 47–8.

36 Keegan, *The First World War*, pp. 162–3.

37 *Ibid.*, p. 251.

38 See Anthony Cross, 'Forgotten British Places in Petrograd/Leningrad', www.russinitalia.it/europa_orientalis/Cross.pdf (accessed 26th November 2012).

39 *Ibid.*, p. 137.

40 See Chapter 1.

41 Christine E. Hallett, *Veiled Warriors: Allied Nurses of the First World War* (Oxford: Oxford University Press, 2014), p. 104.

42 Violetta Thurstan, *Field Hospital and Flying Column: Being the Journal of an English Nursing Sister in Belgium and Russia* (New York: G. P. Putnam's Sons, 1915, p. 175.

43 Jane Potter, *Boys in Khaki, Girls in Print: Women's Literary Responses to the Great War 1914–1918* (Oxford: Clarendon Press, 2005), p. 173. Potter considers the rhetoric and language used by Thurstan in some detail, pp. 171–83.

44 *Ibid.*, p. 177.

45 IWM, 01/17/1, Letter dated July 14th 1915, Miss E. A. Greg, Private papers.

46 *Ibid.*

47 Keegan, *The First World War*, p. 174.

48 Christine E. Hallett, *Containing Trauma: Nursing Work in the First World War* (Manchester and New York: Manchester University Press, 2009), p. 102.

49 Mary Britnieva, *One Woman's Story* (London: Arthur Barker, 1934), p. 15.

50 *Ibid.*, p. 16.

51 *Ibid.*

52 *Ibid.*, p. 18.

53 *Ibid.*, p. 33.

54 *Ibid.*, p. 47.

55 *Ibid.*

56 Florence Farmborough, *With the Armies of the Tsar: A Nurse at the Russian Front in War and Revolution, 1914–1918* (New York: Cooper Square Press, 2000 [1974]), p. 24. Farmborough later discovers that the sugar lumps were used to prevent the opening of the eyes and have no symbolic importance.

57 Mary Borden, *The Forbidden Zone* (London: Hesperus Press, 2008 [1929]), p. 40.

58 Farmborough, *With the Armies of the Tsar*, p. 97.

59 *Ibid.*, pp. 97–8.

60 *Ibid.*, p. 98.

61 *Ibid.*, p. 46.

62 *Ibid.*, p. 132.

63 *Ibid.*, p. 123.

64 Britnieva, *One Woman's Story*, p. 47.

65 *Ibid.*, p. 22.

66 In Erich Maria Remarque's 1929 novel *All Quiet on the Western Front*, a single pair of good boots make their way around a company as each new soldier inherits them from a dead comrade.

67 Henri Barbusse, *Under Fire* (London: Everyman, 1988 [1917]), p. 147.

3

Role call? The female body and gender identity on the Eastern Front

A human soul is peculiarly detached from its fellows. Not another nor a million others will be allowed to make reply. When the Roll Call is made we each must give our own separate answer and show our own method of deduction, the way in which we ourselves have solved Life's problem.[1]

Genders can be neither true nor false, neither real nor apparent, neither original nor derived. As credible bearers of those attributes, however, genders can also be rendered thoroughly and radically *incredible*.[2]

The British women who went to work on the Eastern Front during the First World War were faced with some unique challenges. For those who were not trained nurses or doctors, there was nothing in their previous lives that could have prepared them for the hardships of life at the front, even given that the Eastern Front had a tendency to attract women of an adventurous nature. Mabel St Clair Stobart, for one, had a range of experience of outdoor life, from living under canvas on the South African veldt to ranching with her son in Canada. But even she was tested in the war zone, confronted not only with the wounded, dead and dying, but also the hardships of inclement weather, lack of food and unforgiving landscapes. The female body, as understood in Edwardian myth and culture, should not have been equipped to deal with this level of hardship. Ever since the publication of Coventry Patmore's poem sequence 'The Angel of the House' in 1854, Victorian society had developed a mythologised impression of the ideal woman, and many women had been socialised into the belief system that endorsed this image. It is an image that is thrown into sharp relief when juxtaposed with the Eastern Front experience. Although this may seem like a very strange place to find so many British women, perhaps it is this very juxtaposition that may in part explain the appeal. The Eastern Front enabled women to break out of conventional gender roles, and as Caroline Twigge Matthews puts it, 'give their own separate answer'.[3]

As already noted, Jane Marcus suggests that:

> The 'Balkanization' of British women doctors and nurses in Serbia and Russia may be seen as part of a larger historical repression of the Eastern Front in favor of the story of Western Europe in histories of the war. The Eastern Front is the female 'other' of World War I.[4]

Marcus uses the term 'Balkanization' in its generic sense, but she is also correct in asserting that as a site of conflict, the Eastern Front itself has tended to be marginalised in historical narratives. Here British women found greater freedom to do their bit, supported by the Serbian military. As a site for women's endeavour the Eastern Front becomes a 'female other'; within this arena women were granted many unlikely freedoms. And here, female bodies were put to the test in ways not previously imagined, and some women explored gender roles in unexpected ways. Nurse-turned-soldier Flora Sandes later wrote:

> When a very small child I used to pray each night that I might wake up in the morning and find myself a boy. Fate plays tricks sometimes, so that it behoves one to be careful of one's wishes.[5]

As we have seen, Serbia was the destination of various British women's medical groups, including the SWH, the British Farmers' Unit, the Berry Unit led by James Berry and his wife, F. May Dickinson Berry, and the SRF3 in April 1915, led by Mabel St Clair Stobart. One of the earliest manifestations of the SRF led by Mabel Groutich, linked with the St John Ambulance Brigade, travelled out in August of 1914. All these units included a significant number of women workers of all types. In this chapter the primary focus will be on the experience of two women in particular: Flora Sandes, who went to Serbia with Groutich as a nurse in 1914, but joined the Serbian army as combatant soldier in 1916 and remained in the army until 1922; and Mabel Dearmer, who served as an orderly with the SRF3 from April 1915 until her death in July of that year. These two experienced the war in very different ways and their attitudes to the female body and to gender roles vary remarkably. Each performed war in a unique way, taking on a range of different roles, offering convincing examples of the ways in which women used the war to reinterpret their bodies.

There has been considerable work done on the connections between women's war experience and their sexuality.[6] However the primary focus here is on how these two particular women's case studies altered the ways in which they performed their gender as a result of the war. Their writings engage with this in an overt way. And while the war experience may have offered some women the freedom to explore aspects of their sexuality, it remains doubtful that this would have actually influenced the wartime behaviour patterns of most women. In keeping with almost all written records, neither Dearmer nor Sandes engages with sexuality in their texts; both have clear alternative agendas considered here and elsewhere in this book. One way of approaching the extraordinary impact of the war on the gender roles performed by these women may be to consider the ideas of Louis Althusser in his essay 'Ideology and Ideological State Apparatuses'.[7] Although Althusser is principally concerned with the state, his ideas foreground a way of reading the fluidity of gender in wartime Serbia in a useful way. He argues that:

> [T]he 'ideas' of a human subject exist in his [her] actions, or ought to exist in his [her] actions, and if this is not the case, it lends him [her] other ideas corresponding to the actions (however perverse) that he [she] does perform. This ideology talks of actions: I shall talk of actions inserted into *practices*. And I shall point out that these practices are governed by the *rituals* in which these practices are inscribed.[8]

In other words, it is not the ideas associated with gender and conventions of 'femininity' that define these women, but their actions, the *rituals* that they perform. As we shall see, the experience of the war in Serbia offers Dearmer and Sandes the opportunity to adopt practices and rituals more usually associated with the male subject. According to Althusser's ideas then, this enables the women to adapt their ideology, their subject position, and in the extreme case of Sandes, effectively to 'become' a man. Here Judith Butler is useful. She argues that:

> Gender ought not to be construed as a stable identity or locus of agency from which various acts follow; rather, gender is an identity tenuously constituted in time, instituted in an exterior space through a *stylized repetition of acts*. The effect of gender is produced through the stylization of the body and, hence, must be understood as the mundane way in which bodily gestures, movements, and styles of various kinds constitute the illusion of an abiding gendered self.[9]

Although many of Butler's arguments concerning the performance of gender are bound up with sexuality, they are still interesting in the ways in which they enable us to see Sandes' transformation from nurse to soldier. The '*stylized repetition of acts*', the *rituals* of military life, had an impact so profound that Sandes was able, at times, to quite seamlessly perform the role of a man, her close-cropped hair and uniform completing the picture.

Mabel Dearmer's war story is told in a series of letters written to her friend the MP Stephen Gwynn while she was on active service.[10] She was married to a clergyman, Percy Dearmer, and had two sons at the front. Percy Dearmer was the chaplain to the Stobart unit. Despite having worked as an artist and writer throughout her more than twenty-year-marriage, and indeed achieving some success as a dramatist in the years before the war,[11] Mabel Dearmer seems to have internalised many conventional notions of Victorian and Edwardian 'femininity'. She had been 'wife' and 'mother' for two decades. In her letters it is clear that she sees herself as a 'feminine' woman, weaker and more vulnerable than the rest of her family; and that her woman's body is a potential liability in a war zone. Had she lived to write a retrospective account, as Sandes did, her representations may have been different. But the fact of her early death, without time to reflect, gives her testimonies immediacy and an authenticity that may be missing from some later accounts.

Flora Sandes, who remained single until the end of her army service, never voices any such concerns.[12] Her two autobiographies detail her life as a soldier, *An English Woman-Sergeant in the Serbian Army* (1916) and *The Autobiography of a Woman Soldier* (1927). While both texts acknowledge the fact that as a British woman soldier she is rather unusual, her representation of the experience is much more concerned with the plight of the Serbian nation than with her sex or nationality. Although Sandes wrote her accounts in order to capitalise on her experience, both for herself and for the Serbian cause, her style remains interesting. The self she presents has apparently failed to internalise the rituals of 'femininity'; she quite simply adopts an alternative practice and plays the role of a man to great effect. Butler suggests that:

> Taking on a gender is not possible at a moment's notice, but is a subtle and strategic project, laborious and for the most part covert. Becoming a gender is an impulsive yet mindful process of interpreting a cultural

reality laden with sanctions, taboos, and prescription. The choice to assume a certain kind of body, to live or wear one's body a certain way, implies a world of already established corporeal styles.[13]

War-torn Serbia enabled Sandes to act on an impulse that she herself traces back to her childhood. It presented her with an alternate cultural reality with a different set of sanctions and taboos that in turn offered her the opportunity to perform gender in opposition to the forms prescribed by British culture.

Both women express the physical experience of war. As recent scholars have shown, this is not unusual in writings of the First World War. Paul Fussell's seminal study, *The Great War and Modern Memory*,[14] explores the war as a primarily physical experience on a number of levels, considering the realities of trench life alongside men's preoccupation with the body – their own and each other's – in terms of the hardships of life as well as the homoerotic impressions of a life without women. Joanna Bourke's important book, *Dismembering the Male: Men's Bodies, Britain and the Great War*,[15] examines the relationship between masculinities and the male body in the war through both written and oral media, but she is not concerned with equivalent female experience. In *Touch and Intimacy in First World War Literature*,[16] Santanu Das analyses the writing of the male body in war from a number of perspectives. This includes the examination of the way in which women, and in particular nurses in the front line, react to men's bodies in their records and memoirs. Considerations of the female body at war are more difficult to find. Susan Grayzel's 1999 study, *Women's Identities at War*,[17] does explore the female body, but primarily through the lens of motherhood. She argues that motherhood shapes women's identity more powerfully in war than in civilian life because of the need for women to produce sons as future soldiers on the one hand, and on the other because it is only through the pain and suffering of childbirth that women can gain an experience comparable to the pain of the battlefield. But Dearmer's narrative, in the form of her letters, writes the body at war in quite a different way, one that can be heard echoed in the writings of other women who served in Serbia and Russia. She acts as we might expect a 'stereotypical' Edwardian woman to do and gives an insight into the different ways in which the female body experienced war itself and the way that this experience impacted on her reading of the conflict that surrounded her. Dearmer and many of her contemporaries in Serbia were mothers,[18] but their children were often already grown up, so their bodies cannot be defined through reproduction. Instead, these women identify more with the male physical experience of warfare. Flora Sandes, who was never a mother, writes literally of the pain of the battlefield in all its forms.

Despite her consciousness of her 'femininity', Mabel Dearmer's artistic success led her to a passionate involvement with life, perhaps reflecting an unconscious desire to live life to the full. As Freud suggests, 'Life is impoverished, it loses in interest, when the highest stake in the game of living [life], may not be risked.'[19] Entering the war zone as an Edwardian lady gave Dearmer the opportunity to achieve a kind of heroism only traditionally available to men, including risk to life. In war, Freud suggests, 'Life has, indeed, become interesting again, it has recovered its full content.'[20] What is clear from Dearmer's own words is that she was preoccupied with physical dangers and ready to embrace them regardless. There is an undercurrent of excitement in her letters. She frequently writes, 'I am *so* glad I came.'[21] But the idea of death was never far from the front of her mind.

Flora Sandes never contemplates death, but there is no need to as her account is retrospective. We cannot know for sure how she felt in the heat of battle. But her attitude to notions of heroism and danger seem to have their roots in her earlier life. A clergyman's daughter, born in 1876, Sandes spent most of her pre-war existence successfully avoiding all the trappings of 'femininity' that Dearmer embodies. Always a tomboy, she earned her own money as a secretary, wore pantaloons and spent her time bicycling and camping, implying the 'subtle and strategic project' to which Judith Butler alludes. She was very widely travelled and had spent a lot of time working her way through the United States. Later she was a familiar figure driving her sports car around her home in Suffolk.[22] Her childish desire to be a boy coloured her life into adulthood, encouraging her to explore gendered alternatives. She seems to act out Freud's analysis of the appeal of war.

In fact, Sandes fits into the role of the 'New Woman' at the end of the nineteenth century.[23] With an income of her own and an interest in 'male' pursuits, such as motoring, and a tendency to adopt more 'masculine' styles of dress, she seems to represent that group of women who had begun to rebel against the constraints of 'femininity'. Although Mabel Dearmer does not fit this definition, she had been making an important contribution to the family income for years and had built an independent artistic career that illustrates her sense of her self-worth as a woman. Wife and mother she may have been, but the practices and rituals of her pre-war life indicate that she was less conventional than might be assumed and perhaps ready for the dangers of warfare.

The dangers that Dearmer feared and Sandes relished began to manifest very early. Dearmer's decision to join the SRF3 was taken hastily when she learnt that her husband was to go as the chaplain. Shortly before the unit's departure in April 1915, she attended a farewell service at St Martin-in-the-Fields, arranged by the Church League for Women's Suffrage and presided over by her husband. As she sat in the congregation, her thoughts distracted by the pressing demands of the rehearsals for her latest play, Dearmer suddenly became aware of her husband's address: 'This is only *au revoir*', he was saying, 'for I myself am to accompany you to Serbia. I have this morning been appointed Chaplain to the British units working in that country.'[24] As her husband's words penetrated her consciousness, as she realised that he would be joining her two sons on the front line, Dearmer responded as any self-respecting Edwardian lady might expect to: she cried.

As she wept silently, her tears dropping into her hymn-book, Dearmer realised that everyone whom she valued was to become a part of the war; that she alone would be left behind. Arguably she had already done her patriotic duty by producing two sons to be fighting men. As Nicoletta Gullace suggests, this was all that society really expected of her, military service being the only real legitimate basis for citizenship.[25] But the loss of her husband as well seemed too much. As the final hymn filled the church, she became convinced that only one course of action was open to her. Thus it was, sniffing and with red, swollen eyes, that Mabel Dearmer approached the leader of the unit, Mabel St Clair Stobart, and asked if she, too, might go to Serbia. Stobart's instinct was to say no. She, Stobart, saw before her a slight, fragile-looking, very feminine 'lady' dressed in green silks and furs, with a slightly bohemian air about her, suffering from emotional distress, a great contrast to the businesslike, uniformed women who had already signed up. Stobart believed that Dearmer would not be physically capable of the work that the unit was to undertake nor able to deal with the hardship of life under canvas in all weathers; that hers was a female body that would let the unit down. Nevertheless, Dearmer persuaded her, and shortly afterwards found herself riding in a motor car to a planning meeting, a newly assigned hospital orderly.

Dearmer was fully aware of her difference when she presented herself to Stobart as a recruit. And it was a difference that was overtly physical. The members of the unit were already organised, uniformed women. They presented a marked contrast to her elegantly dressed feminine form. Many of the recruits had a background in the Suffrage Movement. Those who were militant members of the WSPU in particular would have been used to the quasi-military organisational policies of Emmeline and Christabel Pankhurst, an experience that may have helped to prepare them for war both mentally and physically. Their rudimentary uniform was crucial to their identity. Dearmer noted:

> The unit consisted of some forty women of varying ages dressed in a grey uniform and wearing a black hat.... They all looked very businesslike and keen on the undertaking. I had only heard of Serbia as a country penetrated by disease that brought death to those who went to minister to it, and I wondered as I looked at them how many would return at the end of the expedition.[26]

This extract is taken from the memoir that Dearmer began to write. The women in their uniforms, so different from her feminine self, have already moved into a different dimension, taking them towards the war zone.

Susan Grayzel has argued that the notion of women in uniform was a politically problematic one, particularly before the introduction of conscription for men in January 1916, and especially if the women were dressed in khaki, seeming to emulate the soldiers that they could never be.[27] While wearing a uniform could be seen as a significant patriotic gesture, as long as women were unable to make the 'ultimate sacrifice' of death on the battlefield, they could not claim the right to wear the 'sacred khaki' that in its own way denoted citizenship. The women who went to Serbia, however, problematise Grayzel's reading.

Dearmer's understanding of the significance of uniform, of the importance of the way in which the female body at war is presented, develops through her letters and emphasises the importance of belonging. From Paris, *en route* to Serbia, she wrote:

> I *do* wish we had brassards, I should feel so much more heroic with a Red Cross on my arm. Aren't people silly over these things? They don't realize the value of symbols.[28]

Then from Marseilles she wrote:

> Lots of soldiers about, lots of uniform.... We sit in long lines, looking very black in our dark uniforms. The nurses of the British Farmers unit ... are not in uniform at all – we consider them very inferior.[29]

Ellen Chivers Davies, a member of that Farmers' Unit, both echoed Dearmer's judgment and expressed concern that some women had rather over-dressed, not really understanding the significance of uniform.

> We were – and are – divided into two camps: those who wore uniform regardless of expense, either of the wards wardy or of that newer kind, of a khaki shade hung round with many implements, doubtless useful but a little reminiscent of a travelling tinsmith – and those of us who travelled out in mufti, and rightly hung our heads in consequence, being regarded (I hope wrongly) as frivolous by the opposition camp.[30]

Like Dearmer, Davies sees the presence, and indeed absence, of uniform as defining. She herself was no doubt one of those women on the boat who earned Dearmer's disdain for being dressed in 'mufti'. But equally, some of the women who wear uniform don't seem to have quite understood, presenting rather ironic parody figures of soldiers, rather than achieving their goal of fitting in. This is particularly true of those in the 'sacred khaki'.

The SWH did seem to have got it about right in terms of how women at the front should present, although the committee in Edinburgh were less sure of this. Elsie Inglis wrote to Miss Morris in August 1915: 'I don't think you should alter the uniform, for everybody is beginning to know it, here, at any rate, and people come up to you and say – "You are the Scottish Women, aren't you? I travelled with your people on such and such a boat, or met them in such and such a place."'[31] Uniform, identity and nationality merged, enabling the women to present a united front, and to develop a positive reputation to carry with them as they worked across the country.

The sober and unassuming grey uniform of the SRF3 was also a success. It demarcated the women as participants in the war, and in Serbia it became an essential part of their martial identity. Sharon Oudit discusses the significance of uniforms in *Fighting Forces, Writing Women*. She argues that: 'Uniform is crucial to military organization. It also might be said to act as an interface between the individual and institution she represents; indeed it is often the means of transformation from the former to the latter.'[32] Dearmer and her peers, once in uniform, are without history, without individuality, without an easy definition of gender, subject only to the hierarchy of the military or quasi-military regime. As Yvonne Fitzroy puts it, 'Mercifully one feels less oneself in this grey kit, and one's belongings have a super-military air that discourages the civilian emotions.'[33] The anonymity subsumes feminine instinct as well as overt femininity. In most cases, as with the SRF3, the uniforms reflected, rather than copied, those of soldiers, rejecting all conventional 'femininities'.

The symbol of the red cross is equally important. While Dearmer's uniform defines her as 'of the war' it fails to locate her within it. Women in uniform without a Red Cross are a bit of an anomaly. At this early stage of the war, the *only* women in uniform were those associated with medical units such as Stobart's, privately funded and self-designed, creating an identity for themselves that allowed them to be associated with the army, but retaining some of the traits of feminine clothing. The formal women's military organisations such as the khaki-clad Women's Army Auxiliary Corps (WAAC) were not set up until much later, after the introduction of conscription.[34] The symbol of the red cross gave the women an additional credibility because it delineated their connection with an established medical institution. It was, as Dearmer notes, a powerful symbol that carried with it a range of meanings and implications. Writing after the war, Mary Borden, who had herself worked as a nurse near the front line on the Western Front, captured the potency of the symbol when representing a nurse in one of her stories: 'She was a beautiful animal dressed as a nun and branded with a red cross.'[35] In this fragment describing a war-weary regiment marching into a town for inspection, Borden places her nurse with the officiating officers. She is both of the military and separate from it. Borden's imagery suggests the complex position of the medical woman at the front, bearing a seductive femininity,[36] yet retaining the trappings of a chaste femininity. But what really gives her a presence is the 'red cross' 'branded' onto her; she is a uniformed healer with every right to be in the war zone alongside the men.[37]

Uniform was to become even more important for Flora Sandes. While it helped to give Dearmer a credible identity, it helped Sandes to become a 'man'. Friedrich Nietzsche argued that:

[W]hat things *are called* is incomparably more important than what they are. The reputation, name, and appearance, the usual measure and weight of a thing, what it counts for – originally almost always wrong and arbitrary, thrown over things like a dress and altogether foreign to their nature and even to their skin – all this grows from generation unto generation, merely because people believe in it, until it gradually grows to be part of the thing and turns into its very body.

What was at first appearance becomes in the end, almost invariably, the essence and is effective as such.[38]

The Serbian army uniform was more makeshift than the British, particularly when the army was in retreat, but it becomes an important signifier for Sandes once she ceases to be a woman-nurse and adopts the role of a man-soldier. The uniform becomes a symbol of her 'maleness', endorsing the rituals that she will perform, perhaps a type of drag. Butler argues that 'the notion of an original or primary gender identity is often parodied within the cultural practices of drag, cross-dressing, and the sexual stylization of butch/femme identities'.[39] For Sandes, however, cross-dressing has no sexual connotations, merely practical ones. Although her complete adoption of male dress does have a symbolic significance it is no parody; the role of soldier is not one that Sandes was performing, but actually living. After her initial trip to Serbia as a nurse, Sandes returned home at the end of her contract. After six weeks of fund-raising she returned to Serbia in the company of an American nurse, Emily Simmonds, with £2,000 for the Serbian cause. The pair worked in a military hospital in Valjevo treating the typhus epidemic that crippled the country in the winter of 1914–15. Sandes became ill with the disease, but made a full recovery.[40] During the summer lull in fighting she again returned to London, but was back in the country by October, determined to rejoin her hospital. Unfortunately this return coincided with the invasion of the country by the Bulgarian, German and Austrian armies and getting anywhere was extremely difficult. Contrary to the advice of the British consul, Sandes managed to travel into the country and attached herself as a nurse to a Serbian regiment. As the invasion and subsequent retreat of the Serbian army gathered momentum, Sandes found herself as much a soldier as a nurse. This was formalised when the commandant of the 2nd infantry regiment made her a private.

> Colonel Militch, laughingly took the little brass figure '2' of his own epaulettes, and fastened them on the shoulder-straps of his 'new recruit,' as he called me, it seemed a 'fait accompli,' and official sanction came when we reached Bitol [*sic*] before going into Albania.[41]

Again the symbol is important. From the outset a uniform of sorts marks Sandes out as a soldier. The regiment took uniforms from wherever they could: Sandes' was by turns grey, blue or khaki, the sign of the 'English' soldier, the epitome of the taboo identified by Grayzel.

With her cropped hair and breeches she blended in with the other troops. There was no obvious visible difference. She could ride as well as any man and shoot straight. She was, to all intents and purposes, an ordinary soldier. She also problematises Grayzel's argument because from the moment she joined the regiment in retreat she was in significant danger of making the 'ultimate sacrifice'.

Flora Sandes was not the only woman soldier in the Serbian army, nor indeed on the Eastern Front. Sandes herself spent time in hospital with a fellow woman soldier, Milunka Savic.[42] Other British women document encounters with women soldiers, who like Sandes seem to have had no difficulty enlisting. Elsie Corbett records that 'A Serb girl in soldier's uniform came up this evening and wanted to see Dr Banks and asked the way to Major Gashiatz's office, which Rudolph reported with great excitement; and Dr Banks said he had no idea she was not a young man.'[43] Like Sandes this woman seems to have completed the transition to soldier. Ishobel Ross of the SWH had a closer encounter. 'We shook hands with a woman soldier in the Serbian Army who came up to the camp to see us. Her name is Milian and she has such a nice face, so sturdy too. She has been fighting for three years and was so pleased to have her photo taken.'[44] Although Ross concedes to a pretty face, she still notes the 'sturdiness' of the woman soldier, in a kind of expectation of masculinity. Florence Farmborough, too, met women soldiers: 'A woman soldier with a badly contused leg came to us for a dressing: She did not belong to the Women's Death Battalion; she had, however heard of them and from her curt remarks one could understand that she held them in but little respect.'[45] Maria Bochkareva founded the Women's Battalion of Death in 1917. She had served as a soldier throughout the war, but had become disillusioned by the collapse of Russia's combat forces following the first revolution. She encouraged the all-female regiment to replace their men. As a curious postscript, Botchkareva, fleeing the country in 1918, was on the same steamer as Farmborough, the *Sheridan*, which sailed from Vladivostok in April.[46]

But Flora Sandes had the distinction of being the only British woman soldier to serve on any front in the First World War. And as such she could never be an ordinary private soldier. It seems probable that at least part of the reason why the Serbian officers so readily accepted her lay in her potential value for morale. As a British nurse, she represented the British Allies; the army that the Serbians hoped would come to their aid. A little British goodwill was very important. Equally, her medical skills increased her potential value on the battlefield. She was also given an orderly, along with other privileges that would not have been accorded to a private or even a non-commissioned officer, and she was quickly promoted. She was an anomaly, but nevertheless managed to blend in. Julie Wheelwright, whose book *Amazons and Military Maids* is a study of Sandes and women like her, argues that:

> Flora Sandes' ability to straddle these worlds provides insight into how women who masqueraded in the ranks were able to maintain their disguise. The female soldiers who were known to their comrades were accepted once they had 'proved' themselves and in the heat of battle, sexual difference was superseded by the larger, all-consuming struggle for survival.[47]

Sandes learned to play the role of the soldier so effectively that most of the time her comrades forgot she was a woman.

As a hospital orderly, Mabel Dearmer was near the bottom of the hierarchical structure of the camp. Stobart soon gave her the responsibility for all the camp's linen, which alleviated this slightly, but here the social patterns of civilian life were reversed. The orderlies were ladies – the poor useless 'ladies' who had been trained to do nothing – 'we have to take our orders from the nurses'.[48] Generally, the nurses were professionals, trained to do the job precisely because they came from a social class in which they needed to earn a living. Despite this, as the wife of the chaplain, Dearmer, not unlike Sandes, occupied an unusual middle ground; excluded from taking meals with her husband, Stobart and the doctors, she still had the option of sharing his tent instead of staying in the communal tent with the other orderlies. This must have been a great relief to her as her letters indicate that she suffered from a continual string of ailments from the time of her departure from England. Mabel Dearmer was rarely without pain.

Had Commandant Stobart known about these ailments, she might have felt that her first instincts about Dearmer were justified. Any concerns she may have had about Dearmer's fragility, her conventional 'femininity', her inadequacy, were certainly shared by Dearmer herself. Like the men and women who later wrote war fiction and memoirs, Dearmer wrote of the body in distress. Her concerns are like those of other writers and include 'fatigue, sleep deprivation, hunger, rotten food, the invasion of fleas and rats, cold'.[49] Paul Fussell highlights and analyses the impact of all these problems on the men in the trenches; the discomforts of the body are paramount in the experience of this war.[50] Dearmer's letters list a constant string of ailments, all of which threatened her potential efficiency. She embarked upon the journey with an injured knee that plagued her throughout; at times she could not walk because of the pain. In Paris she informed Gwynn that 'the knee is still swollen but not painful, I am still lying low about it'.[51] It would not have done for Stobart to hear of such potential vulnerability. In the same letter she wrote wistfully of the comfy bedrooms and hot baths that she would shortly leave behind. These preoccupations remained with her in Marseilles.

> I am still in bed waiting for the *femme de chambre* to give me a bath, the last until – when? Perhaps it will be smooth and nice though, and I shall have lots of baths. The knee isn't right yet. I have only one prayer now, that I shall have the strength to stick this job.[52]

While her ability to persevere with the job may be in question, she resembles most other women on the Eastern Front in her appreciation of the opportunity for a bath. Florence Farmborough records the building of a bathhouse for her camp with excitement: 'Among other wooden structures erected was one the contemplation of which was hailed with delight by the members of both Units: it was a *banya*, or bathing-house.'[53] Even the boundary-crossing Flora Sandes kept a rubber bath as part of her kit, astounding her fellow soldiers. She did not get to use it as often as she might have liked, but it was always useful to have it around should the opportunity arise.

Dearmer's niggling physical troubles continued. 'I have had a terrible arm from vaccination, which is, however, I am told, usual with some people, and nothing to be surprised at. It has been very painful and I could not move it.'[54] But as if aware that her letters were in danger of presenting her as a weak and vulnerable woman, she devoted a great deal of her correspondence to the art of reassurance.

> I am much better. I am emerging from all my inoculations into health, and it's such a happy feeling. My arm is still stiff and swollen, but I myself am beginning to feel like a bird and ready for anything.[55]

In fact, Dearmer's letters are insistently rhetorical, as though it is herself that she is trying to convince. Her choice of language is interesting. She feels like a bird, suggesting freedom rather than strength. Is it freedom from the physical troubles that hold her back, or excitement at whatever is to come? By the time she reached Salonika, Dearmer was anxious to start work despite a bout of travel sickness on top of all her other troubles, determined to prove that she could do her bit as well as any of the other women.

For Flora Sandes, the physical hardships of army life were even more pronounced, first on the Serbian retreat which led her regiment across the Albanian mountains to the coast, then back to Serbia via Salonika as they moved towards front-line action. For Sandes, as for Remarque's soldiers, getting enough to eat was always a priority. Erich Maria Remarque's *All Quite on the Western Front* illustrates this well, as narrator and protagonist Paul Baumer relates a range of adventures built around the acquisition of food and rituals of eating, blending the military and the domestic, the masculine and the feminine.[56] The soldiers shared whatever food they could find, but Sandes seemed particularly adept at foraging. Local people and army quartermasters alike seemed to be vulnerable to her female charms when it came to giving up food. She seemed able to overcome red tape when it came to feeding her men.

> I managed to pitch them such a pitiful tale of woe about the sufferings of the men, and the awful time I was having trying to get them something to eat, that I quite softened their hearts, and they said they would give me what I wanted without any further signature, but that I must not make a precedent of this unofficial way of doing business. I was overjoyed, and sent my orderly off at once to hunt up a carriage, and we returned to camp in triumph about 9 o'clock with a whole sackful of bread, another of tinned beef, and two large earthenware jars of wine.[57]

The paradoxical nature of Sandes' position is evident here. Although she could live as a man, she could also draw in the characteristics more associated with her as a woman, emphasising how she could use her gender-crossing position to the advantage of her men.

Dearmer spent May and June of 1915 organising the linen for her hospital. Her letters indicate that she enjoyed this job, despite the hard work it entailed. Her accounts of camp life are dominated by the physical challenges that are thrown at all the camp staff. The long days and hard work were something quite new and alien to her. She was constantly foot-sore, '[I] change my shoes three or four times a day',[58] but discovered a range of unexpected strengths. As noted in Chapter 1, Dearmer excitedly wrote, 'I have learned how to pitch my own tent ... and what guy lines are – and also I am much stronger in the arms than I thought I was.... I can hammer in my own tent pegs and lift packing-cases that a month ago I shouldn't have dreamt of touching.'[59] Although this is hardly the sophisticated wooden hut-building that Farmborough mastered,[60] it is a job normally carried out by a man, so Dearmer did learn new 'male' skills, discovering previously unsuspected aspects of herself. She was not as weak as she had imagined, and performed her duties to everyone's satisfaction. Mabel Stobart later wrote of her that 'none of her various roles in life were better played than her role of orderly in a Serbian camp hospital'.[61]

Tiredness and sleep deprivation were her worst enemies. Like the soldiers in the trenches, she had to snatch an hour of sleep whenever she could, but unlike them it was not the sound of the guns that kept her awake during periods of enforced waiting. Instead she was preoccupied by her responsibility to keep her hospital going for the wounded soldiers who were expected very soon. But despite her pity for the wounded and her desire to perform as well as her peers, night watch duty defeated Mabel Dearmer. 'Oh I am *so* sleepy and my feet feel like jelly. I was up at five – so my day to-day has been one of *twenty* hours.'[62] She had finally given in to exhaustion. 'Nothing – too tired. I have been called for night watch again, and refused. I couldn't help it. I'm too tired.'[63]

But it was Flora Sandes who experienced the greatest physical hardship in her role as a soldier. As well as the lice, the mud, the danger of infection and the lack of food, she had to face the enemy guns. On 15th November 1916 she was badly wounded. Her account in her autobiography indicates that her position as a woman entitled her to no special treatment at the casualty clearing station.

> The First Aid Dressing Station was the same in which I had been a dresser when I first joined the regiment, and by the time we reached it, blood was dripping through the stretcher. I was about at the end of my tether, but they gave me hot drinks, warmed me up, and then laid me on the table to probe round and find some of the numerous pieces of bomb. I buried my nose in the broad chest of Doctor B—, who was standing at my head, while the other one worked, and frankly yowled for the first time. But he knew better than to sympathize with an overwrought patient, so he lit a cigarette, thrust it between my lips, and told me to 'shut up and remember I was a soldier', which had more effect than any amount of petting would have done.[64]

Sandes' account acknowledges her twin status as both a woman and a soldier, but the resolution, the plugging of her wounds, and indeed the metaphoric plugging of her 'female' voice with the cigarette, emphasise the notion that her womanliness was forfeited on the battlefield. Established gender is disregarded. Sandes was perhaps fortunate to be discovered by other British women shortly after she was wounded. Elsie Corbett recalls:

> When we got back the following night we heard that Flora Sandes had been brought down, badly wounded, to the Field Ambulance beside which we were camped.... In hand to hand fighting Sandes was hit by a grenade thrown at short range, which broke her arm in several places and severely wounded her side. A snow blizzard was raging; there was no track down from the mountain top; there were not proper stretchers up there; and she had to be partly dragged on a ground sheet down the rocky hillside. The bearers lost their way, and it took them five hours to carry and slide her down to the Field Ambulance. At first she did not want to come to our camp in case it hurt the Serb feelings, but in the end the doctor himself persuaded her, and Edith Harley claimed her for her tent. She seemed to be wounded absolutely all over, but said we moved her much better than the Serbs did, which we felt was a tremendous compliment.[65]

This account suggests that Sandes was lucky to be alive, such was her ordeal after her wounding. Her continued loyalty to her Serbian unit is emphasised by her reluctance to move to the SWH, despite the obvious attraction of her compatriots. Sandes' wounds left her effectively disabled for life, but, as with so many soldiers, her condition did not result in her leaving the army; indeed it did not prevent her from returning to the fighting once she was patched up, just like the men.

While Sandes seems to put a brave face on her physical suffering, Dearmer was much more inclined to dwell on the hardship, to be aware of her potential limitations. Even while she proves what a woman can do, somehow she does not let go of the 'Edwardian woman' in her to the same extent. If the job of hospital orderly tried the female body at war, the conditions under which it must be performed, did little to help. The weather was a constant source of discomfort.

> It has been pelting and pouring with rain. The mud is ankle deep ...
> This heavy rain continues. You would laugh at my costume – breeches and heavy rubber boots, which are not one bit too heavy. I wear my macintosh over this, which has been shortened to the knee and girt round the waist with a luggage-strap ...

> The storms have been simply terrific. I was nearly blown out of my
> bed last night. It was miserably depressing to crawl out in the mud and
> loosen ropes and get soaked through.[66]

The self-image Dearmer offers here is a long way from that of her
pre-war self. Like the soldiers on the Western Front, she is surrounded
by and covered in mud. The language she employs to describe herself
and her surroundings is reminiscent of that found in many soldiers'
accounts. Her makeshift uniform of breeches and macintosh would
make her appear more like her male counterparts than her former self.
As her remarks suggest, Dearmer understands the way the weather
conditions help to transform the female body into something unrecog-
nisable, something more androgynous, a creature of the war. Yvonne
Fitzroy, dealing with the Russian winter of 1917, echoes these sentiments: '[A] frightful blizzard, and collapse of the wood and water supply. The problem seems to be getting serious.... Colder than ever with
a bitter wind. I suffered a severe relapse, and had to stay in bed, tooth-
ache being added to my other woes.'[67]

And when it was not raining, the sun came out.

> It is *very* hot now in the day time, my face and neck are very sore and
> burnt. I have sent into the town to see if a veil of any kind can be
> found.[68]
>
> I am very well – but I am suffering from prickly heat which, I under-
> stand, is a common complaint in these parts. We have all got it, and it
> is *the* most unbearable and tiresome thing you can imagine and takes
> away one's sleep – one's nice comfy sleep I mean, not the sleep of ex-
> haustion which no amount of prickly heat would do away with – and
> it makes one's arms and body look so horrid although it is not on one's
> face.[69]
>
> I am not suffering from anything at present but fleas at night.
> Fleas! – they have snouts like walruses – and sulphur, Keating and ver-
> migelli are just pleasant little tonics to them – and as to the boiling sun-
> shine that is supposed to kill them, they simply revel in it and hop with
> joy when I put my blankets out to air.[70]

Suffering from the heat, Dearmer seeks to once more adopt the trappings of womanhood in the form of a veil. But here the veil is trans-
formed from a symbol of elegant femininity into a practical tool to protect her from the sun, giving it a curious double meaning. Likewise,
Dearmer's descriptions of the trials of prickly heat hold a similar echo
of her past life. She takes some small comfort from the fact that her

face is unmarked, suggesting a kind of limp vanity that feels out of place in the hospital camp. And as if sunburn and prickly heat are not enough, the sun appears to exacerbate the problem of fleas. Dearmer's hatred of the fleas once again parallels the experience of combat soldiers, who often cited lice as one of the worst plagues of the trenches. 'Killing each louse is a tedious business when a man has hundreds. The little beasts are hard and the everlasting cracking with one's fingernails very soon becomes wearisome.'[71] But not all women reacted with such passion as Dearmer. Caroline Twigge Matthews approaches these various types of vermin more stoically, learning to cope with the cockroaches that had previously filled her with fear.

> There is a side to travelling on the vessels which ply the Syrian coasts which used to cause me hours of distress and moments of horror and pathos, but when these beetles and beasties of that ilk ran over my blankets and bit my face and flavoured my food in Serbia I sometimes smiled when I thought of the acute physical suffering it really had once meant.[72]

Dearmer's letters, with their myriad different ailments and injuries, sore knees, and arms, lice, prickly heat, cold, wet and mud, seem to present her body in a fragmented form. The structures of the letters themselves reflect this fragmentation. They are written in an informal, rather chatty style, flitting from one topic to another, often leaving the reader waiting for more information. They are fragmented by interruptions – she was often forced to rush away to the work of the hospital, only to pick up the letter hours later with a completely different thread. As Jane Marcus suggests, 'the body of the text is "not whole"; it is a war casualty'.[73] She had to juggle her multiple roles in her letters to be both woman friend and hospital orderly, to inform but also to protect her reader. The fragmentation of her writing draws a parallel with many other front-line war texts as well as with the physical realities of life in the war zone.

Flora Sandes, on the other hand, tried to tell as much as possible of her war experience in both her published accounts. In a retrospective account there is no need for interruption or fragmentation. But what she describes is often a collective experience rather than simply her own.

> Hill 1212 is a fairly high mountain, and the Bulgars were strongly entrenched on the top of it.

About 10 p.m. my company was halted behind a big pile of rock, some way up, and close to the Battalion Reserve, with the rest of the battalion on the other side facing the enemy, who preserved a dead silence all night.

It was bitterly cold, so we spread our groundsheets on the snow, and slept wrapped in our overcoats. No Serbian carries a blanket, they scornfully contended that a man wasn't a soldier if he couldn't sleep out on the mountains in midwinter with only his overcoat!

Dawn was just breaking when I was awakened by the sudden crackle of rifle-fire, followed clearly, loudly and ominously close, by the wild 'hourra hourras' of the Bulgarian attack.[74]

This kind of detail is typical. She was concerned to recreate as much of the atmosphere as possible, to engage the senses of the reader: sound is almost as important as feeling. The mundane, the ritual, the repeated are all part of the routines of her life. Although she includes personal anecdotes, much of her information speaks of a collective identity, 'we ... slept wrapped in our overcoats', 'no Serbian carries a blanket'. In this interpretation Sandes qualifies as both a 'man' and a 'soldier' because her practice conforms to that of her company. Hill 1212 was in fact the site of her wounding, the location of her final initiation into 'manhood'.

By the time Sandes was facing the bombs on Hill 1212, Mabel Dearmer was long dead, victim of the terrible infectious disease that Sandes had already fought at Valjevo. Many British women succumbed to infectious illness while on active service, and a few, like Dearmer, died. Florence Farmborough was taken seriously ill, like Dearmer, with a strain of typhoid in September 1916. It meant she was unable to retreat with her unit and was instead evacuated to a field hospital. Such was the severity of her condition that she was sent to convalesce in the Crimea. Her physical condition was so poor that she had to have her head shaved. This loss of her hair, one of the most significant trappings of her femininity, had a profound effect on Farmborough's self-image, despite the fact that her nurse's headdress completely covered her head throughout the lengthy period of regrowth.[75] Mabel Dearmer believed in her own physical vulnerability, and was on the defensive from the outset. She *knew* that she might die and spoil it for everyone else. The obsession with the danger of typhus is apparent throughout her correspondence, as she reports the various methods applied by the camp to prevent infection.

The arrangements seem extraordinarily complete. We may not have a cup of tea or a biscuit in our tents without first spreading a cloth so that not one single crumb shall fall to the ground to attract a fly. We may not even clean our teeth and throw the water on the grass – everything has to go to a particular place. We are to have our temperatures taken every morning.[76]

The body must be protected at all costs. The women of the camp would only be of use to the war effort, if they were subject to a strict regime.

Mabel Dearmer saw the suffering in the surrounding hospitals even before the disease penetrated her own. 'I feel it would be horrid to get typhus just now when life is so delightful',[77] she wrote soon after her arrival. But the fear of the disease, combined with homesickness and the physical hardships of camp life, left her prone to depression. And in June, they lost their battle against infection. A number of the camp staff, including Mabel Stobart, were placed in isolation, suffering from typhoid fever. Dearmer's reaction was pessimistic, but once again offering to reassure. She wrote to Gwynn:

If I get it, will you always remember that I am *very* strong with a terrific constitution, and most tremendously alive and well from my life in the open, so that there is every chance of my pulling through....

One has to stop someday, and personally I would rather 'stop' here, doing this work, than anywhere else in the world. There is nothing terrifying or agonizing about typhus – you sleep most of the time, and just drift away into the unknown quite quietly.[78]

The tone of the letter changes significantly halfway through. On the one hand Dearmer appears confident. She tells Gwynn that she will send him a wire if she is taken ill, but wants to get in the reassurance first that even in this event, all will not be lost. But, as the letter progresses, the shift from confidence in her health to the positive nature of such a death is somewhat unnerving. It begins to feel as though this is what she expects after all. Being a part of the war, something far bigger than herself, with national consequences, makes the sacrifice worthwhile. Finally the notion of sacrifice begins to place her on an almost level footing with the soldiers. She begins to assume a role of equal danger, to perform similar rituals.

As illness in the camp progressed, the danger that women might make the 'ultimate sacrifice' became significant. As we have seen, they would not be the first. Nicoletta Gullace argues that 'Women who risked injury or death became an important part of both feminist panegyric and suffrage argumentation. This bravery didn't slip the notice of the general public.'[79] As noted in Chapter 2, on 4th July, a nurse, Lorna Ferriss, died of typhus with complications. When Dearmer was actually taken ill, in early June, she attempted to keep it from the camp authorities, as she wanted to continue with her work and did not want to be isolated. She made light of her illness: 'I simply feel hot and "soppy" and dissolve into tears at intervals during the day and night. My prickly heat sticks to the blankets (oh for sheets!) and my hair is in wet lumps, and I don't feel lovely or heroic or anything – which just means that I am not really ill at all.'[80] She trivialises her symptoms, teasing herself for this 'feminine' reaction. The camp staff, many of whom felt unwell, laughed and joked about these petty illnesses, while surrounded by so much genuine suffering.

As June progressed, the very hot weather brought with it further disease and there was growing concern for those in the camp who were considered seriously ill. Dearmer eventually gave in to the illness. 'Yesterday I knocked under with this fever – typhoid – but mild, owing to inoculations. Don't worry about me – it may mean, though, that I come back to England at the end of three months. I should be no help unless quite fit.... Good-bye. M.'[81] This was to be her last letter, typically self-effacing.

Mabel Dearmer did not die for almost a month. Indeed, she appeared to be making a recovery. During that time, Gwynn had only telegrams to inform him of her progress. He wrote, 'On the 9th [of July] they still hoped to save her. But I am sure that long before this her face was set for the last journey, and she would not willingly have turned back.'[82] She died of typhoid (enteric fever) with pneumonia on 11th July 1915. Stobart wrote:

> From the first I had misgivings about her; I felt that she had not the physique to withstand this type of illness. It was partly on this account that I had been unwilling to accept her services when first offered.... My first instinct about her suitability had only been right in regard to her physique.[83]

In terms of Dearmer's ability to adapt, to reject the internalised gender constraints of her home life, Stobart had been quite wrong. Mabel Dearmer is buried at Kragujevatz next to Lorna Ferriss, her fellow unit member, and Dr Elizabeth Ross from the fever hospital, who had died a little earlier.

But a great many British women, a great many Edwardian 'ladies', apparently equally as fragile on the outside as Mabel Dearmer, also survived the war in Serbia and Russia. As the 'female other' front of the First World War, the Eastern Front offered many women the opportunity to be much more closely involved with the war than the British government would allow. It enabled them to escape from the conventional 'female' identity of war, that of motherhood, and take on roles that brought them much closer to the male war experience. Individually, they each found their own way to adapt and survive, or otherwise. Mabel St Clair Stobart, who went on to lead her hospital unit on the terrible retreat across Serbia, Montenegro and Albania, was a small, 'feminine'-looking woman, a similar physical type to Dearmer. Stobart and many women like her worked very hard to prove that women could contribute just as well as men in wartime.

Flora Sandes became a career soldier in the Serbian army, promoting the cause of Serbia around the world, rising to the rank of lieutenant, only demobbed in 1922. She recorded:

> I cannot attempt to describe what it now felt like, trying to get accustomed to a woman's life and a woman's clothes again; and also to ordinary society after having lived entirely with men for so many years.
>
> Turning from a woman into a private soldier proved nothing compared with turning back again from soldier to ordinary woman. It was like losing everything at one fell swoop, and trying to find bearings again in another life and an entirely different world.[84]

Her difficulties settling back into 'female' civilian life demonstrate how comprehensively she had been able to change her gender in the first place. As Butler suggests, changing gender is a laborious project, throwing on a dress is not enough in the first instance to alter the essence of the subject. What Sandes has been 'called' is more important than what she 'is'. Whereas for Dearmer the female body had seemed to be a liability in the war zone, for Sandes it is almost as though the female body ceased to exist, as though she had found a space in which she could literally become a 'man', so completely was she assimilated into the rituals of army life. Her story is, admittedly, unique. But it does nonetheless suggest that traditional arguments against women's involvement in conflict could be invalidated. It also supports the notion that Serbia, the 'female other' of the First World War, did indeed provide a theatre of war in which, for a woman, anything was possible. As Caroline Twigge Matthews states, 'When the

Roll Call is made we each must give our own separate answer and show our own method of deduction, the way in which we ourselves have solved Life's problem.'[85]

Notes

1 Caroline Twigge Matthews, *Experiences of a Woman Doctor in Serbia* (London: Mills & Boon, 1916, p. 25.

2 Judith Butler, 'Bodily Inscriptions, Performative Subversions', in Sara Salih (ed.), with Judith Butler, *The Judith Butler Reader* (Oxford: Blackwell, 2005), p. 114.

3 *Ibid.*

4 Jane Marcus, 'Corpus/Corps/Corpse: Writing the Body in/at War', in Helen Margaret Cooper, Adrienne Munich and Susan Merrill Squier (eds), *Arms and the Woman: War, Gender and Literary Representation* (Chapel Hill and London: University of North Carolina Press, 1989), p. 135.

5 Flora Sandes, *The Autobiography of a Woman Soldier: A Brief Record of Adventures with the Serbian Army 1916–1919* (London: H. F. & G. Witherby, 1927), p. 9.

6 For example see the work of Laura Doan, 'Topsy-Turvydom: Gender Inversion, Sapphism, and the Great War', *GLQ: A Journal of Lesbian and Gay Studies* 12:4 (2006), 517–42, and 'Primum Mobile: Women and Auto/Mobility in the Era of the Great War', *Women: A Cultural Review* 17:1 (2006), 26–41.

7 Louis Althusser, 'Ideology and Ideological State Apparatuses' in Julie Rivkin and Michael Ryan (eds), *Literary Theory: An Anthology* (Oxford: Blackwell, 2004), pp. 693–702.

8 *Ibid.*, p. 696.

9 Butler, 'Bodily Inscriptions', p. 114.

10 Mabel Dearmer, *Letters from a Field Hospital* (London: Macmillan & Co., 1916), p. 60.

11 Mabel Dearmer had worked as an illustrator for *The Yellow Book*, and published six novels before establishing herself as a respected dramatist in London.

12 Flora Sandes married Yurie Yudenitch, a Russian artillery colonel, in May 1927.

13 Judith Butler, 'Variations on Sex and Gender', in Salih, *Judith Butler Reader*, p. 26.

14 Paul Fussell, *The Great War and Modern Memory* (Oxford: Oxford University Press, 1977), particularly ch. 8.

15 Joanna Bourke, *Dismembering the Male: Men's Bodies, Britain and the Great War* (London: Reaktion Books, 1996).

16 Santanu Das, *Touch and Intimacy in First World War Literature* (Cambridge: Cambridge University Press, 2005).

17 Susan R. Grayzel, *Women's Identities at War: Gender, Motherhood and Politics in Britain and France during the First World War* (Chapel Hill and London: University of North Carolina Press, 1999).

18 Mabel St Clair Stobart was the mother of two adult sons.

19 Sigmund Freud, 'Our Attitude towards Death', in *Civilisation, Society and Religion* (London: Penguin Books, 1985), pp. 8–9.

20 *Ibid.*, p. 80.

21 Dearmer, *Letters*, p. 121.

22 Julie Wheelwright, *Amazons and Military Maids* (London: Pandora, 1989), p. 34. For more detailed information about Sandes' early life, see Louise Miller, *A Fine Brother: The Life of Captain Flora Sandes* (London: Alma Books, 2012), ch. 2.

23 For full discussion of the 'New Woman' see Ann Heilmann (ed.), *Feminist Forerunners: New Womanism and Feminism in the Early Twentieth Century* (London: Pandora, 2003).

24 Dearmer, *Letters*, p. 60.

25 Nicoletta Gullace, *The Blood of Our Sons: Men, Women and the Regeneration of British Citizenship during the Great War* (Basingstoke: Palgrave Macmillan, 2002), p.110.

26 Dearmer, *Letters*, p. 60.

27 Susan R. Grayzel, '"The Outward and Visible Sign of Her Patriotism": Women, Uniforms, and National Service during the First World War', *Twentieth Century British History* 8:2 (1997), 145–64.

28 Dearmer, *Letters*, p. 74.

29 *Ibid.*, p. 77.

30 Ellen Chivers Davies, *A Farmer in Serbia* (London: Methuen, 1916), p. 4.

31 Mitchell Library, Glasgow, SWH Archive, Large Trunk, Letter dated 16th August 1915, from Elsie Inglis to Miss Morris.

32 Sharon Ouditt, *Fighting Forces, Writing Women* (London: Routledge, 1994), p. 17.

33 Yvonne Fitzroy, *With the Scottish Nurses in Roumania* (London: John Murray, 1918), p. 1.

34 Lucy Noakes, *Women in the British Army: War and the Gentle Sex, 1907–1948* (London and New York: Routledge, 2006), ch. 4.

35 Mary Borden, *The Forbidden Zone* (London: William Heinemann, 1929), p. 34.

36 See Sandra M. Gilbert, 'Soldier's Heart: Literary Men, Literary Women, and the Great War', *Signs* 8:3, Women and Violence (Spring 1983), 422–50, for a full discussion of the idea of the empowerment of nurses in the First World War.

37 For further discussion of Borden's work in this context, see Angela K. Smith, *The Second Battlefield: Women, Modernism and the First World War* (Manchester: Manchester University Press, 2000), ch. 3.

38 Friedrich Nietzsche, *The Gay Science* (London: Vintage, 1974), p. 58.

39 Butler, 'Bodily Inscriptions', p. 111.

40 For more details, see Miller, *A Fine Brother*.

41 Sandes, *Autobiography*, p. 13.

42 Miller, *A Fine Brother*, p. 349.

43 Elsie Corbett, *Red Cross in Serbia 1915–1919* (Banbury: Cheney & Sons, 1964), p. 39.

44 Ishobel Ross, *Little Grey Partridge: First World War Diary of Ishobel Ross Who Served with the Scottish Women's Hospitals Unit in Serbia*, ed. Jess Dixon (Aberdeen: Aberdeen University Press, 1988), p. 23.

45 Florence Farmborough, *With the Armies of the Tsar: A Nurse at the Russian Front in War and Revolution, 1914–1918* (New York: Cooper Square Press, 2000 [1974]), pp. 306–7.

46 *Ibid.*, p. 408.

47 Wheelwright, *Amazons and Military Maids*, p. 61.

48 Dearmer, *Letters*, p. 75.

49 Marcus, 'Corpus/Corps/Corpse', p. 142.

50 Fussell, *The Great War and Modern Memory*, ch. 2.

51 Dearmer, *Letters*, p. 76.

52 *Ibid.*, p. 78.

53 Farmborough, *With the Armies of the Tsar*, p. 78.

54 *Ibid.*, p. 83.

55 *Ibid.*, p. 91.

56 Erich Maria Remarque, *All Quiet on the Western Front* (London: Picador, 1991 [1929].) Remarque's novel raises similar questions about the significance of the domestic from a male point of view.

57 Flora Sandes, *An English Woman-Sergeant in the Serbian Army* (London, New York and Toronto: Hodder and Stoughton, 1916), p. 45.

58 Dearmer, *Letters*, p. 111.

59 *Ibid.*, p. 121.

60 'In the forest, we learnt to build woodland houses, and so skilled did we become in the art that we grew to despise tent-life.' Farmborough, *With the Armies of the Tsar*, p. 78.

61 Mabel St Clair Stobart, *The Flaming Sword in Serbia and Elsewhere* (London, New York and Toronto: Hodder and Stoughton, 1917), p. 53.

62 Dearmer, *Letters*, p. 125.

63 *Ibid.*, pp. 126–7.

64 Sandes, *Autobiography*, pp. 67–8.

65 Corbett, *Red Cross in Serbia*, pp. 86–7.

66 Dearmer, *Letters*, pp. 131–2.

67 Fitzroy, *With the Scottish Nurses in Roumania*, p. 111.

68 Dearmer, *Letters*, p. 119.

69 *Ibid.*, p. 151.

70 *Ibid.*, pp. 167–8. Keating's powder was a widely used insecticide. Vermigelli was a jelly or ointment smeared on to the body and clothes to deter lice.

71 Remarque, *All Quiet on the Western Front*, p. 54.
72 Matthews, *Experiences of a Woman Doctor*, p. 29.
73 Marcus, 'Corpus/Corps/Corpse', p. 146. Jane Marcus is actually discussing *Not So Quiet: Stepdaughters of War* by Evadne Price, but her analogy works equally well for Mabel Dearmer's writing.
74 Sandes, *Autobiography*, p. 61.
75 Farmborough describes her illness in detail, *With the Armies of the Tsar*, pp. 238–46.
76 Dearmer, *Letters*, p. 101.
77 *Ibid.*, p. 113.
78 *Ibid.*, pp. 150–1. Dearmer's description of the symptoms of typhus is quite inaccurate. 'At first they were stricken with a severe headache, cough and chills. Within twenty-four hours they could hardly move, prostrated by soaring fever and excruciating muscle pain in their legs and back. Sticky white mucus began to accumulate in their mouths and throats, coating their tongues thickly. Four or five days later a pink rash spread from their chests across their bodies and rapidly developed into purplish-red slightly elevated spots. Often its victims became delirious or writhed in agony from the wracking pains in their limbs; many suffered from diarrhoea and became incontinent. After about a week the high fever dropped away suddenly while its victims sweated profusely, only to rise and fall two or three times over subsequent days. Those who survived were often reduced to near skeletons.' Miller, *A Fine Brother*, p. 59.
79 Gullace, *The Blood of Our Sons*, p. 157.
80 Dearmer, *Letters*, p.156.
81 *Ibid.*, p. 173.
82 *Ibid.*, p. 175.
83 Stobart, *The Flaming Sword*, pp. 51–3.
84 Sandes, *Autobiography*, p. 220.
85 Matthews, *Experiences of a Woman Doctor*, p. 25.

4

Waiting for the Allies: prisoners of war

> Little grey ghosts are walking to-night among the oak trees, the moon
> is overshadowed and there is a chilly wind that makes a small moaning
> noise around the tents. I am cold and very sad, and I shall not write
> any more.[1]

On 30th September 1915, Ellen Chivers Davies said goodbye to the
Serbian troops who had been stationed with her unit throughout the
summer. It was three days after they received the news that Bulgaria
had joined the war on the side of Germany and Austria. The phoney
war was over and all those in Serbia prepared to face the worst. It had
been a quiet summer, after Serbia's perhaps unexpected military success in repelling the Austrians the previous autumn. But Bulgaria's
entry into the war was to change everything for the Balkan state.
The Allies and the Central Powers had been competing for the allegiance of Bulgaria for some time, both understanding its strategic
importance. But as Misha Glenny argues, 'No Balkan nation joined in
the Great War because of any special sympathy for either of the two
power blocs.... Bulgaria attacked Serbia not to open up supply lines
from Berlin to Istanbul, but to regain Macedonia.'[2] It was, Glenny suggests, effectively a Third Balkan War, drawing once again on the unavoidable histories of conflicts in the region. It is hardly surprising that
Davies ends her diary with such a sad entry. The only consolation, as
the Serbian army headed off for war, was the reassuring pledge of support from her allies, the British and the French, already stationed at
Salonika. Lady Paget takes up the story.

> Then the storm burst. The Germans and the Austrians advanced from
> the north; the Bulgarians swept into Macedonia from the east. It was
> known that all available regiments had been sent north and that,

relying on the Allies, the military authorities had left the southern portion of the Bulgarian frontier practically undefended. Thus there were the makings of panic and disaster on a colossal scale.[3]

Paget's account of the invasion of Serbia was printed for private circulation some months after her return to England in 1916. As she would also go on to record, the Allies never came. Tim Judah suggests that there was every reason to expect support from Britain.

[I]n the wake of all that has happened since, it is difficult to imagine just how glorious was the Serbian name during and after the First World War. The Serbian Relief Fund in Britain boasted no lesser figure than Queen Mary as its patroness and its president was the Bishop of London.[4]

But in military terms, the Allies did not regard Serbia as strategically important enough to risk troops; they had other priorities. When the country was flooded by the invading armies in late 1915, the Serbian army, weakened after three years of warfare,[5] had no chance at all of holding them off. Tens of thousands fled, both soldiers and civilians, and among them, most of the British women who had been working in hospital and relief units for various organisations since the beginning of the war. Lady Paget's husband, Sir Ralph, was the Commissioner for British Relief Units in Serbia. He had been appointed by the Foreign Office in April 1915 when it became clear to the British government that a significant number of British units were already in Serbia.[6] Working under the joint auspices of the Red Cross and the Order of St John, he had spent six months trying to co-ordinate the work of the British. With the invasion he personally undertook to ensure that staff from all the units had the opportunity to leave the country; a significant proportion of these were women. Some headed for Salonika, the gateway held by the British. Others, like those attached to Mabel St Clair Stobart's SRF3, accompanied the fleeing armies across the mountains of Montenegro and Albania to the west. Their adventures will be explored in the next chapter. Some women, however, mostly doctors and nurses, but Lady Paget as an administrator among them, simply refused to leave. Their sense of duty and their patriotism was too strong. Despite the fact that the British army did not come to Serbia's aid, or perhaps because of it, the women who stayed behind to run their hospitals, who chose to be prisoners of war, turned to their 'Britishness' both to protect their medical charges and to make their own personal stand against their captors. If they were the only Allies prepared to fight for Serbia, they were determined to make their presence felt.

In this chapter, I wish to argue that these British women saw themselves as serving the British war cause, despite their location in a very alien land. Although Serbia was an ally, it had a reputation for being a rather wild and savage territory, and was culturally very different from their British home. But it was an innate patriotism, a commitment to their Britishness that motivated the women to remain, even as Serbia fell. I also suggest that it was the culture of Empire in which these women had been raised that stimulated this patriotism, giving them a sense of duty that was deeply embedded in their sense of personal identity. Julia Bush has argued that 'The British Empire was a subject of interest, and even a source of pride and enthusiasm, for a great many Edwardian women.'[7] But it was more than this. The culture of Empire enabled these women to see themselves as beacons of Britishness in all foreign lands, and that duty extended to representing their country if there were no men around to do it. This led to their being placed in a complex position. As doctors and nurses, as carers, they needed to prioritise their sick and wounded. But as British women, representing their country in a war zone, they often needed to assert themselves in other ways, leading to a need for twin identities that did not always sit comfortably together.

Serbia was an ally partly by default. Many saw the Serbs as responsible for triggering the war in the first place, as it was a Serbian nationalist who had effectively fired the first shot. The assassination of the Austrian heir to the throne and an old allegiance with Russia brought her into the conflict on the Allied side. While the conquest of Serbia offered Germany a useful communication route with her Ottoman allies to the south, its defence was seen as less of a priority by the British, who had other important battles to fight in 1915 with the attack at Gallipoli, as well as on the Western Front. As Louise Miller notes:

> The British Naval Mission, under the Command of the Rear Admiral Ernest Troubridge, had arrived in Serbia in early 1915. Although it was tiny, only seventy men, the Serbs put their faith in them and the even smaller French and Russian Missions to defend their northern border, and transferred the greater part of their thin forces to the east to face the Bulgarians.[8]

But the British women based in Serbia had no way of knowing the extreme limitations of these forces. Like the Serbs, they had no access to military strategy. They knew only that they were working with an ally, embroiled as they were in the daily life of the country. Paget's SRF1 at Skopje had been set up in mid-November 1914. Throughout the winter of 1914–15, they had seen little fighting, but instead, as discussed in Chapter 2, had been on hand to provide medical support and nursing care during the shattering typhus epidemic that raged across the country until the late spring of 1915. It had been a difficult winter.

The terrible winter led into a long and relatively quiet summer. But they must have had little idea of what was going on elsewhere in the war. As they waited for the war to find them, they, like the Serbians around them, expected that the allies would repel any attack on Serbia as a matter of course. Mabel St Clair Stobart passed through Nis just after the invasion, and remarked that:

> [T]he town was indeed beflagged in honour of the arrival of the Allies!! We guessed that they would not arrive now, and for many weeks to come, those flags of welcome drooped metaphorically in our hearts, reproducing that indescribable feeling of mingled hope, disappointment, and humiliation that we felt as we rode into Nish [*sic*] that day.[9]

Stobart's mobility and military position gave her insight into the true situation. It was less clear to those women working in static hospitals. When the expected invasion came in September 1915, they began to take in the new casualties of war. But there was no response from the allies. The situation in Serbia reached a crisis very quickly. As the invading armies advanced, Lady Paget travelled to Salonika to try to impress upon the British and French generals stationed there that the situation facing her hospital was very urgent. But her pleas fell upon deaf ears. She discovered to her astonishment that the Allies really had no immediate plans to intervene. As she returned to her unit, Paget began to see at first hand the exodus of the Serbian people as they fled.

> The station [at Veles] was in great disorder, the platform being packed with refugees and wounded who had crawled from the battle-field, and before the train finally drew up wounded and unwounded alike tried to rush it, hanging on the roofs, the one idea of the crowd being escape no matter how. Little children were trampled under foot and others hurled by their parents over the heads of the affrighted crowds into the horse

boxes where the sick and wounded soldiers huddled together. Willing hands were out stretched to catch these little ones but many were injured. The scene was horrible. Women were screaming, children crying, men shouting, and it was impossible to help them as the frenzied mob was too intent on fighting its way into the train to pay attention to us, and we tried in vain to make ourselves heard above the din.[10]

Although Paget's account is retrospective, she manages to convey the chaos of the retreat. It echoes events witnessed and recorded by British women across Serbia at this desperate time. Society is out of control and in panic. The failure of the women to make their voices heard in the chaos seems to be an ironic reflection of Paget's failed meeting with the Allied generals. Nobody was listening to their pleas for quiet, for order, for assistance: all fell on deaf ears. Her focus on the plight of children gives the account an added poignancy. It is clear that she believes the weakest will suffer the most in a situation where nobody listens. This vulnerability reinforces her need to offer aid. It is almost a patriotic duty.

However, when she returned to her hospital the situation was even worse. In her absence the decision had been taken to evacuate all British medical and nursing staff. Two hundred of the Austrian prisoners of war, who represented the legacy of the autumn military successes and had since then been doing vital work as orderlies, had also been removed. The walking wounded had joined the throng. But the hospital was full to bursting point with wounded men who could not be moved. And the invaders were approaching.

Of all the Allies, Serbia was one of the hardest hit by the First World War. John Keegan has argued that Serbia was:

> The worst proportionate sufferer ... of whose pre-war population of five million, 125,000 were killed or died as soldiers, but another 650,000 civilians succumbed to privation and disease, making a total of 15 per cent of the population lost, compared with something between two and three per cent of the British French and German populations.[11]

The 1915 invasion made a significant contribution to this devastation as it shattered the country and its population. It took six weeks for the combined Bulgarian, Austrian and German forces to occupy the country. Once occupied, the interim rule was divided between the Austrians and the Bulgarians. As Tim Judah suggests, 'Conditions under occupation were appalling. In addition to those despatched to concentration camps in Hungary, some 30,000 Serbs were sent to Austrian camps or used as forced labour. Factories were plundered of their machinery and a devastating typhus epidemic stalked the land.'[12] Thousands of women and children were left behind to face this chaos. Thousands of prisoners of war were on the move, carrying with them infection and despair. And no Allied armies appeared to help them out. The Bulgarian armies quickly settled into occupation. Glenny states that 'the Germans were soon to learn to their cost that Bulgaria was interested only in its narrow war aims. Once the Bulgarians had occupied southern Serbia and northern Macedonia and helped the Germans and Austro-Hungarians drive the Serbian army south-west through Kosovo and Albania, their commitment to the Central Powers faded.'[13] While in the longer term this narrow view would eventually pave the way for the return of a triumphant Serbian army, it was not good news in the short term for the conquered people who remained.

Many British women had been welcomed and accepted and had become part of the Serbian communities during 1915. No doubt conscious of the absence of their own armies, they were reluctant to leave now, when the need for relief seemed at its greatest. Lady Paget decided to stay. Despite the best efforts of her husband to get all the British women out, she understood that if she, as an upper-class British civilian woman, retained command of the hospital it might offer the wounded Serbians some protection. And if she could save the hospital stores, she would be in a position to offer aid to the stricken town as well as to the soldiers. A well-equipped hospital was a bargaining tool in wartime. The Serbian generals agreed to her staying, although all the other nurses were told to go; only male medical staff were to be allowed to stay on. But Paget and some of her nurses refused to comply and argued that if they stayed and continued to serve the Serbian people, they might alleviate some of the bad feeling caused by the failure of the Allies to step in. They won the argument, but their decision was not an easy one.

> It is impossible to give a clear account of the next two or three days, of the increasing nightmare of horror that descended upon Skoplje, [sic] sweeping us into alternative moods of feverish activity and sullen lassitude, as rumour after rumour held sway. Our nerves and tempers varied like a barometer before a typhoon, the unceasing rain chilled our bodies and souls, and mud plastered all and everything with ugliness and desolation.[14]

Paget's metaphor of the barometer before a typhoon suggests a woman used to travel, a woman of the world. She had certainly spent time in the Far East, as at the time of her marriage Sir Ralph Paget was Extraordinary Envoy and Minister Plenipotentiary to Siam. She had also lived in Germany before he was given the same role for the Kingdom of Serbia. Her weather imagery, her use of pathetic fallacy, emphasise the despair of those waiting. She had seen a lot, but nothing had prepared her for this situation of defeat. All evacuating staff left by 21st October 1915. The Bulgarians marched in on 22nd October.

Because the Allies failed to come to Serbia's aid, the relationship between the British women and the country grew even more complex. The hard military reality was that, for the British and the French, the timing of the invasion of Serbia was quite wrong. The intention had been to deploy Allied troops from Gallipoli as needed. But the Gallipoli campaign had not gone according to plan and there were no troops available. However, no one in Serbia understood this so the expectation remained. The British women, who already stood out from the crowd because they were so clearly Western European, came to represent, for the Serbian people, the Allies upon whom they were so depending. The women internalised this expectation of their patriotic duty, and as representatives of their country, some would not leave despite the grave danger they now faced.

Although by October 1915, many of the British women working in Serbia were in flight, along with most of the army and a good proportion of the civilian population, Lady Paget was not the only one to refuse to leave her wounded. The founder of the SWH, Dr Elsie Inglis, also refused to leave her post at Krushevatz, which was taken by the Germans in November 1915.

> The German occupation of Krushevatz was heralded in proper form by bombardment. The Serbs blew up the railway bridge, which attracted their fire and they threw bombs and several shells into the town. We felt that we had had our baptism of fire....
>
> Their entry next morning, 7th November, was almost in the form of an anti-climax. We turned into the principal street to find a German regiment lined up there. The best of the Serbs had left, white flags were hanging out of most of the occupied houses, and Krushevatz was taken.[15]

Like Lady Paget, Inglis and her contingent of nurses became prisoners of war. And like Paget, they were very conscious of their 'Britishness' in that time of crisis.

Inglis knew exactly what she was doing when she opted to remain with her patients as the invasion began.

It seemed to some of us impossible to leave her [Serbia] in her hour of catastrophe. We had come out to help, and now that help was most needed it was our clear duty to stand by. Sir Ralph Paget gave his consent to those staying who wished to. It was the good fortune of some of us that we were able to work for Serbs in a Serbian hospital as long as there were Serbs to work for. Others of us, who desired the same lot, were fated to spend dreary weeks as prisoners in Austria.[16]

When Inglis subsequently wrote about her time in Serbia, she took care to record the history of her intervention from a Serbian point of view. It was very clear that the bond established between the women and their Serbian Allies was extremely strong. She does not concern herself with the absent British, but with doing all she can to alleviate suffering in the face of that absence.

Sir Ralph Paget did endeavour to evacuate as many British women as possible and his attempts elsewhere were more successful, but equally they reveal a great deal of unwillingness on the part by women to accept the Allied abandonment of Serbia to the enemy. The unit of the SWH under the control of Dr Alice Hutchison was evacuated from Valjevo; however, moving them was not easy. Hutchison refused to leave anything behind to fall into enemy hands, but the nurses had only ox-carts as a means of transportation. The slow trek with all their equipment meant that they did not move fast enough to outrun the armies and were still in the town of Vrinjatcha Bania when it fell to the Austrians on 10th November 1915. They were only 50 miles away from their colleagues, Inglis' unit, in Krushevatz, but all lines of communication had been severed. Making use of both her nationality and her civilian status, Hutchison was quite determined to stand up to her captors. When the Austrian army commandeered all her hospital equipment before sending her on to Krushevatz, she refused to give it up without a receipt, insisting that after the war the Austrian government would be required to pay for it all under the terms of the Geneva Convention. Hutchison had made a point of ensuring, and indeed making it known, that she understood her rights as a civilian in the arena of war, and was determined that her captors would respect those rights.[17]

Hutchison's attitude, along with the responses of Paget, Inglis and their nurses, was clearly influenced by the extent to which she confidently assumed and projected her identity as a British woman of high social status. These socially elite and highly educated women were products of a particular, imperial, kind of European culture, which, as

Edward Said has noted, 'gained in strength and identity by setting itself off against the Orient as a sort of surrogate and even underground self'.[18] And although Serbia was not the 'Orient' in the accepted sense, it was alien enough in the setting of the First World War to inspire this kind of imperial confidence. As Julia Bush has argued, despite the primarily patriarchal nature of Empire:

> The spiritual creed of Empire was as attractive to many British women as it was to their male counterparts. It was an improving, self-reinforcing faith, designed to assert national vigour in an increasingly competitive world, but ultimately dependent on the personal qualities of the individual.[19]

'The personal qualities of the individual' can be seen at work in each of these women as they draw on their upper-class status to assert their authority over their captors. Bush also suggests that 'Intrinsic to the imperial outlook was a self-definition of the British (often, inter-changeably, "Englishmen") as a peculiarly gifted race with an insa-tiable need to exert their colonizing genius for the benefit of less for-tunate others.'[20] Although there is no real sense that these women were 'colonizing' Serbia (despite the fact that many stayed on after the war), there is nonetheless something of this imperial benevolence in their determination to help the less fortunate, less developed and substantially 'different' Serbian people. Said suggests, further, the importance of:

> the idea of European identity as a superior one in comparison with all the non-European peoples and cultures. There is in addition the hegemony of European ideas about the Orient, themselves reiterating European superiority over Oriental backwardness.[21]

Lady Paget notes that Serbia had been lost to Christendom for 500 years. Its non-European characteristics were at the forefront of the women's consciousness. As the invaders swept in, the women began to see themselves as the protectors of their Serbian charges, bolstered by that innate sense of British superiority. Of course, some of the invaders were Western Europeans too, but they were not British, and were demonised as 'barbarian', uncivilised and brutal. The Bulgarians were another Balkan nation with a history of conquest in the east to match the Serbs. The Austrians, too, had a reputation for barbarity that did not sit comfortably with the British moral code. This may have been one of the reasons behind the women's strong sense of self-righteousness, which enabled them to stand up for their rights and the rights of their patients. For women like Hutchison, the mere fact that the enemy troops were prepared to take civilian women prisoner indicated the level of their barbarity and transgression of 'civilised' wartime codes of behaviour. The existing treaties of the Geneva Conventions (1864 and 1906), together with the stipulations of the Hague Conventions (1899 and 1907) made it clear how (military) individuals should be treated in a war situation and Hutchison was able to interpret these to ascertain her rights.[22] However, it was not until the third convention in 1929 that the rights of prisoners of war were addressed and it took the horrors of the Second World War to trigger the 1949 Convention that finally addressed the issue of the civilians. The British women, products of an imperial society, understood that 'right' was on their side, nonetheless; they must have been quite a daunting prospect for their captors.

Hutchison's move to Vrinjatcha Bania brought her into direct contact with many other British units threatened by the invasion. Ellen Chivers Davies of the Second Farmers' Unit wrote, 'there are so many English now that the Serbs have christened this place an "English town"'.[23] Elsie Corbett, then working for the Red Cross, recalls that 'There were by this time [26th October 1915] at least seven British Hospital Units in Vrinjatchka Banja [*sic*] including two of the Scottish Women's Hospitals, and several with curious names like "the Wounded Allies" and "the Farmers". These newcomers took over such empty buildings as remained.'[24] Although many of these British relief workers followed the Serbian troops as they headed for the mountains, many others became captives. Davies describes the wait for the invading armies thus, 'This is really very like waiting in a dentist's chair to have a tooth out. I wish they'd hurry up!'[25] For her, the suspense turns out to be worse than the actual experience of captivity. Unlike Hutchison, the women of the Farmers' Unit did not protest too much to their captors.

> All our medical stores have now been commandeered, and one felt really rather sorry for the Hungarian doctor whose unpleasant duty it was to superintend their removal – he did not like the task at all, though we gave them up with a very good grace and tried not to look as if we minded too much when the great rolls of cotton-wool, piles of gauze, and packets of bandages went down the stairs![26]

Davies does react bitterly to the idea of captivity, 'But it is a bitter pill to be a prisoner with a sentry in front of the hospital and another at one's door, and to know that one can't bolt ten yards if one wants to without being brought down like a rabbit!'[27] But the reality of her day-to-day experience is not that uncomfortable. Indeed, she and her colleagues spend much of their 'captivity' walking in the nearby hills and developing friendships with the Serbian peasants. Much of this part of her diary reads rather like a travelogue, focusing on local customs and culture rather than the behaviour of her captors. But as I have already suggested, these relationships were very important in establishing the status of all the women as beacons of Britishness at a most difficult time. This increased interaction with the local population caused the women to take on a rather symbolic status as the representatives of the absent Allies, symbols of hope against all the odds.

Dr F. May Dickinson Berry, who with her husband, the surgeon James Berry, headed the Berry Unit stationed very close to the Farmers at Vrinjatcha Bania during this period of captivity, echoes some of Davies' sentiments. On the one hand, there was a pleasure in their enforced leisure time, which offered the opportunity to really engage with the local communities on a different level. 'Many of us felt that these latter weeks at Vrntse [*sic*] enabled us to gain an insight into Serbian life and character which we should otherwise not have obtained.'[28] For Berry, the hardships of captivity came not from deprivation, but from isolation.

> But there was another side to the picture, and one which was very trying to most members of the Unit. Absence of any news from home, uncertainty about our own fate, whether we might not be retained as prisoners to the end of the war, were causes of much anxiety to most; and the feeling that we were no longer in any way free agents, that however well treated, we were really at the mercy of the conquerors, was not exactly pleasant.[29]

For independent doctor Caroline Twigge Matthews, the declaration of war by Bulgaria resulted in the realisation of her dream, as it finally persuaded her Serbian military employers to post her to the front line. As a result, she was sent to the Bosnian frontier, a long way from any of her female compatriots. Perhaps as a consequence of this, and perhaps also because of her own highly patriotic and imperial attitude, Matthews had a rather more troubling experience of captivity than any of the other women. In October 1915, the hospital in which she was working was evacuated of all patients who could be moved. The army left too. Matthews was left in charge of what remained of the hospital with only the local peasants for support. Her descriptions of the Germans give as much an indication of her own attitude as they do of the enemy.

> The looks I received are hard to define. It was not an enemy's contempt of his foe. There was something fiendish, something horribly suggestive of the most evil side of human character in the bold looks directed at me. The evil was so real, so vivid as to feel almost like a blow in my face, and as if after a blow, I felt sick and stunned.[30]

This is an extreme reaction, much less balanced than any of the other women's records, and one cannot help but feel that if Matthews allowed it to influence her interaction with her captors, it may have impacted on the way she was treated. Certainly they seemed out to scare her. She is also assured that she is the only Allied woman prisoner in the whole country and she has no reason to disbelieve this. But she uses this false information to feed her own patriotic inspiration and sees herself as the ultimate beacon of Britishness representing the allied cause.

> I am English. A very insignificant unit of the empire but I was all there was of it out there. I stood for England, Scotland and Ireland and the Dominions beyond the Seas!
>
> ... I think it was this realization of my nationality that upheld me. Fear? One could not show the white feather to Britain's foe. Afraid of the enemy who would tear down our Flag by foul means, when they cannot play fair? A thousand times No!
>
> To some of us who have heard the 'Call of the Wild,' who have chummed with strange peoples, and walked along untrodden paths and seen the glory of the Infinite untouched by man, to us is given the real valuation of the British Flag. We have learnt what the Empire means and our love for our King is a very real and personal matter.[31]

This is patriotic, indeed jingoistic rhetoric in the extreme, no doubt embellished for publication in 1916, and reflecting her isolation. It suggests a real and tangible engagement with the cultures of Empire and emphasises the importance of this background in Matthews' understanding of her own identity. It reinforces the idea of the importance of both nationality and imperialism to these women, as they struggled to represent their absent male comrades.

For the rest of 1915, these British women prisoners survived as best they could and dealt with their captors in the most diplomatic ways possible. They all determinedly held on to their 'Britishness', and wherever they saw an opportunity, they used it as a kind of beacon as they continued to give aid to the other victims of the invasion. Initially, after the Bulgarians had taken Skopje, Lady Paget noted that 'The English were now questioned more closely as to why the Allies so long delayed their coming. In those evil days old Serbian friends, with whom we had faced death all through the typhus-scourge of the previous winter, turned away from us, hardly knowing whether we were friends or foes.'[32] In order to combat this kind of thinking, the women worked hard to demonstrate British goodwill. They were faced with a disturbing paradox, which may be described by adopting Homi Bhabha's phrase the 'impossible unity of the nation as a symbolic force'.[33] The women were seen by many as the physical embodiment of Britain and therefore, by extension, the Allies. They were perceived as representing the 'unity' of the British nation and so needed to carry the full symbolic weight of the Allies as they went about their daily tasks. In reality, their situation was much more complex than this. They were not formal representatives at all, however much their imperial upbringing may have instilled the importance of nationality in them. They were not really part of a 'united nation', but one fractured by war; they too were waiting for Allies who would never come. They carried out this complex role principally by distributing aid to the local residents, most of whom had been left with nothing, as well as by continuing to treat both Serbian and Bulgarian wounded. But at the same time, Paget used her British citizenship and civilian status to ensure that the unit received the best treatment and that they were not detained for too long. It was one thing to make a stand, to remain and to ensure that their patients were not ill treated, but ultimately they should not be kept long as prisoners of war. By the end of 1915 the women were confident that they had done all that they could.

> I pointed out quite clearly to [the Bulgarian Chief Medical Officer] ... that we might have escaped, but had chosen to stay and be made prisoners rather than abandon our work. I explained that we were a unit supported by a public fund raised in England to help the Serbians, and that I should have to account both to my Government and my committee, as soon as I got home, for everything I had done. I said we were willing to give help to the wounded Bulgarians until they could make their own medical arrangements, but that I formally demanded as soon as it was practicable, to be sent home with my entire staff.[34]

Paget's tone here implies that sense of imperial superiority, no doubt endorsed by her status as an upper-class British woman.

A 'democratic' public fund, specifically English, supports this: they cannot let down the ordinary English people who have invested in them. She draws upon the higher authorities of the British government and her committee as evidence of the importance of their commitment. Surprisingly, the 'committee' almost seems to carry more weight than the government, highlighting the importance of the notion of British women's imperial or benevolent societies in Paget's frame of reference. The institutional support for the activities of the women remains strong. This situation brings out the real paradox of the twin roles performed by these medical women. On the one hand, they were doctors and nurses, dedicated above all things to the care of their wounded, Serbian and Bulgarian alike. On the other, as British women, envoys of the Allies, they needed to assert their patriotic, imperialist sense of superiority that enabled them to take the moral high ground with their enemies. The demand to be sent home places authority firmly back in the hands of the leader of the unit, not the invading soldiers, but it is not without its moral complications for their position as doctors and nurses.

The other captive women made similar demands, but it appears that their value was as great to their captors as it had been to the Serbian army. At Krushevatz the Germans took over Inglis' hospital, forcing all the nurses to move to the Czar Lazar, the Serbian military hospital named after the legendary martyr of the 1389 battle of Kosovo. This hospital was intended to accommodate 900 patients but the number rose to 1,200 during the women's time there. In addition to this, the hospital was surrounded by thousands of prisoners of war, being moved to the concentration camps of Hungary, for whom they felt obliged to care. 'The existence of misery they led was indescribable, as was the filth amongst which they lived.... The hospital itself possessed the most villainous sanitary appointments it has ever been my lot to behold.'[35] With sanitation such a problem, typhus was a significant threat, but the nurses adapted a disinfection machine to heat water and managed to avoid the disease completely.[36] Clearly this was very important in altruistic terms, but equally it was necessary for the women to demonstrate their understanding of humanitarian treatment for all prisoners of war. Again, this understanding enabled them to occupy the moral high ground. In her discussion of POWs, Sibylle Scheipers has argued that:

> During the twentieth century, prisoners became an increasingly important aspect of war propaganda. Emphasizing one's own humane

treatment of prisoners and condemning the opponent's treatment of prisoners was often intended to enhance the international reputation of a state.[37]

While the women were busy ensuring that they did the absolute best for all patients no matter which side they were on, Elsie Inglis certainly had firsthand experience of this concern from the point of view of her captors. When the Germans moved out in late November, handing the town over to the Austrians, they asked her to sign a document testifying to their good behaviour. Despite being threatened and harassed, she refused. She was concerned that the propaganda value of such a document would be too great, particularly with regard to women prisoners. The 1915 shooting of British nurse Edith Cavell, in Belgium, was still fresh in everyone's minds. The Germans had received a good deal of international criticism for this execution, despite the fact that Cavell had pleaded guilty to the charge of helping British and Belgian soldiers to escape occupied territory. Inglis was very conscious of this. She was not prepared to do anything that might inadvertently improve the international reputations of her captors.

In late November, her captors allowed Inglis to write to her committee in Edinburgh, no doubt as a demonstration of their humanity.

> We are told we may send letters home – open of course, so this is to tell the Committee that Dr Holloway's Unit and mine are here working in the Serbian Military Hospital. I enclose a list of people here – so you may tell their friends. Dr Hutchison's Unit is at Vrnatskbania [*sic*] and Dr McGregor's went Southward – possibly you may have heard from her. Some of our people also left with Mr Smith.
>
> I am sure the committee would approve of our work here. We have charge of the 'Magazine' where the overflow of patients from the Hospital are taken about 300 wounded (there are 900 altogether)[.] We are working in the dressing-rooms and certain wards in the Hospital – and the Director has put all the sanitation and laundry work into our hands.
>
> We live in the Hospital. There are two rooms given to us ...
>
> This is just a bare report for the committee. I cannot tell you what our next move will be. At present the prisoners are being sent through in thousands. They stay in the Hospital grounds, and leave their sick and wounded, and pass on northward.
>
> The Committee must not worry about us. We are well and very busy, and doing the work the committee sent us out to do.[38]

As this is an open letter, Inglis plays down the negative aspects of their captivity, instead emphasising their continuing medical and relief work. This is understandable given the fact that their actual living conditions were quite shocking. It is most likely that Inglis felt that the Germans did not deserve her endorsement, but at the same time she would not have wished to antagonise them unnecessarily. Dr Helen McDougall later wrote:

> Black sour bread – we might have sugar in coffee if we liked, but no sugar elsewhere – thin soup and bean mess, with limited rough meat at lunch, and as often as not the bean mess again at night.... There was no milk, no eggs, nothing at all of the lighter sort. It may sound all right to those who have never tried it, but for myself the black bread was sometime scarcely eatable, yet from experience I knew it was better than none.[39]

Nothing in their medical training had prepared the women for privations of this sort, just as nothing had prepared them for imprisonment. Alice Hutchison noted:

> I came across Dr Inglis and her Unit. If I had up till then felt that we in no way merited the title of 'the heroic band of women', I came away from Dr Inglis' hospital feeling that they *had* earned it. Picture over twenty people – including the head of the hospital – dining and sleeping and eating and washing in one room; picture all their equipment gone, and them looking after Serbs in the best way they could in hospital corridors. They were however, wearing no air of martyrdom.[40]

Hutchison is very aware of the way the women may be perceived from the outside, that their being prisoners of war might earn them a particular heroic reputation. While determined not to accept any such accolade for herself, as this is a kind of heroism usually reserved for male combatants, and she is clearly uncomfortable about it from her position as a civilian woman, Hutchison acknowledges that Inglis and her nurses really have earned this status of martyr-heroine. However, it is also clear that the women have internalised and modelled the behaviours of the British imperial heroine here, as they continued their hospital work under extreme conditions. Again, this is reflective of notions of the heroism of work 'against the odds' in the empire. As Bush puts it, 'duty and responsibility, interest and honour impelled the British to sustain their imperial burden',[41] and for decades British society had internalised the heroic qualities associated with this duty.

While the nurses tended the wounded in Krushevatz and Paget and her company worked to restore the tarnished British image in Skopje, Alice Hutchison's unit was forced to join the thousands of prisoners of war being herded towards Hungary. Their encounter with Inglis took place after they had been removed from Vrinjatcha Bania. A brief stop-over in Krushevatz showed them what they might expect on their own journey. When they reached their destination, Kevevara, thirty-two of them were accommodated in two rooms. They were held there for five weeks, but unlike the women in other locations they were not given any work, so for them the monotony was as great a trial as the black bread. Days were spent 'waiting for the Allies', or at least waiting to be restored to them. Hutchison continued to argue that, as a civilian woman, it was a breach of the Geneva Convention for her to be held as a prisoner of war at all, but for a while her argument fell on deaf ears.

In December there was an outbreak of cholera among the Serbian prisoners. Hutchison was instructed to take charge. She remembered the directives of the Hague Conventions relating to prisoners of war and work: 'They could be employed in work, so long as it was not related to war operations, nor should it be exhausting or humiliat-ing.'[42] Nursing the sick Serbian prisoners, their Allies, did not count as inappropriate war work as such, but exposing themselves to the acute danger of sickness or death did contravene the dictates of the Conventions. She drew on her authority as an educated British civil-ian woman, and she refused to allow her nurses to work unless they were all first vaccinated against the disease. 'Then came a torrent of the most uncontrolled abuse and threats that I have ever been sub-jected to – incarceration to the end of the war, starvation, treatment as ordinary prisoner, &c.'[43] But Hutchison stood firm and the nurses were never forced to work in the cholera hospital, another moral vic-tory for the women prisoners.

Christmas found all the units still in captivity. A determination to celebrate it regardless of their circumstances provided Hutchison's unit with a sense of patriotism that helped to carry them through. Celebrating Christmas became a kind of symbol of their Britishness, particularly as their Christmas did not fall in line with the Serbian Orthodox calendar. Alice Hutchison notes that their guards, who would have shared their festive season (unlike the Serbs), had become quite friendly by Christmas Day and they were able to celebrate far bet-ter than they had expected.

On Christmas Day we had quite a jolly time, with a Christmas tree and a first-rate dinner. We went out and got some live geese from the mar-ket, which were killed and cooked, and we had all kinds of cakes, and even butter.... In the evening we sang carols and drank toasts. We even ventured for the first time to sing 'God Save the King' under our breath. After this we sang it every night, and it cheered us up wonderfully.[44]

In comparison with the usual diet of black bread, this seems quite luxurious. However, what is most significant here is the singing of the national anthem, the reclaiming and celebration of national identity. This freedom, gained through the occasion, becomes a part of their daily ritual, an assertion of their nationhood, the British Empire and, by implication, their superiority. Their captors were not to be allowed to forget their Britishness. This refusal to forget who they are unites all these women, and helps them to face the extraordinary challenges to their identities, both personal and national.

In contrast, Caroline Twigge Matthews' Christmas was very austere. Suffering from diphtheria that severely weakened her, Matthews received no rations at all on Christmas Day. She records that she was often deprived of her rations, and she was regularly subjected to violent and rough treatment. When she questioned her treatment, as Hutchison had done, in terms of the Geneva Convention, she was curtly informed by her Hungarian guard, 'There is no Geneva Convention now.'[45] She took consolation in displaying the only image of the British flag she could find, a tiny picture from the inside of tin of sweets. 'In pure defiance, in sheer delight, I nailed that badly drawn specimen of the old Flag on my door!'[46] It became a symbol of her determination to survive and return home.

The assertion of a morally superior, an imperial brand of British womanhood appears to have worked. With the dawning of 1916, the German, Austrian and Bulgarian armies seemed determined to rid themselves of the British women prisoners in their midst. Lady Paget had enjoyed the patronage of Eleanora, Queen of the Bulgarians, with whom she had worked in the Balkan Wars. The Queen's history of war nursing and these previous associations with British medical women during the Balkan Wars made her very sympathetic to the work of the various hospitals.[47] Although there is no direct evidence to suggest that this was why Paget's unit was released, the Queen may have had some influence. But Paget had adopted a policy of gentle negotiation with her captors and later believed that this, in the end, led to a smoother passage home for her party. She also disassociated herself publicly from anyone she defined as 'pro-Serbian' during their return journey, because she thought any such connection would lead to their being detained for the duration of the war. She endeavoured to remain as neutral as possible, foregrounding her medical role and its intersection with her 'British' one throughout the process of her release, adopting an impression of British calm, reserve and, above all, control, throughout.

SRF1 left Skopje on 17th February 1916.

> It was not very easy to leave the hospital, though it held for us the memory of so much pain and hard work. It had been brought forth in sorrow, when typhus held the land in its grip. It had risen up out of the filth and disease in which we found it, by the labours of a few, till by degrees it had become one of the best-equipped hospitals in Serbia....
>
> I had not realised till the moment came to leave how much I had hoped to hand it back to the Serbians. Never had the mountains looked more serene or more beautiful than in that early morning light, but it was a sad leave we took of the poor Serbian captives, and tears rolled down the faces of our faithful Austrians.[48]

Imperial benevolence appears to play its part here. The 'poor Serbian captives' and the 'faithful Austrians' are still presented as needing the protection of the women and, by proxy, the Allies. But, as Allies, they have failed their charges, leaving them in the hands of their captors. It was to be a long trip home. The group were detained further in Sophia for four weeks. Paget refused to travel home through Germany, and their progress was hampered by continual reports from German officials that they were all spies. When the Swiss border was closed to them, they were forced to travel home via Russia and did not arrive in London until 3rd April 1916. Despite her determination to uphold her Britishness and to represent the absent Allies, or perhaps because of it, Paget and her nurses were criticised on their return for getting on too well with the Bulgarian Queen. Perhaps because of her previous connection to the Queen, it had been inaccurately reported that they had been her guests in Sophia, whereas in fact the Bulgarian Red Cross had accommodated them. Here again is the paradox, the 'impossible unity of the nation as a symbolic force'. The women had symbolically embodied Britain and the Allies, and had put themselves at great personal risk in order to uphold the international reputation of their nation. Yet the nation, in its most formal sense, seemed blind to this endeavour. Because the women could be deemed to have transgressed in their dealing with the enemy Queen, the nation distanced itself from them, belying notions of 'unity'. Sadly, this is fairly representative of the formal British attitude to this work in Serbia, despite its popularity as an abstract cause. At home the hard work of the women went unappreciated, and they were even criticised for their efforts. Unlike the trained and volunteer nurses who went to other fronts, they had not been sanctioned. The Serbians, however, awarded Lady Paget the Order of St Sava, First Class. For them, her twin roles both deserved formal recognition.

Elsie Inglis' unit left Krushevatz on 9th February 1916. They were escorted to neutral Switzerland by an armed Austrian guard with fixed bayonets. 'Great care was taken that we should not communicate with any one *en route*.'[49] Perhaps Inglis had appeared to her captors to be a little more recalcitrant, a little more threatening. They were handed over to the American embassy in Vienna and from there received safe passage home. Having spent nearly four months waiting for the Allies, Inglis had not yet given up hope. 'When we reached Zurich and found everything much the same as when we disappeared into the silence, our hearts were sick for the people we left behind us still waiting and trusting.'[50] The silence may be a strange way to describe a war zone, but it gives an accurate impression of that zone in the eyes of the British and French military. Since their capture, Inglis had continued to await the rescue of the Serbian nation. She had never given up hope. Eva Shaw McClaren notes that 'Those who know her best feel that it was here, going in spirit with her beloved Serbs through their time of extremest woe, that Dr Inglis' "heart broke" and the "beginning of the end" came upon her.'[51] Later that year, Elsie Inglis led another unit of the SWH to Russia; she died from cancer shortly after her return home on 26th November 1917. In death, however, Inglis did receive the recognition of her homeland. Her funeral in Edinburgh was attended by thousands and was followed by the founding of the Elsie Inglis Memorial Hospital in the city. Another was also founded in Belgrade. This legacy will be discussed in more detail in Chapter 7.

While her unit was held captive in Budapest, Alice Hutchison encountered Caroline Twigge Matthews. Matthews had met with this particular SWH unit several times and was delighted to see them. Her experience had gone from bad to worse. Alone and isolated, she had, like Paget, fallen to victim to charges of espionage but without an institutional support network she had trouble denying them. Starving and ill, she was transported from Serbia to Hungary to meet these charges. In one poignant memory, she recalls how some Russian prisoners of war had found a way to give her a bar of chocolate. Recognising her starving condition, they assumed she was on her way to inevitable execution. In Belgrade her situation worsened. She was repeatedly interrogated as a spy, but determined to remain silent. Accommodated at an inn, her guard was relaxed slightly, but this led to an even worse situation.

> Someone was creeping up behind me, of that I felt convinced. It is a horrid feeling, the feeling that something is going to spring out of the darkness and at one's back.... Then, the next moment, I was in the embrace of a German soldier. A great broad-shouldered, helmeted man was holding me in his arms, kissing me, or, rather, trying to do so, again and again. It was not quite the easy job he had anticipated!
>
> ... Down we came together. I tried hard to bang his head against the stones. Two could play at that game and he was bigger. Crack went my occiput and I saw stars. I tried to get my fingers into his eyes and failed.
>
> ... But I was decidedly getting the worst of the fray. How long could I hold out?[52]

The landlord of the inn rescued her: fortunately he had been made responsible for her safety. However, this is a startling attack. Although idea of rape has always been attached to conquest, this kind of sexual attack against a British woman seems to have been quite unprecedented. Women as nursing staff were covered by the international agreements of the Geneva Conventions, on the one hand, but also by their own femininity. The combination of their British imperial superiority and their rather nun-like status seems to have been sufficient to protect them. Matthews, a military doctor, wore a uniform that more closely resembled that of a male officer than a nurse. Under interrogation, Matthews defies her captors to shoot her. However, while she may be one of the few people who had not heard of Edith Cavell and the subsequent international outrage as a consequence of her isolation, her captors would certainly have been aware and were no doubt reluctant to make the same mistake twice.

By the time Matthews was reunited with Hutchison, she was in a shocking physical condition and regretting her isolated involvement.

> No woman should go out as a Free Lance unless she is fully accustomed to fighting her battles alone, to suffering in silence, prepared for any emergency. Else let her be one of many and a worker with some Unit.
>
> The cold, the want of sleep, the preceding months of privations, fatigue and rough usage with a scanty diet, denuded of sugar or fat, had left me a shivering wreck not ill but simply a parcel of unwarmable bones.[53]

Hers was probably the worst prisoner of war experience of any British woman in Serbia. No doubt if there had been many more, their plight would have been much better known. After her release, Matthews continued to be pursued by agents determined she was a spy until she managed to return safely to England, via Switzerland, in the spring of 1916.

Throughout her captivity, like Matthews, Alice Hutchison secretly preserved the unit's Union Jack flag. The flag held the same symbolic importance for her as it did for Caroline Twigge Matthews. When they left Budapest for Vienna on 4th February 1916, she wound it around her body, underneath her clothes, for safekeeping, determined not to see it trampled and insulted. As their train passed over the Swiss border, the unit produced the flag, waving it from the train windows in triumph, shouting 'God Save the King'. They had retained, or perhaps reinforced, their 'Britishness' in the face of oppression and were prepared to shout about it to the world. Their British identity remained dominant despite their adoption of a more transitional, humanitarian identity as doctors and nurses. The combination of these twin strands enabled them to prevail and secure their release while continuing to give as much support to their Allies as possible.[54]

These operations of British women in Serbia in the First World War were an extraordinary phenomenon. Serbia presented British women with a theatre of war in which they could be active, could 'do their bit', when the British government had made it clear that independent women on active service, even medical women, were undesirable. It was a paradoxical situation from the start. The culture of Empire, and imperial sensibility, internalised since childhood, fed these women's desire to play a part in a war that threatened the whole of society and, indeed, the empire itself. This unquestioning adoption of a particular brand of 'Britishness' gave them the confidence to face up to and overcome dangers, retaining and upholding their national identity despite being isolated by their own countrymen, and having to watch the nation to which they had committed themselves in service fall into despair and defeat. Despite the disappointment, waiting for the Allies brought out the best in these women, and, for many, being able to stay on and support Serbia as it fell must have made up, in some small way, for the failings of a male military machine that could regard so small an ally as being not quite important enough to save. It also offered them the chance to explore a further aspect of their identity as prisoners of war. They were Edwardian women, they were nurses and they had used the experiences of both these roles take control of their situation, remaining beacons of Britishness throughout their captivity. The next chapter explores the various roles and survival strategies adopted by those women who did not stay on as prisoners of war, but instead joined the thousands of refugees on the great retreat through the mountains of Montenegro and Albania.

Notes

1 Ellen Chivers Davies, *A Farmer in Serbia* (London: Methuen & Co., 1916), p. 111.
2 Misha Glenny, *The Balkans 1804–1999: Nationalism, War and the Great Powers* (London: Granta, 2000), p. 333.
3 Imperial War Museum, London (hereafter IWM), 34602, 9, Lady L. Paget, *With Our Serbian Allies: Second Report*, printed for private circulation, 1916.
4 Tim Judah, *The Serbs: History, Myth and the Destruction of Yugoslavia* (New Haven and London: Yale University Press, 1997), p. 90.
5 The Serbians had been at war with the Ottoman Empire in the two Balkan Wars of 1912–13. See Introduction.
6 *The Times* (13th April 1915), issue 40827, p. 10, col. D.
7 Julia Bush, *Edwardian Ladies and Imperial Power* (London: University of Leicester Press, 2000), p. 16.
8 Louise Miller, *A Fine Brother: The Life of Captain Flora Sandes* (London: Alma Books, 2012), p. 80.
9 Mabel St Clair Stobart, *The Flaming Sword in Serbia and Elsewhere* (London: Hodder and Stoughton, 1917), p. 139.
10 Paget, *With Our Serbian Allies*, p. 12.
11 John Keegan, *The First World War* (London: Pimlico, 1999), p. 7.
12 Judah, *The Serbs*, p. 99.
13 Glenny, *The Balkans*, p. 335.
14 Paget, *With Our Serbian Allies*, pp. 19–20.
15 E. Inglis, 'The Tragedy of Serbia', *The Englishwoman* 30 (1916), p. 166.
16 *Ibid.*, quoted in Angela K. Smith (ed.), *Women's Writing of the First World War: An Anthology* (Manchester: Manchester University Press, 2000), p. 270.
17 The position of these British women as prisoners of war was highly unusual. As a consequence there has been no scholarly work carried out on their experiences as yet. Indeed relatively little work has focused on prisoners of war in the First World War generally. The work of Heather Jones provides a good starting point, particularly *Violence against Prisoners of War in the First World War* (Cambridge: Cambridge University Press, 2011). This book also provides a good reference sources for other work in the area. Very little of it addresses the Balkans.

18 Edward W. Said, *Orientalism* (London: Penguin, 2003), p. 3.

19 Bush, *Edwardian Ladies*, p. 2.

20 *Ibid.*, p. 1.

21 Said, *Orientalism*, p. 7.

22 For further information see Alan R. Kramer, 'Prisoners in the First World War', in Sibylle Scheipers (ed.), *Prisoners in War* (Oxford: Oxford University Press, 2010), pp. 76–7.

23 Davies, *A Farmer in Serbia*, p. 154.

24 Elsie Corbett, *Red Cross in Serbia 1915–1919* (Banbury: Cheney & Sons, 1964), p. 41.

25 Davies, *A Farmer in Serbia*, p. 160.

26 *Ibid.*, p. 167.

27 *Ibid.*, p. 160.

28 F. May Dickinson Berry, 'Captivity', in James Berry, *The Story of a Red Cross Unit in Serbia* (London: J. & A. Churchill, 1916), p. 255.

29 *Ibid.*, p. 256.

30 Caroline Twigge Matthews, *Experiences of a Woman Doctor in Serbia* (London: Mills & Boon, 1916), p. 36.

31 Matthews, *Experiences of a Woman Doctor*, pp. 41–2.

32 Paget, *With Our Serbian Allies*, p. 20.

33 H. K. Bhabha (ed.), *Nation and Narration* (London: Routledge, 1990), p. 1.

34 Paget, *With Our Serbian* Allies, pp. 36–7.

35 Dr Helen McDougall, from an article published in *The Instructor: Journal for the Children of the Free Church in Scotland*, April 1917, quoted in Leah Leneman, *In the Service of Life: The Story of Elsie Inglis and the Scottish Women's Hospitals* (Edinburgh: Mercat Press, 1994), p. 42.

36 For more details see *ibid.*, pp. 42–3.

37 Scheipers, *Prisoners in War*, p. 8.

38 Mitchell Library, Glasgow (hereafter ML), SWH Archive, Box B, Letter from Elsie Inglis, 30th November 1915.

39 McDougall, quoted in Leneman, *In the Service of Life*, pp. 42–3.

40 Alice Hutchison, quoted in Eva Shaw McLaren, *A History of the Scottish Women's Hospitals* (London: Hodder and Stoughton, 1919), p. 164.

41 Bush, *Edwardian Ladies*, pp. 1–2.

42 Kramer, 'Prisoners in the First World War', p. 76.

43 Hutchison, quoted in Leneman, *In the Service of Life*, pp. 44–5.

44 Hutchison, quoted in McClaren, *A History* of the Scottish Women's Hospitals, p. 165.

45 Matthews, *Experiences of a Woman Doctor*, p. 52.

46 *Ibid.*, p. 49.

47 Eleanora, Queen of the Bulgarians had worked with Mabel St Clair Stobart and her field hospital units who had participated in the Balkan War of 1912.

48 Paget, *With Our Serbian Allies*, p. 93.
49 Inglis, 'The Tragedy of Serbia', p. 71.
50 *Ibid.*, p. 171.
51 McClaren, *A History of the Scottish Women's Hospitals*, p. 172.
52 Matthews, *Experiences of a Woman Doctor*, p. 70.
53 *Ibid.*, p. 78.
54 Dr Hutchison continued to serve with the SWH until the end of the war. After the war she devoted herself to children's medicine, working in a number of hospitals, including Great Ormond Street.

5

Domestic survival strategies: the Serbian retreat, 1915

> November 5th was full of rumours. Men were passing through all morning, thousands of them like ants against the sky when they had climbed the hilly road and reappeared on the crest. For some curious reason it did not occur to any of us that what we were watching so calmly was our entire army starting on their retreat across the snowy mountains of Albania to the Adriatic coast.[1]

Bulgaria entered the war at the end of September 1915, joining forces with Germany and Austria, and, as we have seen, the invasion of Serbia commenced at the beginning of October. Despite expectations, so poignantly illustrated by the streets of Nis decorated with welcome flags, the British and French Allied armies did not come to Serbia's aid. The Serbian army was exhausted from years of war and weakened after the terrible scourge of the winter epidemics; it quickly failed. Rather than surrender, the army fled west over the mountains, towards the sea. Elsie Corbett, who remained in Vrinjatcha Bania with her Red Cross unit, witnessed the beginning of that flight without realising the full extent of the tragedy. As the armies fled, they were joined by thousands of civilians, all trying to escape the invaders. John Keegan suggests:

> Only an army of mountaineers could have survived the passage through Montenegro, and many did not, dying of disease, starvation or cold as they fell out of the line by the wayside. Of the 200,000 who had set out, however, no less than 140,000 survived to cross in early December the frontier of Albania, independent since 1913 and still a neutral, and descend into the gentler temperatures of the Albanian Adriatic ports.[2]

Huw Strachen's figures differ slightly. He suggests that 'of the original strength of 420,000 men in September, some 94,000 had been killed and wounded in action and a further 174,000 were captured or missing. Civilian deaths have not been calculated. The Serbs suffered the greatest losses in relation to population size of any participant in the war.'[3] It is perhaps telling that there are no figures for civilian deaths. Leah Leneman relates the story of 30,000 Serbian boys aged between twelve and eighteen, sent over the mountains with the armies in the hope of saving their lives. But only 7,000 survived.[4] However these figures, or indeed the lack of them, are interpreted, the great Serbian retreat was a tragedy on an epic scale. And one in which some of the British women who had been working in Serbia played an important part.

In late September 1915, Mabel St Clair Stobart was invited to the office of the Serbian Army Medical Department. As we have seen, Stobart had been successfully running the SRF3 field hospital at Kragujevatz since her arrival in the country in April and had spent the summer of 1915 setting up dispensaries in the surrounding countryside to offer medical care to the local population. Now she was asked to take on a different task. The Army Medical Department must have been impressed with her work because they invited her to take charge of a flying field hospital to be attached to Schumadia division of the Serbian army. The unit was to be the First Serbian–English Field Hospital (Front) and Stobart was also to be given sixty soldiers to be attached to the hospital and under her direct command. She was to be given the rank of major. This was the first time that such a position had been offered to a woman by any army. Stobart, as a feminist and suffragist, was fully aware of the extent of the opportunity to show that women could perform as well as men under extreme circumstances. Always looking for a new challenge, she was quick to accept the job. Not everyone was as excited as she was. Sir Ralph Paget would probably have tried to dissuade her, but he was absent at the time of her appointment, trying to make arrangements with the Serbian authorities for the evacuation of the many British medical units serving across Serbia. Paget's priority was to get British citizens away from the dangers of the invasion. His temporary absence enabled Stobart to go ahead and form the column that would take her and her women dangerously close to it.[5]

Although the flying field hospital was initially sent to the front line, the soldiers here were soon forced to retreat in the face of the invading armies. This put Stobart and her women on a path that would eventually take them across the mountains with all the other refugees, once the last resistance collapsed. In the face of extraordinary hardships, the women would have to use all the survival skills they could muster to complete the journey successfully. Stobart kept a diary throughout the retreat, a tiny, pencil-filled notebook that is barely decipherable now. It is written in the staccato style of many diaries, recording ideas rather than sentences. Diaries were forbidden by the British military because of concerns about the potential leak of military information so it was not unusual for diarists to lack specificity.[6] Equally, much of what a woman might choose to record in a war diary was difficult to articulate in such a small space. Additionally, the conditions of the retreat were far from conducive to diary writing; it is perhaps astonishing that the document exists at all. Upon her return to England in 1916, she used this dairy as a basis for her record of her time in Serbia, *The Flaming Sword in Serbia and Elsewhere*. These two documents give a fascinating insight into the survival strategies Stobart and her fellow travellers adopted and, in particular, the ways in which they used the domesticity of their 'feminine' backgrounds as a means of getting through.

> At sunset I climbed a hill with Major A., and on three sides we saw the battle – many battles – raging.... On the fourth side ... we saw a small white camp. Moving in and out, quietly, and leisurely, amongst the tents, were some women, who seemed to have no concern with the tumult that was raging around them. One of them was cooking supper over an open wood fire. She was apparently joking with the Serbian cook-orderly and threatening to hit him on the head with a frying pan.[7]

On 2nd November 1915, Stobart took a moment to survey the situation of the hospital. It did not look good. The invading armies were closing in, driving them towards the mountains. 'Can't see how we going to escape surrounded on all sides but one already', she noted in her diary.[8] But when she reinterpreted her diary in the published account of the experience a year later, Stobart embellished this entry with the details of what lay on the fourth side, quoted above. The pessimism of the diary is gone. She adopts tropes of conventional heroism that still influenced the public view of the war in early 1916. Now Stobart knows they will escape and she believes she knows why. Stobart believes it is *because* of these women, who go about their everyday business so serenely in the face of the enemy guns, *because* they will continue to do so for the next two months, carrying with them the Serbian soldiers attached to the unit, ensuring that they are the only military column in the retreat who do not lose a single man to death or desertion. Stobart believes that these women bring alternative skills to the front line, by playing out the roles that society has defined for them; carrying with them domestic order amidst the chaos of war, it is they who ensure that the column will survive.

By 1915, Stobart was already relatively experienced in warfare. Her work in Bulgaria with the WSWCC had taught her a lot and helped to shape her political and feminist thinking. She did not believe that women should be the same as men; on the contrary they were naturally, essentially different. But Stobart believed that it was this very difference that made women's participation in warfare and then in politics all the more important. She was convinced that what women could bring, which men could not, was an essential 'womanliness' that was fundamentally pacifist, and would benefit mankind in the longer term. With the outbreak of the First World War, Stobart transferred control of the WSWCC to the Red Cross and began a new project. She travelled to Belgium with a view to setting up a hospital there in the face of the German invasion. However, she and her travelling companions, who included her second husband, retired judge John Greenhalgh, were caught up in the invasion and imprisoned as spies. The only reason they were not shot was that the military judge presiding over their trial recognised Greenhalgh and could vouch for him. It was a very near miss, but instead of putting Stobart off war work, it inspired her further, motivating her to work in France before the move to Serbia. She had experienced enough hardship already to know that discomfort did not matter. She had begun to understand what could be achieved with a little determination.

The First Serbian–English Field Hospital (Front) contained two women doctors, four women nurses, a woman cook and two women orderlies as well as Serbian interpreters, several Serbian officers and the sixty soldiers, with Stobart as the commandant and John Greenhalgh as the secretary. The presence of so many women in close proximity to the firing line was radical, particularly in British terms, but Stobart was committed to showing that women were as capable of 'doing their bit' as any man. Stobart was now in a position to really prove her argument that women had skills to offer that made them every bit as valuable in wartime as their male comrades. By the beginning of October they were on the road, but when they reached the front line it became clear that the line would not hold. They were forced to join the retreat, but staying with their regiment and acting on orders rather than joining the free-for-all rush for the mountains. For the next two and a half months, the women's unit followed the soldiers backwards and forwards across the country as the situation worsened and a full-scale retreat turned into a mass exodus, with all those who could do so fleeing the country and the invading armies. The unit, with its soldiers, received orders to move on a daily basis, making it difficult to set up a hospital for very long. They were often frustrated by their inability to help the wounded, as soldiers were simply left to die on abandoned battlefields. Their lives were in constant disorder as they struggled on through appalling weather conditions, across rugged and mountainous countryside, with the threat of capture or death close behind. They dispensed medical care wherever they could, looked out for each other and finally delivered the unit to Scutari, reaching the coast beyond just before Christmas 1915.

Because of their relation to the front-line troops and various communication hitches, Stobart's unit travelled with the last retreating Serbs, but other British units were successfully evacuated earlier and accompanied the many thousands of civilian refugees on the road from early October onwards. Kathleen Royds, a nurse serving with the SWH at Salonika, described the flight in a letter to her mother.

> A party of refugee nurses arrived here three days ago who had been fleeing for a month, from north Serbia, the last week they walked a hundred miles. They set out with what they could carry themselves & on 30 donkeys. Seven of the donkeys died on the first day & others got tired on the way & were left, then some luggage had to be discarded. The nurses slept in all sorts of places often just as they were on stone floors, often wading through streams & walking all day. They had only very gritty black bread & some tinned meat & porridge; but in spite of all they went through, they all look & seem fit.[9]

Royds' women had taken a different road from that taken by Stobart. By the time her unit joined the retreat the route to Salonika was blocked. But like Stobart's party, these women seem eminently capable. Royds emphasises their ability to make the best of things and cope despite their difficult situation. Her account focuses on the way in which the women deal with the everyday realities: how they travel, what they eat and where they sleep – domestic survival strategies in an anti-domestic space. They were accompanied of course by many Serbian refugees: 'We have had 800 at the hospital, but there are said to be 10,000 in the town.'[10]

Stobart's route took her west, across the mountains, towards the Adriatic Sea. Stobart's diary gives an extraordinary insight into the experience as it was happening. Given the lack of time, the external pressure and the extreme suffering that surrounded her, some of the ideas recorded there are rather surprising. From her location at the very heart of the matter, she addresses the enormity of the combat situation, the defeat of the armies and the plight of the refugees. But in equal measure, the diary locates much of the experience within the language of the domestic, a language which articulates Stobart's concept of the woman's perspective. As in Royds' letters, more important than the movement of armies is where the next meal is coming from, the making of soup with whatever they find, while waiting for the soldiers to get the hay for animal feed. The poor condition of the horses, the oxen and the men's boots are issues of primary concern. Embedded within this blend of the everyday and the tragic, Stobart touches on deeper questions. Her diary highlights the politics of the war and the importance of women's role within it, what will become her political message. And always the plight of the Serbian nation is at the forefront of concerns.

> Terrible situation. Where are French & Eng. Troops? Serbs badly beaten this morning & retreating. Road unending stream of refugees in carts kukurus straw on which babies frying pans bread troughs etc. Women drag oxen, old men drive sheep.... Sitting up on top of straw looking hurt expression at leaving fav. Pastures.[11]

Like the British women POWs, Stobart looks out for the allied armies, but they were still delayed at Gallipoli: they had what they perceived as more pressing matters to deal with. But Stobart, like the other British in Serbia, did not know that. In the face of so much disruption, the total destruction of everyday life all around her, Stobart strove to maintain some kind of order within the unit itself. From the outset, the maintenance of this order depended on her establishing control and patterns of military discipline, despite the fact that, because she was a woman, this might have been difficult for the men of her command to accept. Here Stobart showed great initiative. She understood that although she may hold the rank of major, she most certainly did not look the part. A small, feminine, slim, even fragile-looking woman, she needed to establish her military bearing in a less conventional manner.

> In the hospital at Kragujevatz, and at all the dispensaries, the soldiers and the people had always called me 'Maika'.... I quickly determined to

remain 'Maika.' The word 'Maika' is already, to Serbian hearts, rich in impressions of the best qualities of the old-fashioned woman; it would do no harm to add to this a few impressions of the qualities of authority and power not hitherto associated with women.[12]

Stobart had already demonstrated her concern for the ordinary people of Serbia throughout the summer of 1915, with the setting up of her dispensaries. During this exercise she had established a kind of authority that was recognised by the Serbian civilians and military alike. 'Maika' (Mother) was a name bestowed on her out of respect. Isabel Emslie Hutton notes that 'It is a strange relic of feudalism that the mother is the most loved and honoured woman in the family, and that wife and children have to take second place. The most appreciative thing they could say to us was that we had been as a *Maika* to them.'[13] Like Flora Murray and Louisa Garrett Anderson, who eventually earned the respect of the RAMC by running their hospitals so successfully on the Western Front, Stobart had made herself into an authority figure to be respected. Unlike them, however, she was not a doctor so did not have professional training to fall back on to justify her position. She had to develop a different strategy. In some ways Stobart resembled some of the distinctive and authoritative suffrage leaders. Emmeline Pankhurst, for instance, used her role as mother and matriarch, blended with that of a quasi-military leader of the WSPU, to embody a range of aspects of power. Pankhurst's femininity, her 'womanliness', was as important to her image as that of the suffrage 'general' and the combination enabled her to command respect across the ranks of her followers.[14] During the retreat, Stobart, like Pankhurst, combined the patriarchal authority of military rank with the matriarchal authority of the domestic sphere, and a dose of feminism thrown in. She could thus embody wisdom, enabling her soldiers to come to her for advice, and justice, dispensing discipline to any who threatened the order of the column. Additionally, she took on the role of provider, of nurturer, ensuring her men were fed and clothed just as a mother in the home might do. Through these attributes, Stobart was able to bring the domestic and the familiar to an extraordinary situation, but maintaining this through the hardship of the retreat proved to be a very difficult task indeed.[15]

Much of the time, this combination of patriarchal and matriarchal authority was very effective. 'Lecture to soldiers & lash re fire & food. Not up till I called them at 4a.m. Pulled them up sharp.'[16] 'Find Nicola kitchen boy playing cards in mali shatro after told to fill lamps. Take Narednik [sergeant major] put my whip in his hand & make him whip all 4 & tear up cards.'[17] Stobart is the voice of authority, and very formidable, leading by example in the first diary entry here. In the second, she retains the power, but as one might expect of a lady, does not sully herself with the actual administration of punishment. Her soldiers were always aware that she had the might of military discipline behind her. No doubt this and the sight of the whip were enough to get her the results she needed. But the additional layer, the maternal associations, inspired a loyalty that made all the difference. In late October, several weeks into the job, she began to experience difficulties with the Serbian dispenser, who had an unfortunate liking for drink. When drunk, he was less receptive to Stobart's authority than he might otherwise have been.

> Yankovitch (Dispenser) drunk & made ass of self. Called soldiers & talked rubbish. Got up on horse & when I told him dismount brought out loaded revolver. Did this twice. Blagovich ... induced him get off go to his tent. Took away revolver & gave me. Loaded with 5 cartridges. Sent courier to Popovitch who came but dealt weakly. I gave him revolver. Apoteker [dispenser] then threatened if not given him in ½ hr. Destroying nation Serbs & steal anything he could. Soldiers & Narednik angry with him put double guard round my car at night.[18]

The drunken dispenser with a gun was more than Stobart could deal with because he did not accept her authority. At the same time she was very disappointed by the response of her male comrade Major Popovitch, who had 'dealt weakly' with the situation. Perhaps what is most telling here, however, is the support she received from the men of her command and their anger that she had been threatened. Although she did not personally obtain the loaded gun, it was immediately surrendered to her. And it was the soldiers who chose to put a double guard around her as she slept. In *The Flaming Sword*, Stobart suggested that the dispenser ran away when she interrupted his drunken tirade. He later vowed vengeance because she had confiscated the revolver and sent it to the major: 'He would smash the cars and destroy everything we had, etc. but I got rid of him.'[19] She does not say how she got rid of him, but with soldiers around her car, nothing more was heard of him. It was the only case of drunkenness that she encountered and she explained it by suggesting that the dispenser was an Austrian Serb, an ethnic difference of some significance under the circumstances.

Stobart was a woman whose dedication to a cause was absolute. By late 1915 she was totally committed to the cause of the Serbian people. She was painfully conscious that the Allies had let them down in a military sense. As a British woman she was determined to do all she could to make up for what she saw as the failure of her country-men. Consequently she set out to ensure that all of the Serbians in her care reached safety, and did whatever was needed to achieve this. Part of the reason for Stobart's success, through her role as 'Maika', was that she prioritised the domestic and everyday needs of the men, always doing her utmost to ensure that they had enough to eat and somewhere to shelter if possible. Each day Stobart noted these every-day details in her diary, juxtaposed with observations about the sound of the pursuing guns and the appalling weather conditions. Food is, after all, one of the most important issues in wartime. Getting enough to eat is always the priority of the soldier. Like Remarque's soldiers, like Flora Sandes, Stobart took on this dual role: as both 'Major' and 'Maika' she oversaw food provision and production, a difficult task while they were on the road with so many thousands of others all in the same position. Olive Aldridge, a nurse from Stobart's hospital at Kragujevatz, later recorded:

> Maize bread and meat were our stock foods. The bread was so full of sand which got between our teeth and was not only very unpleasant but caused dysentery amongst many of our members. If at any time other bread could be obtained, it was given to those who suffered these ill effects. A deep craving for fruit and sugar was experienced by all, but these were only very rarely obtainable.[20]

The poor quality of the food available during the retreat led to a range of illnesses. Stobart herself suffered badly from diarrhoea towards the end of the journey. She suffered particularly at night and the result-ing lack of sleep was very debilitating. However, this is recorded only in the diary. She makes no mention of her illness in her public record of events.

With food, particularly good food, so difficult to come by, rituals of eating also became very important. 'Supper, 2 turkeys spitted over open fire. Excellent.'[21] 'Make fire in tent for meals. Spit 5 chickens for supper.'[22] Stobart's diary entries are reminiscent of the later passage in Remarque's novel where his soldiers, Paul and Kat, kill and cook geese together, an event that takes on symbolic significance and one that feminises the men over a domestic experience. But as the retreating army left the boundaries of Serbia behind the role of provider became a harder one to fulfil. 'No food all night & day.... [C]amp on road. Rain in night make swamp. No house poss. No kitchen arr.'[23]

The column was plagued by bad weather. It would rain on them so hard one day that the roads would flood and they would be coated in thick mud; the next it would be hot sunshine; the next bitter blizzard conditions. Additionally, they were just one small part of a very large convoy: As many as 500,000 people were struggling across the mountains that winter, soldiers, civilians and prisoners of war. There was a lot of competition for the small amounts of food stored by the peasants of Montenegro and Albania, who were often understandably reluctant to part with any as winter set in. Gertrude Pares, an administrator with the SWH and also part of the retreat, recorded:

> Long after dark we were still struggling along, hardly able to stand for very weariness and constantly falling on the slippery ice. At last we saw a light, and at nine o'clock, after thirteen hours' walking, we thankfully threw ourselves down on the mud-floor, round the blazing logs, in a peasant's cottage. With great difficulty we took off our frozen boots, and then sat contentedly gnawing the remains of frozen bread and meat from our bread-bags, and drinking with relish our milkless and sugarless tea till we fell asleep, so closely packed that we could not turn over, too thankful to be under cover to be critical of our neighbours, or of the state of the floor, or even of the acrid wood-smoke that filled our nostrils and made our eyes stream with tears.[24]

The relief to be out of the snow is the overwhelming emotion. None of the other discomforts can impinge on this. The local peasants have every right to be resentful: 500,000 people passing through looking for food and shelter must have put an impossible strain on the ordinary people who lived in the mountains.

It was here, on the last leg of the journey, as the winter closed in around them, that Stobart really showed her worth as a provider for her men and for the animals essential for their final trek. She found food, shelter and, whenever possible, even clothing, to protect them against the forces of nature surrounding them.

> Dark in rain & then sleet & hail. No hay for ponies but find some after 3 hrs. up mountain to fetch & make soup in cottage woman (& sucking child) cooking. Trek ox for sale, ponies etc. went on while V & I bargaining for hay, & had to search for them. But thankful for hay. Very cold and unpleasant mud again. Make soup while waiting for hay. No bread.

Go on after 2 hrs road good & scenery grand & rugged, bare rocks grey & mossy.[25]

Stobart managed to cram so much into her diary despite its size.[26] In this brief extract she gives a real sense of the everyday life of the retreat for her. It begins with the terrible weather and absence, 'no hay for ponies'. But with a detour and an effort she finds both animal fodder and the means to make hot soup for her people. High up on the mountainside, the peasant woman suckles her child as she bargains, no doubt getting a good price for all she has to offer. Stobart was used to this kind of negotiation. She and her first husband, St Clair Stobart, had run a farm on the South African veldt at the beginning of the century. During this period of her life, Mabel had set up a 'Kaffir' store as a business of her own, selling produce and offering services to the local population.[27] No doubt this experience served her well when she came to bargain with locals for the supplies on which many lives depended. And the hay for the horses was just as important as the soup for the men.

Often, rooted in the domestic, Stobart was able to persuade people to sell food to the unit where her male comrades failed to do so: 'Told Commissaire to buy sheep for men but when come to it kept making excuse of expense etc, so finally when he said man had gone to bed, I went with Vooitch [interpreter] & found sheep in his bedroom & pay him.'[28] Perhaps the owner of the sheep had hidden it for fear that the refugees could not or would not pay for it. In the event, unlike her men, Stobart was either confident enough or determined enough, or both, to dismiss any concerns for the man's privacy and, upon receipt of the poor sheep, certainly did pay him, ' "20 dinars" (about 11s. 8d.)'.[29] This anecdote resembles one recorded by Flora Sandes in her account of her war experience in Serbia, in which she is able to procure food for her men where other soldiers have failed to do so.[30] Additionally, Stobart not only worked to feed and support her own men, she was also quick to offer hospitality to any passing comrades who might need it. Hers is an almost classical notion of hospitality that operates to strengthen the bond between her British unit and the land and culture they have sworn to serve.

We were, of course, happy to offer these officers hospitality, and were glad to be able to show, even in a tiny way, British sympathy with the Serbian nation. But now our little stock of stores was coming to an end, and there was no prospect of renewal, and on this evening we shared our last pot of jam with these Serbian friends. Could they, we asked, have a more practical proof of sympathy than that?[31]

This is a gift indeed, given the craving for sugar, noted by Aldridge, and shared by all the refugees. But hospitality is, of course, reciprocal. As Stobart correctly understands, the favour will be returned to her party on many occasions when they are in need of nourishment, even if it is only through a cup of coffee. Her actions tap into the camaraderie of the retreat that helps them, in turn, to survive.

One of the most extraordinary features of Stobart's diary is the way in which she slips in lines and passages that illustrate the landscape through which they travel; the diary becomes a sort of travelogue in its own right, feeding the way in which she adopts the tropes of travel writing in her published text as discussed in Chapter 1. Stobart was only too aware of the significance of the Balkan landscape in determining experience. Mark Mazower has noted the way in which Balkan geography and topography differs from other European regions: 'Unlike the mountain chains guarding the necks of the Iberian and Italian peninsulas, the Balkan ranges offer no barrier against invasion, leaving the region open to easy access and attack from the north and east. On the other hand, their irregular formation hinders movement between one valley and the next.'[32] Stobart was of course, very aware of these geographic difficulties, but she is much less prosaic in her illustration of the problems they present to the retreating armies. For example, even as she treks away from the advancing enemies, she notes, 'Moonlight plain with snow like a foamy sea with mountainous waves & islands (hills interspersed) waves breaking both sides of road to swallow one up.'[33] Despite all the suffering and the pressure on her to alleviate it, Stobart not only has an eye for landscape, for colour, for the sensuality of the world around them, but also manages to find a form of poetry to interpret what she sees. She is not satisfied with simply describing the snow-covered landscape. Instead she finds a way to make us see, feel and hear the landscape using the extended metaphor of the sea. It is both beautiful and threatening: the fear of being swallowed up seems to reflect more than just the weather, but the whole experience of the retreat.

She also uses colour very effectively. 'Colors [*sic*] in mountains other side Morava green-grey-yellow beech leaves caught by setting sun. Rainbow unwilling to touch blood sodden earth. Is it a wonder? Dispersed in clouds. Along road everything drab dying or dead.'[34] Here it is possible to see Stobart evaluating as well as describing. There is conflict between the natural world and the war that influences her broader intellectual response to the war, developed in *The Flaming Sword*. Diaries of experience in Serbia, like this one, tend towards describing the alien, if beautiful nature of the landscape. In contrast women's diaries of the Western Front, while still often concerned with the beauties of nature, have a propensity to highlight what is familiar, what reminds the diarists of England and home.[35] At times Stobart's diary has a poetic quality that is totally unexpected, as she finds ways to describe the landscapes and the life and the death that surrounds her. One clear effect is pathos. Her rainbow imagery embodies the tragedy of war. But another effect of these injections of colour and landscape is to firmly locate the experience in the physical and the present. The record of the retreat is rooted in the everyday world, a world that contains beauty as well as tragedy, a landscape that she is only passing through but one that will nonetheless remain with her.

She was not the only one passing through.

> Sent Marko to find room. Got small one & kitchen for cook food, 2 little refugee girls lost parents on trek left here by officers who gave them lift in kola & couldn't wait.... Nightmare getting places for ponies in stables ... too late for bread but hope for some tomorrow. Two ponies left en route ... but picked up another on mountainside when fetching hay. Sleet all day till 2 p.m. & very cold. My pony done, can't ride him, another man dead on roadside. No one's business to bury him.... All slept in small room on floor & Vooitch etc. in kitchen. Ill as usual in night sleet & cold turning out twice in slippery mud.[36]

The diary is full of references to the victims of the retreat; civilians like these lost girls cry out for help from the pages. And while there is the impression of humanity found in the officers who gave them a lift, no one has the resources to do anything more substantial. This was an impression shared by other British women involved in the retreat. Another SWH nurse, Elizabeth Bertram, wrote of:

> Crowds of people, soldiers, oxen, guns, pack ponies, mules, all trying to form a line as it were, to ascend a height of 7000 ft. To add to the difficulty it was snowing hard, and, to all appearance every thing was a perfect wilderness of white – for four days we were in this wilderness. The 1st day we walked on until dark. The path, for there was just one path to follow, became steeper & steeper, & more slippery and as ponies, mules, guns, soldiers & civilians were practically all mixed up, our ascent was slow. The ponies and oxen slipped about, and many fell down exhausted. I cannot relate some of the sights, they were too awful.[37]

Bertram's landscape is all about people. The snow, the altitude and the narrow path operate to give a meaning to the various people and animals that populate the mountainside. The retreat for Bertram is all about this flowing mass of humanity travelling as one. Although her writing is more prosaic than Stobart's, it is equally poignant. Yet finally language fails her; she cannot describe all that she sees, the sights are too awful. It is that old difficulty of war writing: how does one articulate the unspeakable? Stobart attempts to do it by focusing in as well as out; her language remains peopled with individuals rather than crowds: 'Another man dead on the roadside. No one's business to bury him.' 'Ill as usual in night'. The small stories evoke the tragedy, the crowd and the individual work together in these writings to present an overall impression of the horrors of the retreat. It was such a significant event in First World War history and yet one that has been systematically ignored in most Western narratives since.

The final part of Stobart's *The Flaming Sword* is dedicated to spelling out the political lessons learnt during the time in Serbia. It is here that she finds the space to publicise the Serbian cause.

> The story should show, if only, alas! in a small way, something of the courage and the dignity, and spirit of the Serbian people. It is difficult for those who have not had first-hand evidence, to realize the heroism of the Serbian nation, not only during their defeat and their retreat, October to December, 1915, but also during the summer of political temptation in 1915.[38]

While the 'heroism' of the Serbian people, the victims of war, is rarely questioned, other accounts of the retreat are far more critical of the Serbian authorities and the way they managed, or failed to manage, the invasion of their country. Sir Ralph Paget, in his 'Report on the Retreat of Part of the British Hospital Units from Serbia',[39] submitted after the event, expresses frustration at broken promises of the military; they assured him that carts would be available to transport the units and their equipment, but when the moment arrived, none were forthcoming. Others are more critical still. One report of the retreat, possibly written by Miss M. Barclay, states:

> But I doubt if even the retreat will ever be written of. It was practically hopeless from the start....
>
> From the date the Serbian retreat began there was never any real plan of campaign undertaken. The whole actions of the Serbian Headquarters were based on haphazard movements of armies....

... [F]rom that moment the retreat became not that of an army, but of a country, hampered as they were both with their families and by the flight of the people which was not in any way controlled.[40]

These thoughts appear prophetic. Although people did write of the retreat, their records quickly disappeared from public view and have remained hidden for decades. All the accounts of the retreat seem to identify this overriding confusion, Stobart's included. Back in Britain, real understanding of the events of the retreat remained sketchy. J. H. Kemp wrote to the SWH, generalising and glossing over the experiences of the members, even a fatality.

Forty-six members of our Serbian Units have now returned to this country....

The journey across the hills of Montenegro, though attended with great hardships, was accomplished without any casualty, except in the case of Dr Macgregor's party, in which several Nurses were travelling. We greatly regret to say that, as a result of this, Mrs Toughill – one of the nurses – lost her life.

We learn from the return party that all members were given the choice of leaving Serbia or of remaining; but as the dangers of the journey were great, those leaving were asked to sign a paper stating that they did so of their own will.[41]

This letter is extraordinarily matter-of-fact in tone. The 'great hardships' are not explored. It is not even mentioned that Mrs Toughill was killed in an automobile accident. The idea that the nurses were required to sign a disclaimer before beginning the journey is almost sinister. The choice between the dangers of the retreat and the dangers of captivity cannot have been an easy one.[42]

For Mabel Stobart it was important to try to bring order to chaos. It was in no one's interests to criticise the Serbian HQ, when there was food and shelter to be found. Domestic survival strategies took priority. In 1916 and 1917 Stobart promoted the publication of her book with a series of lecture tours across Britain and later the United States, during which she sought to raise awareness of the country's plight and to raise money for the SRF. While in Serbia she embraced national culture as well as forging an identity for herself within the military. It was a relationship that remained important to her throughout her life.[43] 'I am proud if I have been able to render to this Serbian Army, and to the Serbian people whom I love and respect, even the smallest service.'[44]

In the end, despite the failings of the Allies to provide the country with military support, and despite the lack of campaign plans from the Serbian military, it is the state of warfare itself that is seen by many of the women involved as being to blame for all the suffering. Olive Aldridge wrote:

> All this misery and all the many roadside tragedies were happening not because anybody was going deliberately out of their way to be unkind to anybody else, but it was the inevitable result of war and invasion. And so long as countries recognize war as a legitimate means of settling their differences, so long as countries are greedy for their neighbours' territory, these tragedies will be re-enacted.[45]

Also a member of the First Serbian–English Field Hospital, Aldridge's view echoes Stobart's, but for the 'Major/Maika' the argument went a stage further. By 1916, she understood herself to be a feminist. She understood that all her work of the previous fifteen years has been focused on demonstrating the need for equality and the potential of women. While her feminism was not radical in the militant suffragette sense, it was radical in terms of the extent to which she was prepared to go to illustrate the abilities of women to play their part in time of crisis. This had been her undertaking since the founding of the WSWCC in 1909. Women could play a useful part in warfare, in the defence of the nation and as such they were entitled to full citizenship. But her experiences convinced her of more than this.

War was the direct result of women's exclusion from politics. War was caused by the unchecked growth of militarism and 'militarism is maleness run riot'.[46] It was male dominance of the world that had culminated in the First World War: 'To this end has the wisdom of Man brought Man. Could the wisdom of woman bring us to a worse abyss than this? However desperate the remedy, must not the help of woman be hailed to save life from the abyss?'[47] Stobart and her women entered the male arena of the battlefront and survived, more than survived, demonstrating how women could contribute to, even lead an army in wartime, but by 'saving life from the abyss', rather than by seeking to take it. This formed the basis of all Stobart's political campaigning after the war.[48] She opposed war and determined to help the victims of war, including soldiers as well as civilians, because she understood that war was fundamentally wrong. Her views in many ways echo those of other feminist pacifists active during the war.[49] Where Stobart differs profoundly is in her front-line experience. And crucially, throughout all their undertaking, Stobart and her women remained *women*. Unlike Flora Sandes, who took on the 'man's' role of the soldier and experimented with conventional gender identities, these women nurtured, nursed and provided for the men, extensions of the domestic role that they might have been expected to fulfil in civilian life. They succeeded as women in a man's world. They gave Stobart her vision of what the future should be, a future in which women's contribution might make all the difference. For now, a few men at least, had begun to understand.

> You brought, successfully, with your energy and splendid behaviour, all your staff to Scutari. It was a tremendous task to achieve on account of the many difficulties and inconveniences through which the Serbians had to pass. Your hospital was the only one that knew how to save the staff and bring some to Scutari. That can be explained by the fact that you did not give up your command for one moment and shared all the war difficulties and inconveniences. You have made everybody believe that a woman can overcome and endure all the war difficulties, and as a Commander of a Medical Unit, can save all staff and at the same time doing useful work while going back to your Motherland.
> Colonel Dr Laza Geuich
> Scutari, January 9th 1916[50]

Stobart's experiences during the Serbian retreat influenced the rest of her life, politically, intellectually and spiritually.

> ([A] few yrs. above ground, eternity beneath. Diff aspects in war. Trees not trees but fire-wood, men only soldiers to be killed & maimed, oxen only machines etc. And women?)[51]

In war, all things seemed to lose their value, trees, oxen, men, 'a few years above ground, eternity beneath', and yet still such waste. 'And women?' Women represented the subtle difference between Stobart's column and all the rest. For her, women represented domestic order surrounded by turmoil and chaos. Women participated in war to alleviate suffering and to emphasise its futility. Empowered women could do more than this: they could help to prevent future wars and to protect nationhood. To contemporary readers, this is an essentialist view, perhaps. But Stobart believed it absolutely, and believed that her actions and achievements endorsed it. Despite the many trials presented by the Serbian retreat, the invading armies, the weather, the lack of food and shelter, the physical suffering, Major Stobart's unit made it through to a man (and woman), the only unit to do so. Why were they different? Perhaps luck was on their side: a solution always turned up for every problem, the regular 'miracles' that Stobart refers to in her 1935 autobiography, *Miracles and Adventures*.[52] But perhaps they did have something else that the other columns didn't have, something that held them together even through the toughest times: 'Moving in and out, quietly, and leisurely, amongst the tents, were some women, who seemed to have no concern with the tumult that was raging around them.' Such calm in the face of a storm must count for something. Domestic survival strategies based on the established 'feminine' role in life. And at the helm, guiding them through in a way that no man ever could, they did have the 'Maika', Mabel St Clair Stobart.

The next chapter will consider a different chaos, that of revolution, and explore the ways in which the British women working in Russia coped with the tumult that enveloped them in 1917.

Notes

1 Elsie Corbett, *Red Cross in Serbia 1915–1919* (Banbury: Cheney & Sons, 1964), p. 44.
2 John Keegan, *The First World War* (London: Hutchinson, 1998), p. 273.
3 Huw Strachen, *The First World War* (London: Simon & Schuster, 2006), p. 154.
4 Leah Leneman, *In the Service of Life: The Story of Elsie Inglis and the Scottish Women's Hospitals* (Edinburgh: Mercat Press, 1994), p. 42.
5 Imperial War Museum, London (hereafter IWM), 8761, Sir Ralph Paget, 'Report on the Retreat of Part of the British Hospital Units from Serbia October–December 1915', records Stobart's presence in the country but makes no mention of her breakaway 'Flying Column'.
6 No doubt the Serbian military, to which Stobart was answerable, would have been more relaxed about this.
7 Mabel St Clair Stobart, *The Flaming Sword in Serbia and Elsewhere* (London: Hodder and Stoughton, 1917), pp. 173–4.
8 IWM, EN1/3/COR/015, Mabel St Clair Stobart, Unpublished diary.
9 IWM, 12811, Letter from Miss K. E. Royds, of the SWH, to her mother, 30th November 1915.
10 *Ibid.*
11 Stobart, Diary, Tuesday, 19th October 1915.
12 Stobart, *The Flaming Sword*, p. 124.
13 Isabel Emslie Hutton, *With a Woman's Unit in Serbia, Salonika and Sebastopol* (London: Williams & Northgate, 1928), p. 85.

14 For further information on Emmeline Pankhurst see June Purvis, *Emmeline Pankhurst: A Biography* (London: Routledge, 2002).

15 For a discussion of a proposed inversion of the gender power dynamic during the First World War, see Sandra M. Gilbert, 'Soldier's Heart: Literary Men, Literary Women, and the Great War', *Signs* 8:3, Women and Violence (Spring 1983), 422–50.

16 Stobart, Diary, Monday, 11th October 1915.

17 Stobart, Diary, Tuesday, 9th November 1915.

18 Stobart, Diary, Saturday, 23rd October 1915.

19 Stobart, *The Flaming Sword*, p. 157.

20 Olive Aldridge, *The Retreat from Serbia through Montenegro and Albania* (London: Minerva, 1916), p. 92.

21 Stobart, Diary, Tuesday, 26th October 1915.

22 Stobart, Diary, Saturday, 30th October 1915.

23 Stobart, Diary, Monday, 15th November 1915.

24 Gertrude Pares, 'With the Serbian Retreat', *The Englishwoman* 29 (1916), p. 237. Quoted in Leneman, *In the Service of Life*, p. 41.

25 Stobart, Diary, Tuesday, 14th December 1915.

26 The actual size of the diary is approximately 100mm × 50mm.

27 As well as running the store, Stobart was considered something of a medicine woman and took responsibility for conducting church services on the veldt.

28 Stobart, Diary, Friday, 17th December 1915.

29 Stobart, *The Flaming Sword*, p. 278.

30 See Chapter 3.

31 Stobart, *The Flaming Sword*, p. 196.

32 Mark Mazower, *The Balkans: From the End of Byzantium to the Present Day* (London: Phoenix Press, 2001), p. 19.

33 Stobart, Diary, Wednesday, 17th November 1915.

34 Stobart, Diary, Thursday, 4th November 1915.

35 See discussion of women's diaries in Angela K. Smith, *The Second Battlefield: Women, Modernism and the First World War* (Manchester: Manchester University Press, 2000), ch. 1.

36 Stobart, Diary, Tuesday, 14th December 1915.

37 IWM, Miss E. Bertram, 'Experiences in Serbia,' First World War Papers, quoted in Leneman, *In the Service of Life*, p. 41.

38 Stobart, *The Flaming Sword*, p. 308.

39 Paget, 'Report on the Retreat'.

40 IWM, 4320, Anonymous report written in Scutari, possibly by Miss M. Barclay, who may have been associated with the SWH, 7th December 1915.

41 Mitchell Library, Glasgow (hereafter ML), SWH Archive, Large Trunk, Letter to SWH from J. H. Kemp, Honorary Secretary, SWH Personnel Committee, 24th December 1915.

42 For a further discussion of the way the participation of British nurses in the retreat was represented in the British press, see Christine E. Hallett, *Veiled Warriors: Allied Nurses of the First World War* (Oxford: Oxford University Press, 2014), pp. 120–6.

43 The experience of war-torn Serbia had the same impact on a number of British women who served there. See Monica Krippner, *The Quality of Mercy: Women at War, Serbia 1915–18* (Newton Abbot and London: David & Charles, 1980), for discussions of the range of women involved. Also see Leneman, *In the Service of Life*, for full discussion of the SWH, and Julie Wheelwright, *Amazons and Military Maids* (London: Pandora, 1989) and Louise Miller, *A Fine Brother: The Life of Captain Flora Sandes* (London: Alma Books, 2012) for further discussion of Flora Sands.

44 Stobart, *The Flaming Sword*, p. 292.

45 Aldridge, *The Retreat from Serbia*, pp. 77–8.

46 Stobart, *The Flaming Sword*, Preface.

47 *Ibid.*, p. 313.

48 Stobart had hoped to stand for Parliament, but the opportunity never arose.

49 For example see Catherine Marshall, 'Women and War', in Margaret Kamester and Jo Vellacott (eds), *Militarism versus Feminism: Writings on Women and War by Catherine Marshall, C. K. Ogden and Mary Sargant Florence* (London: Virago, 1987).

50 IWM, EN1/3/COR/015A, Letter from Serbian colonel to Mabel St Clair Stobart, 9th January 1916.

51 Stobart, Diary, Saturday, 27th November 1915.

52 Mabel St Clair Stobart, *Miracles and Adventures* (London: Rider and Co., 1935).

6

The road to revolution: Russia, 1916–17

This war is the crucifixion of the youth of the world.[1]

Before 1916, there were relatively few British women working in Russia, certainly away from the major cities. Florence Farmborough's involvement as a 'sister of mercy' from as early as 1915 was quite unusual and her active work at the front particularly so. Mary Britnieva, as an Anglo-Russian, was in a slightly different position, but both were long-term residents of the country. Whereas Serbia had been only too pleased to welcome all the various British hospital units formed in the early months of the war, Russia was a less obvious recipient of their services, coming to the war fresh as she did. But there was one notable exception, the Anglo-Russian Base Hospital in Petrograd. The initiative for this project came from Lady Muriel Paget, an established philanthropist who had spent years working in the East End of London, setting up kitchens to feed the poor, particularly women and children. Although this work became even more pressing with the outbreak of war, in the spring of 1915 she heard from a family friend of the acute suffering of the Russian army and determined to do something to help.[2]

Lady Muriel was the Honorary Organising Secretary of the Executive Committee, but intended to go to Russia to run the hospital herself. In the event, ill health delayed her and she was not able to take on the role until April 1916. The hospital, under the temporary leadership of Lady Sybil Grey, was opened by the Russian Dowager Empress on 31st January 1916, and operated under the auspices of the Russian Red Cross.[3] Sarah Macnaughtan, who had been actively involved with the war since 1914 when she had formed part of the first Stobart unit to journey to Belgium, travelled to Petrograd to work at the Anglo-Russian Hospital. She noted the different ways in which the Russian system operated as well as the horror of the sheer numbers of wounded from the Eastern Front.

> There are 25,000 amputation cases in Petrograd. The men at my hospital are mostly convalescent, but of course their wounds require dressing. This is never done in their beds, as the English plan is, but each man is carried in turn and laid on an operating-table and has his fresh dressings put on, and is then carried back to his bed again....
>
> Yesterday one saw enough to stir one profoundly, and enough to make small things seem small indeed![4]

British women like Macnaughtan, experienced in a very national model of professional practice, had to adjust to new ways of operating in Russia. There were presumably no chintz curtains in the Anglo-Russian Hospital, either. And just as the Serbian national character was embedded in her fighting men, so the Russian soldiers seemed different to Macnaughtan.

> After the blind came those who had lost limbs – one-legged men, men still in bandages, men hobbling with sticks or with an arm round a comrade's neck, and then the stretcher cases. There was one man carrying his crutches like a cross. Others lay twisted sideways. Some never moved their heads from their pillows. All seemed to me to have a splendid dignity which made the long, battered, suffering company into some great pageant. I have never seen men so lean as they were. I have never seen men's cheek-bones seem to cut through the flesh just where the close-cropped hair on their temples ends. I have never seen such hollow eyes; but they were Russian soldiers, Russian gentlemen, and they were home again.[5]

Macnaughtan's imagery is interesting. She is drawn towards Christian symbolism in her representation of these men: 'There was one man carrying his crutches like a cross'; 'This war is the crucifixion of the youth of the world.' This endows the foreign soldiers with an aura of martyrdom, implying that they are victims of some greater evil, sacrificed for the greater good. At the same time they are a 'great pageant', which evokes ideas of celebration, commemoration and spectacle, each of which in turn carries with it multiple ways of reading and interpreting the soldiers.

As soon as Muriel Paget arrived in Petrograd she began to organise a field hospital unit of the Anglo-Russian Hospital. The field hospital was up and running by June and was transferred to the Galician

Front, close to Florence Farmborough in July 1916. Although this campaign saw a relative Russian success, casualties were still very high on both sides. keeping all the hospital units busy. Inevitably the civilian population got in the way as well. Paget wrote in a letter to her husband on 12th August, 'I don't turn a hair at all the horrors seen in the operating and dressing room, but when children are brought in wounded I can't bear it.'[6]

Margaret H. Barber travelled to Russia in April 1916 with the Lord Mayor's Armenian Relief Fund party led by the Rev. Harold Buxton. Over the next three and half years her relief work took her across Russia, working both in the cities and the countryside, wherever the need of the refugees was greatest. Barber saw the old regime and the new at first hand, always from the perspectives of the least privileged members of society, giving her another unique perspective.

Not far away, Florence Farmborough was in the midst of the battle, continuing to use her diary to record the stories of the voiceless Russian soldiers. 'Here is a man with half-a-dozen fatal wounds on his body and his strength of will is such that he can ask the time of day, the exact location of our Red Cross unit, even the latest news from his sector of the Front. And having received the answers, he turns his face to the wall and quietly surrenders his wounded body to Death.'[7] Farmborough exhibits the same levels of admiration for the Russian soldier as Sarah Macnaughtan. The presentation of his heroism seems to add to his 'otherness'; the personification of Death, his conqueror, echoes the notion of martyrdom found elsewhere. 'Is there in our language no greater, more laudatory word than "hero" for a man of this calibre?',[8] she asks, questioning the limitations of her own language to articulate the soldier's behaviour patterns. Farmborough contrasts the stoicism of the dying soldier with her own inability to cope with the fallout of the battle. 'I feel terribly tired today and my back aches; I am afraid that there is not much of the "hero" about me – not a scratch on my body and yet I can scarcely walk!'[9] While conventional notions of heroism are inadequate to describe the soldier and his ability to engage with the situation, the same language cannot be used for a mere woman whose physical discomfort does not have the same dignity that can be attributed to a real wound.

Farmborough also notes that the relative success of the army has a significant downside. Many of the soldiers celebrate their victory by drinking and destroying property. This results in the need to tell a very different kind of story, one that rejects all notions of Macnaughtan's

Christian symbolism and pageantry. 'Soldiers were lolling idly about the streets; some of them so drunk that they were reeling.... It was a long time since we had seen a drunken soldier; the sight saddened us.'[10] The drinking leads to a terrible accident. There is a fire in a distillery filled with soldiers, the casks of alcohol leading to a shocking explosion resulting in death and some very severe burn cases. The treatment of these wounded, the acute suffering of two of the burn victims, causes Farmborough extreme trauma. Her ability to cope with witnessing great suffering seems to decrease as the war progresses in 1916. It is as though she herself becomes victim to what we would now call post-traumatic stress disorder.

Farmborough's desire to alleviate suffering at all costs results in her questioning hospital regulations. She cannot comprehend the practice of reviving and treating dying men who she believes should be left to die in peace. Despite acknowledging that the doctor must be right, she seems to have little conviction. This is later tested when she gives in to the temptation to give water to a man dying of a stomach wound, understanding that such an action may hasten his death. The doctor's reaction shocks her: 'Then you have killed him', the doctor tells her. 'Quite simply, you have killed him.'[11] Although Farmborough's fellow nurse assures her that she would have done the same thing, Farmborough struggles with guilt following this incident. The diary pages of 1916 are filled with traumas of this type, each indicating a small decline in Farmborough's ability to deal with her war experience. After an amputation she needs help to remove a leg from the operating room.

> [A] Brother helped me carry it to the tiny shed where a stack of amputated limbs awaited burial. I had not been in that shed before and I turned hastily away; I went to our room, drank some water and swallowed two aspirins; the choking feeling disappeared and I was myself again.[12]

An encounter with the fresh dead on a battlefield compounds her changing impressions of warfare: 'So this was ADVANCE! Wherein lay its glory? Only these forsaken, mouldering bodies could testify to the Russian Victory.... Oh! One *must* believe and trust in God's mercy, otherwise these frightful sights would work havoc with one's brain; and one's heart would faint with the depth of its despair.'[13] After two years of close experience of front-line warfare, the evidence suggests that Farmborough was close to breaking point. It was perhaps no surprise that she soon became very ill with paratyphoid, her own symbolic wound, and had to remain hospitalised when her unit moved on. 'I had thought that an English constitution would have come to my aid in this hour of need.'[14] But it was not to be. She was sent to convalesce in the Crimea and had to have all her hair shaved off as it was in such bad condition, her symbolic scar, to be disguised by her nurse's head-dress when she returned to the front.

Farmborough's state of mind and body in late 1916, perhaps somewhat coincidentally, seems to reflect the state of Russian society as rumours of political unrest grew and social and cultural uncertainty spread. This was the climate that greeted some British women as they came to work in Russia for the first time. Margaret Barber, arriving in Petrograd, recorded:

> Although I saw no injustice under the old *regime* I felt a constraint, which may have been caused by the repeated warnings of my friends against making enquiries about conditions in Russia. The dvorniks or house porters also gave one a feeling of suppression and suspicion. They were very punctilious about all passports, and were said to be Government spies on the look out for suspicious persons holding meetings.[15]

The nurses had to be careful even when trying to help. Following the fall of Serbia, many SWH staff had returned to England looking for new opportunities, while writing their memoirs of their time in retreat or as POWs. So Elsie Inglis once more looked east.

The remnants of the Serbian army who had survived the invasion were stationed on the island of Corfu, much to the consternation of the Greek government, which was in turmoil for much of the war, with opposing political factions lobbying for involvement on both sides.[16] The Serbian government and many civilian refugees accompanied the soldiers. They brought with them another unwelcome guest: typhus. In early 1916 those suffering from typhus were moved to the island of Vido. Duson T. Batakovic states that 'At least 7,000 Serbian soldiers died in Vido, of whom the majority were buried in the Ionian Sea which later became known among Serbs as a "blue tomb".'[17] SWH doctor Mary McNeil, visiting Corfu after the war, noted that 20,000 Serbs were buried there.[18] There was an urgent need to get the Serbian army back into the field. While some were slowly moved to Salonika in preparation for the push to retake the country, others were moved further north and east to Romania and Russia. Romania joined the war on the Allied side in August 1916, applying pressure to Germany and opening up another battlefront. As the Serbian troops prepared to go to Romania, the Serbian government asked the SWH to provide a field hospital unit to go with them. Inglis was happy to agree, but was very aware that this would be a completely different experience.

> As regards the field Hospitals for Russia – I find that the whole organisation and personnel for there is quite different to the Hospitals we have carried so far.
>
> Colonel Gentitch kindly came up and explained the whole thing to me as it is worked in the Russian and Serbian armies. They have no Field Dressing Stations as our Army does. Each regiment has its regimental surgeon who does the field dressings.
>
> Behind there are the Flying Field Hospitals, which are something like our Clearing Stations, but more fully equipped. The men stay there longer than they do in a Clearing Station and the Hospital is more fully equipped. They evacuate, as our Clearing Stations do, to the Base Hospitals.[19]

Inglis' unit and the transport, led by Evelina Haverfield, arrived at Archangel on 10th September 1916 and took the train south to Odessa. It took nine days. They then moved on to Medjidia where they were given a barrack hospital as a base (Hospital A), led by Inglis, and split the unit to form a separate field hospital, led by Dr Lilian Chesney and to include Mrs Haverfield's transport (Hospital B). In the event, the Germans together with the Bulgarians attacked Romania with a much greater force than had been expected. The SWH were busier than they had anticipated and quickly became part of the mass retreat along the Romanian line. Katherine Hodges noted that:

> [T]o those of us who were inexperienced in matters of war it was a good thing that we were flung into the awful chaos existent in Roumania [*sic*]. We had no time to get upset or nervy. We went straight from the feeling of 'Oh, what an exciting adventure' into dreadful horrors and very hard continuous work, which made things easier.[20]

Bucharest fell in December 1916 and the retreat continued for Romanians, Russians, Serbs and British women alike.

Lady Dorothy Kennard was a British woman working at the Military Hospital in Bucharest when the city fell. She had been visiting the city independently since October 1915 and had watched the gradual evolution of the war as it spread through the neighbouring countries, pushing refugees into Romania. As the crisis worsened, it became clear that there was a severe shortage of nurses and women were effectively conscripted to help. Kennard recalls that 'We Englishwomen can go and work where we like, and I have offered myself to one of the big military hospitals.'[21] Bucharest was quickly under fire from the attacking Germans making daily life difficult. She notes the first real bombardment:

> ... and then for half an hour I was really in the war, for there were six Taubes overhead all dropping bombs.
>
> As I neared the hospital, shrapnel began to fall. The bombs, of course, fell all round. I picked up one man wounded and unconscious and took him on in the car. A woman was killed at the gate of the hospital, and one man died on the doorstep. There are barracks just near by, and all the soldiers got out of hand and fired their rifles madly in all directions. Two men wounded by their own comrades were carried in to us afterwards.[22]

What seems to strike Kennard continually as she writes in her diary is the way she is able to adjust to the horror that surrounds her. 'Curious! A month ago I felt faint when I saw blood or smelt a nasty smell.... Sometimes I can hardly credit the fact that this woman, indifferent to blood and white bones and gangrene horrors, is myself.'[23] But like the women in the organised units, Kennard quickly finds a real sense of fulfilment in this unexpected occupation. 'All the wounded in my pavilion call me "Little Mother" now, and I have grown to love each individual man.'[24] While many women nursing on the Eastern and other fronts experience this maternal investment, it is something that seems more connected with the British women, here echoing Mabel Stobart's role as 'Maika'. This identification may perhaps have been a consequence of the women's shared Imperial sense of self, as women of Empire, mothers of the world.

Yvonne Fitzroy, an orderly with the SWH at Medjidia, describes her first encounter with death as the wounded poured in during October 1916. It betrays her affinity to the English culture that had produced her.

> I don't know if the others have ever tried to imagine what coming face to face with Death would be like; I have often wondered how they took the initiation, and whether they had associated it almost inseparably as I had with the order and discipline of an English Hospital. Something inextricably mixed up with privacy, relations, flowers, and fat black horses.[25]

The actual experience of death is, of course, not as she had imagined, but she still endows it with a rather British sense of calm. Alerted to the imminent death of a patient she imagines a sort of lull in the chaos of the ward, as though time stands still for him. 'I wondered how, in this world in which he walks so familiarly, Death had still the power to make men stop and look.'[26] Like Florence Farmborough and Mary Borden, Fitzroy personifies Death. The lull she imagines echoes the strange tranquillity of Farmborough's first encounter with the late Vasiliy.[27] Both women seek to endow death with a kind of dignity the war situation does not allow.

The women of the SWH at the base in Medjidia were soon evacuated. Hospital B, under Dr Chesney, based initially at Bul Bul Mic,[28] had to retreat with the armies. Margaret Fawcett, an orderly with Hospital B, found the whole experience rather exciting.

> We got out about 9.30 last night after a somewhat exciting ride; we were all perched on top of the carts carrying our equipment, of which we have five. There was a nasty thunderstorm on the way along, but luckily Turner had her mackintosh and ground sheet with her, so that we didn't get too wet. We are supposed to have gone within three miles of the firing line, which I can quite believe. We seemed to see the flashes of bursting shells on three sides of us, and the roar of guns was far more distinct than we had heard it before.[29]

In 1993 Fawcett's war papers were published, including her actual diary and a retrospective rewriting of the same events. Fawcett's immediate account of the retreat, above, betrays a real excitement. She seems to have enjoyed her night in the thunderstorm, no doubt the drama of the storm adding to that on the road. Her retrospective account plays further with this sense of adventure. On reflection, the thunderstorm contributes to the 'thrill of things', and the guns blaze instead of roar, adding to the fires on the horizon. In both accounts, Fawcett describes the retreat as though she is a traveller rather than a participant; the war is spectacle, dramatic, exciting and alien, an encounter with alterity that hints of danger while keeping the dangers of the firing line firmly at bay. Student doctor Ellie Rendel, working with Dr Chesney, recorded the retreat rather euphemistically in her letters home, presumably to avoid the censor. Here the retreat becomes the 'tour', literally adopting the language of travel. 'Many other people were making the tour with us so we were not at all dull. The roads were rather like the road to Epsom on Derby day.'[30] The metaphor of the typically English holiday event is surprisingly efficient at capturing the impression of the roads crowded with soldiers and refugees, if not the real atmosphere of the retreat. There is a touch of excitement about both women's accounts despite the severity of the situation.

Although all the parties were in retreat, the British women certainly made a good impression on their Romanian and Russian Allies, perhaps because of the stoic way that they dealt with the dangers around them. Fitzroy records that 'Nothing can beat the tales about us in Odessa ... the best story tells of how the Scottish Women leapt into the sea at Constanza [*sic*] so as to escape the pursuing Bulgar.'[31] She includes a press cutting from an Odessa newspaper that gives a clear indication of the respect the women commanded and it is worth quoting in full, despite its length.

> Rumanian refugees arriving from Medjidia tell about the work of the British Women's Hospital. Immediately upon their arrival they arranged an exemplary Hospital for 200 beds. The Unit divided, and a part of the Nurses went to the nearest firing-line; the Rumanians call the work of the British Women ideal, and in fact the fearlessness and energy of the British Women is beyond praise. Four British Nurses of the Transport stayed in Medjidia till the last moment, picking up the wounded soldiers and taking them back. When the foe got hold of Medjidia, the British Women had scarcely time to jump into their motors and go out of the town. The Rumanian Army and convoy were already out of sight and the British Women had to stray in the mountains in abandoned places without knowledge of the country or food three days. Nevertheless, they forced their way on to the good roads, and in three days came to Reni. The first thing they asked of Admiral Vosselkin, who heartily met them there, was to give them a bath, and only after a good wash in the Russian baths they asked for food. They were given a good meal and taken to Galatz.[32]

The media representation of the women is simply heroic. They administer help until the last minute with no thought for their own safety. They brave the dangers of the alien territory without fear and when they return to civilisation they want nothing more than a bath, like the English ladies that they are. As with Mabel Dearmer, Florence Farmborough and Flora Sandes, there is no substitute for a good bath, the one thing that is most difficult to find in the front line.

Beneath the surface, however, things were starting to crack up for the SWH. The pressures and strain of the retreat and the constant moving around were beginning to fray the nerves of the leaders. Testimonies suggest that Lilian Chesney was a short-tempered woman; Evelina Haverfield seems likely to have had some sort of breakdown; and Elsie Inglis was already ill with the cancer that would kill her a year later.[33] Again, there is an ironic parallel here. The difficulties experienced by the women in Russia and Romania seem to reflect the gradual cracking open of Russian society as 1917, the year of revolutions, dawned.

By 1914 Russian society was ripe for revolution. The war was the catalyst that finally gave revolutionaries, waiting in the wings since 1905, the right environment to make their move.[34] After the series of defeats and retreats, as witnessed by the British women, the Russian peasantry who formed the bulk of the army were ready to listen to alternatives. Peter Gatrell argues that:

> The changing fortunes of war had profound consequences for Imperial Russia. Defeat encouraged and emboldened critics of the old regime, since they could point to the capture and imprisonment of Russian men and abandonment of territory to the enemy. However, more than national pride was at stake. By unleashing an unstoppable displacement of civilians, defeat helped bring war into the daily lives of provincial Russia. In these ways the war changed the contours and conduct of Russian politics.[35]

Rumours of unrest began to penetrate the diaries of British women. Florence Farmborough, so embedded in Russian society, was one of the first to hear them.

> Tuesday 23rd August [1916], Volitsa [Ukraine]
> Newcomers have told us many stories of life in the heart of Russia. In some places there is such a shortage of foodstuffs that, unless the authorities build up sufficient stocks, there could be famine during the coming winter. Dissatisfaction is still rife in many cities. There have been rumours of strikes and even riots in Moscow, but nothing officially confirmed. In the city of Petrograd, there is such unrest; and there is severe criticism regarding the Imperial Family.[36]

Farmborough notes that the German descent of the Empress, coupled with her growing attachment to the monk, Rasputin,[37] aggravated the bad feeling. The rumours she heard proved to be true. 'In 1916, large-scale strikes, often political and economic, erupted once more. On 9 January 1917, 145,000 workers went on strike in St Petersburg in commemoration of Bloody Sunday. "Down with the Tsar" was the ominous cry beginning to be heard.'[38] As Trotsky put it, 'Enormous fortunes arose out of the bloody foam',[39] and people were not prepared to tolerate the hardships of the old regime any longer. Under growing pressure, the Tsar abdicated in favour of his brother in March 1917, but he was not replaced and for a short while Russia was completely without real government of any kind. A provisional government based on the Duma soon emerged and remained committed to the war. Alexander Kerensky became the Minister of War and soon began a disastrous new offensive on the Galician Front.

British women greeted the first revolution in different ways. Yvonne Fitzroy found herself to be a supporter. 'There is the wildest enthusiasm and confidence everywhere, and they claim the whole Revolution to be the work of the Army and people united. Splendid – *splendid*.... Everyone is beaming, and one cannot even in these early days but rejoice at the change of attitude.'[40] Fitzroy's response is perhaps not surprising as a product of British democracy. Florence Farmborough, however was much more sceptical, her sympathy much more firmly placed with the Tsar, who was, after all, closely related to the British royal family. Farmborough was a self-confessed royalist, which of course in Britain was not at odds with her democratic principles. She does, however, express relief that the revolution appeared to be 'bloodless', at least in March 1917, but she seems to find the whole situation difficult to deal with. For everyone involved, a sense of uncertainty about what the future holds is an overriding concern. All of a sudden Russia had become quite a different place.

To some extent the SWH women seem to have been cushioned from the greater changes of the first revolution. Their diaries and letters contain relatively few references to Russian politics. As members of British units they seem to have been surrounded by compatriots, and most closely linked with the seconded Serbian army. By March, however, news was beginning to filter through. 'The state of things here is very exciting, no one seems to know what will happen next. Proclamations are published every day which we buy and read with great difficulty with the help of dictionaries', wrote Ellie Rendel in Odessa to her mother in mid-March.[41] The language, of course, was a barrier for the women that long-term residents like Farmborough did not share. The rumours of rioting in Petrograd were more sinister.

As the year moved on, Farmborough continued to record in her diary, in great detail, everything that she heard, providing a comprehensive record, albeit one coloured by her own conservative opinions. She tried to also record the responses of the ordinary soldiers to the revolution, to continue to give a voice to those who might not otherwise be heard. At first this proved very difficult. 'We were anxious to hear what was going on in the trenches and how the men received the news of the abdication.... We could not get them to talk.'[42] They were not the only ones trying. In the months following the revolution, activists wanting to secure the support of the large peasant army frequently held mass meetings near the front line. Margaret Fawcett and Yvonne Fitzroy attended one in Reni market square in late March 1917. In a letter dated 26th March, Fawcett observed that 'the general opinion seems to be divided between the desire for a constitutional monarchy or a republic. Most of the officers we have spoken to are in favour of the former; they say that Russia is not yet ready for a republic.'[43] Fitzroy's diary gives a clearer impression of her own feelings.

> We have been making history by attending a Free Speech Revolutionary Meeting in the market square. The crowd was almost entirely composed of and addressed by soldiers and Officers....
> Judging from this afternoon the only people in Russia who are not free-born are the people who disagree with you. They had a short way with hecklers!
> Freedom of speech, letters, and religion is granted. So far so good. It is a big task for those responsible. The men are just beginning to realize the change, though to our eyes they seem slow to grasp it, and they are terribly dangerous material for the agitator.[44]

Fitzroy's assessment of the situation at the meeting is interesting. She uses irony to hint at criticism. Freedom of speech either is or it isn't; it can't be modified according to whether the speakers agree with each other or not. In this sense she is somewhat prophetic, seeing the problems with the new regime before they are fully understood by the protagonists. Again, coming from a society that encourages freedom of speech, Fitzroy can observe from a position of authority. She also demonstrates considerable foresight in her understanding of the sleeping giant represented by the ordinary men of Russia, ordinary men who, as they began to awake, would present unexpected dangers for some of the women.

Margaret Barber, however, seems to have weathered the revolutionary years without too much trouble. Stationed in a village in the Samara from October 1916 until May 1918 she recalled:

> The Revolution affected us very little. We were simply told by the peasants one morning at our dispensary that there was no Tsar, and this

was afterwards corroborated by the local paper. The returning soldiers held meetings in the market place, assuring us that the millennium had come, and that we were now all free.[45]

Away from the cities and the battlefront, Barber was able to work with ordinary people and present quite a balanced view of the consequences of revolution. For example, she later observes, 'Bolshevism certainly has an ideal side, which its present system of education is fostering. Bolshevik Russia may be the most barbarous country to-day, but her children are having the best opportunity to prove her the most enlightened country of to-morrow.'[46] Barber spent a great deal of her time in Russia working with the Bolshevik armies and developed a much more positive view of their grass-roots policies. However, when she returned to Moscow later things seemed less positive.

Ysabel Birkbeck, a member of the transport, was on her way back to England in March 1917 when she became caught up in the unrest in Petrograd. For several days she was a firsthand witness of events in the city. On Sunday 11th March, while out walking in the city, they encountered riots caused by a general strike, with Cossacks and the police firing into the crowd. The following day she noted:

> All shops shut. All day we prowled about. We have just realised the importance of things, viz: neither bread riots or anti-war motives are putting through the rebellion and it is all right. To-day the soldiers have gone over entirely and are only seen scattered through the crowd. All officers had their swords taken from them and soldiers and civilians alike are armed with rifles, revolvers and daggers.[47]

The women seem to wander about the city unaccompanied and unaware of any sense of personal danger. Like Fitzroy, Birkbeck instinctively sees the revolution as a good thing, offering an opportunity for a more liberal regime. But the action does get a little closer to home when the revolutionaries unexpectedly take over their hotel.

> Congratulating the Russians on having got through their troubles very quietly and ourselves on having kept whole skins when a great deal of noise outside our hotel and an absolute fusillade at the corner made us wonder what was coming next. We leapt up and dressed in record time. Then the revolutionaries poured into the hotel. Every room was searched. Someone had fired from one of the windows and they meant business. Such a mob as poured into our room, soldiers, factory hands, old men and young, all of them carrying arms and knives. We cordially

welcomed our visitors and gave them cigarettes. After a glance round
the room they saluted and clattered off.

Several times the room was searched by similar parties. It was not
till the evening when a second shot was fired, that the police officer was
discovered on the third floor. He shot himself.[48]

Their hotel remained occupied for several days. Although it is probable that the women were not in any danger, and they were a little
battle-hardened, this must have been a frightening experience. On
14th March, Birkbeck notes that a proclamation from the new government ordered everyone back to work and she was impressed at
the effectiveness of the command. The whole incident seemed to be
an entertainment, an opportunity to demonstrate their British pluck.
Her lasting impression was one of admiration helped along by the way
in which the new Republic treated the women.

On returning [to the hotel] we were hailed with much enthusiasm, and
told that England and France had wired they were in accord with the
new government. (As English we were hugely popular). Who could fail
to be in accord with a government that stands for Freedom of Speech,
Freedom of Religion, Liberty of Conscience, Universal Suffrage and the
Responsibility of Ministers. Rumours abound – the abdication of the
Tsar rumoured.[49]

The answer of course, was that any confirmed royalist might not be
in accord. Florence Farmborough was much slower to understand
any potential benefit to the country and, remaining at the front, she
began to get an insight into potential dangers quite soon after the revolution. In May she begins to articulate anxiety about the potential
repercussions of Alexander Kerensky's army reforms.[50] She expresses
particular concern at his abolition of the death penalty at the front
and the general reduction in army discipline. She shares the fears
of the officers around her that their authority will be dangerously
undermined. Kerensky himself, however, makes a different impression on her when she hears him speak during a visit to the Front.
His accomplished oratory and powerful words of freedom convince
her that the country is in safe hands after all. However, the issue
of the death penalty eventually led to a dispute between Kerensky
and General Kornilov, in August 1917, which undermined the fragile coalition and opened the way for a second revolution.[51] But for
Farmborough, the writing already appears to be on the wall much
earlier despite Kerensky's charisma.

We notice a strange apathy about them [the men]; they lack the spark of loyalty, of devotion to God and their mother-country which has so distinguished the fighting-men in the previous two years. It worries us; we do not need to be told that the Russian soldier has changed; we see the change with our own eyes.[52]

The February revolution had begun to illustrate that change was possible to the various dissatisfied groups across Russia. The war was taking its toll on the rural peasants, the industrial workers of the cities and, perhaps most of all, the Russian army, which was significantly destabilised by the army reforms of the summer. Many officers felt humiliated that they were no longer allowed to address the men as 'thou', a rather demeaning term which emphasised their difference and seniority. Many disillusioned ordinary soldiers were deserting in the face of reduced discipline and the removal of the death penalty. Kerensky's summer offensive was intended to heal these rifts in the army and encourage the feelings of patriotism over the newfound freedom. It failed. By June Farmborough's diary is full of reports of insubordination and desertion. '*Thursday, 29th June.* We heard that many soldiers of the 91st regiment had refused to return to the trenches; some of them had left their regiment and were making their way eastwards towards Russia.'[53] As the offensive began to fall apart and the army was once again in retreat, Farmborough was struck by the general bad behaviour of the Russian soldiers, committing acts of violence against the local people and looting. As if this was not enough, their attitude towards the nurses also changed.

All night long there was loud, chaotic movement. Artillery and troops were constantly overtaking us. Now and then when soldiers saw us in our open transport-van, they called out and some of their remarks were far from agreeable. It was the first time in three years of war work that we had met rudeness from our own men; we felt dismayed and humiliated.[54]

Many of the women of the SWH were still working with the Serbian army even though they were now involved in the Russian offensive, so were spared some of this kind of insubordination. Some of the women came to the end of their contracts in the summer of 1917 and returned to England. Yvonne Fitzroy reluctantly returned in June because her mother had been taken ill, so she was spared the revolutions to come, but had the foresight to understand that things were very complex. 'The trouble is that instead of one clear impression of the Revolution one comes away with half a dozen contradictory ones', she noted.[55] Elsie Inglis spent the summer concerning herself with the future of her Serbs, despite her now failing health. The Russian authorities wanted to keep the Serbs there to set a good example to their own faltering armies. But Inglis saw that it could only end in disaster for her men, as the Russian armies seemed to be falling apart all around them. The committee of the SWH wanted her to leave Russia, but she refused to go until the future of the Serbs was secure. 'If there were a disaster we should none of us ever forgive ourselves if we had left. We *must* stand by. If you want us home, get *them* out', she wrote.[56]

Some members of the unit got away earlier, leaving Inglis with the Serbs. Ellie Rendel passed through Petrograd in September 1917 and found it on the verge of further crisis.

> We are stuck here for the present while our passports are being stamped etc. There are many forms to be filled up before they let us leave this country or land in England. Petrograd is not a pleasant place to be in just now. The price of everything is ridiculously high & many things are not to be had for any money. People have to wait for seven hours to get bread for one day. There is no meat & no eggs to be bought. No food may be brought into the town by private people by order of the food controller who is a Jew! People are searched in trains as they come in for fear that they are bringing white bread, eggs, milk etc.... All English who can are leaving.[57]

The optimism expressed by Birkbeck six months earlier seems to have been misplaced. Rendel perceives that Russia will be a difficult place for foreigners. Indeed it proves to be even worse than she imagines following the Bolshevik revolution, but by then she and the rest of the SWH had all gone.

In September, together with the Serbian soldiers, Inglis and the remaining SWH were relocated to a village in Romania, their last posting. By the end of the month, Inglis had collapsed and was too ill to leave her tent.[58] They returned to England at the end of October, taking the Serbs with them and just avoiding the Bolshevik red tape that would later prove so problematic for Florence Farmborough. Inglis has been credited with saving the lives of the Serbs by insisting that they were redeployed back in their own region and refusing to leave without them.[59] In her 1951 novel *Daylight in a Dream*, former SWH orderly E. M. Butler recalls the memorialisation of Inglis (loosely veiled as Dr Everet in the novel) by the Serbs for this final act of courage.

She had become the hero of one of those epic folk-songs which men chant at night, sadly, interminably, monotonously, to the sound of the *gusle*; she had become a legendary deliverer, a saviour arising in the west, a stranger from the land of the setting sun, who had snatched a whole people (this was the refrain) from the jaws of death. None of those who unexpectedly and accidentally heard a group of soldiers singing that song one moonless night will ever forget the experience.[60]

The journey home was a difficult one with appalling weather conditions on the voyage out of Archangel. They arrived in Newcastle at the end of November. Inglis, despite her weakness, insisted on dressing and wearing her decorations to watch the Serbian soldiers disembark. She died the following night. Margaret Fawcett wrote: 'Tuesday November 27 1917. The Wilton Hotel, London. We heard last night that Dr Inglis was very dangerously ill, and now this morning there is a telegram to say that she died last evening. Isn't this a sad ending to our unit?'[61] As Fawcett's words suggest, Inglis had successfully managed to keep the severity of her condition from most of the unit.

For Florence Farmborough, embedded in the Russian army, the summer of 1917 had become even more sinister. She wrote that 'the soldiers who had always been our patient, grateful men, seemed to have turned against us. Now for the first time we realised that our soldiers might become our enemies and were capable of doing us harm.'[62] These are not the soldiers whose stories Farmborough wished to tell. Her concern was to move through the retreat without being noticed, certainly not wanting to hear their voices. In August she bore witness to the endeavours of the ill-fated Women's Death Battalion, formed by Maria Bochkareva to try and plug the gaps left by all the deserting soldiers; the formation of the battalion seems to have been a direct response to the impact of the revolution on the war. But the women were not adequately trained; unprepared for the reality of the battlefield, they were unable to make any significant difference. Simultaneously, Farmborough and her fellow nurses began to encounter the Bolsheviks as both speakers and propaganda literature infiltrated the front line. By September she was beginning to despair.

> I was feeling far from well. But I knew what was wrong with me. It was that my love for my Red Cross work was slowly fading; I was becoming sick of wounds, illness, dirt and filth. That was the dreadful truth, and I had to face it. The daily fears about Russia; her ghastly predicament;

the wholesale desertion by her soldiers; the hatred and insolence of the deserters; the unfriendliness of the Roumanians [*sic*]; the absence of news from home – all had combined to unnerve me.[63]

By this point Farmborough had been involved in the front-line war for nearly three years. She had only been away from the Front once, as a result of her very serious illness, and during the Christmas period of 1916 she had learnt of the death of her father, and also the death of her 'Russia' father, without having the time to grieve for either. For her, the revolutions had brought only disaster. She decided it was time to go back to Moscow. But in the autumn of 1917, that was no easy undertaking.

This section of Farmborough's diary makes good use of the tropes of travel writing discussed in Chapter 1. It certainly proved to be an interesting journey, and although filled with difficulties, it was not without its uplifting side. Seeing her off on 3rd November 1917, her chief doctor told her that 'travelling by train nowadays must be like purgatory'.[64] He was not wrong. Facing a constant battle with Bolshevik red tape, she travelled first by horse and carriage, then by train to Moscow with many changes. Despite the fact that her papers were in order, it was not easy to find suitable accommodation. 'At last I found a place in a third class carriage near a broken window,' she remembers.[65] On this and the other trains that carried her to Moscow, Farmborough stood out in the crowds. Firstly, and most obviously, she was a lone woman. The trains were packed with troops, all men, Russian, Romanian and Polish, travelling home. Many were probably deserters. The soldiers were often drunk and argumentative and at times threatening. Although Farmborough was accompanied part of the way by one of her hospital orderlies, he also soon got drunk and slept for most of the journey. She recalls that the journey was very slow, cramped and noisy.

> Although I had entered the train soon after 4 p.m. it did not stir from the station of Botushany [Moldova] until 9.30 p.m. Soldiers were coming and going all night long; the chatter of hoarse voices never ceased. They quarrelled; they swore; they shouted with anger; they roared with laughter; there was not thought of sleep.[66]

This created a potentially threatening atmosphere for the lone woman traveller. So Farmborough had to find a way to win the sympathy of her travelling companions. She was able to do this in a number of ways, firstly by adopting a humour that she probably didn't feel. Her narrative employs some of the sense of irony and self-parody that Paul Fussell identifies.[67] She allows the soldiers to see her discomfort, inviting them to sympathise with her situation. Here the orderly came in very handy, as she uses him to endear herself to her fellow travellers.

> For to my consternation he slowly inclined towards me and in a moment I found his head resting on my shoulder. I wanted to push him away with disgust: his drunken face so near to mine sickened me. One or two of the younger soldiers began to giggle and I saw faces of the older ones turned towards me, wondering how I should treat this disagreeable situation.[68]

Farmborough turns the 'disagreeable situation' to her advantage. Accepting the laughter of the soldiers, she immediately becomes a less serious figure herself, and in so doing becomes less 'different'. She compounds this by using the situation to diminish her own alterity. The orderly's condition, she suggests to the other men, is excusable given all that he has been through at the front. And as she has been stationed with him, she too has seen it all during her three years of service. 'Three years, *sestritsa?*', the soldiers ask her. 'They listened attentively, like children: those younger ones loved to hear a story.'[69] Here Farmborough draws upon all that she has shared with the soldiers, but with the vital added assistance of her difference. As '*sestritsa*' she is one who shares their experiences, but equally she has the additional status of a feminine caregiver, a nurturer, perhaps even a mother figure, and she exploits this, too. Simultaneously they are her comrades and also the 'natives' of whom Fussell speaks.[70]

As the journey continued, the trains became more and more crowded as the soldiers occupied every inch of space. They sat and stood everywhere, they lay in the luggage rack and Farmborough even found one under her seat. They filled the inside of the trains and hung precariously on to the outside. Faced with this at Kiev, she did not know how she would even be able to get aboard the Moscow train. She recalls:

> The Moscow train was already full to overflowing. I poked my head in an open window and met the curious gaze of many eyes. 'Listen,' I said, 'I have to go to Moscow. If you will let me in, I promise not to inconvenience you in any way.' They nodded their heads but made no movement. 'It is impossible to enter by the steps; so many soldiers are

clinging to them. I must come through the window,' I told them. Again
they nodded their heads, but again no movement was made. I turned
to my porter and gesticulating towards the window said loudly: 'Lift
me up and push me through.' The miraculous happened! I sprawled
through, pushed from behind and pulled from the front. It was not a
dignified posture for a Red Cross Sister, but I was *in the train bound for
Moscow!*[71]

Again, Farmborough makes herself into a rather comic figure, a
parody of a nurse.[72] But she achieved her desired end and was able
to continue her journey. On the way back to Moscow she used her
difference, her womanliness, to interpret her situation and thus find
acceptance. Instead of being intimidated, she found a way to view
the soldiers who surrounded her as vulnerable and, in return, to offer
a small taste of domestic comfort. Once she arrived in Moscow however, she found the troubles created by the revolution were only just
beginning.

In late October 1917 the Petrograd Soviet established a
Military-Revolutionary Committee, including Lenin, recently
returned from hiding, and Trotsky. The committee had the support
of 20,000–25,000 insurgent troops and planned a military takeo-
ver of the government on 6th–7th November. They met no resistance. It was the beginning of the Bolshevik revolution that would
change the shape of Russia for decades to come.[73] Although initially
a bloodless coup in Petrograd, the revolution quickly spread, resulting in the complete capitulation of the army, a peace settlement with
Germany and civil war. Farmborough returned to the Romanian
front after a short stay in Moscow, and she quickly became involved
in the final collapse of the army. Her flight from the front line back
to Odessa was a terrifying experience. 'How can I describe what
has happened in these last tragic days? I feel as though I have been
caught up in a mighty whirlpool, battered and buffeted, and yet
... I am still myself, still able to walk, talk, eat and sleep.'[74] As the
Bolshevik revolution spread, the officers at the front completely
lost control of their men. Many were shot. The Russian soldiers
abandoned their posts, leaving the war to the Romanians. On 13th
December 1913, Farmborough's unit received orders to disband
and get to Moscow any way they could. Fearing for their lives in
the face of the now hostile army, they began a long and difficult
journey. They often found themselves hiding from drunken bands of
their own soldiers. Keeping together at all times, and travelling on

foot, they joined the throng of people heading for Russia. The group of six women kept hold of each other for safety. Then all of a sudden disaster struck for Farmborough.

> Something was pulling at the hem of my skirt; it had been caught by one of the hooks of my boot; so I released Mamasha's arm for a moment and bent down to free it. I managed it, but when I looked up Mamasha and Anna had disappeared. I tried to force my way through to them but I could cut no passage through that thick wall of uniformed men! I felt frightened, for I had lost my companions. In my fear, I began to shout 'Anna!' 'Anna!' an answering voice called 'Florence!' and to my indescribable relief I saw Dr Rakhil edging back towards me. She seized my arm; I held on to her tightly; we were *together*; jostled backwards and forwards, but *together*! I could not speak, for my relief was so great. At last, I gasped: 'the others?' 'All together; they know I am with you.' I was overwhelmed with thankfulness.[75]

Although Farmborough was able to accompany the doctor as far as Odessa, and then make her way once again to Moscow, she never saw Anna or Mamasha again. Nor was she able to find out what had happened to them. They had been together since 1915. This was clearly one of Farmborough's most distressing experiences. Nearly six decades later she described it again in an interview for a BBC television documentary, and her emotion at the fear and the loss was still vivid in her words and her trembling voice.[76]

The atmosphere of chaos continued into the next year. E. Agnes Greg had worked for the Russian Red Cross in 1915, having travelled there from Belgium via Denmark in late 1914 (probably with Violetta Thurstan). In 1916 she moved to treat Russian soldiers in Persia and Kurdistan, but had returned to the Caucasus in early 1918. She was shocked by what she saw of post-revolutionary society.

> I have got into a kind of Cul de sac. Revolution, bloodshed, murder all round, but here so far it is safe. Robberies after dark and a certain number of murders. But people – mostly refugees from the big Russian cities speak calmly of having their throats cut. It's only a question of who cuts them.... But I have already made up my mind not to nurse the Russian soldier any more. He ceased to play the game last summer and indeed his own too if he only knew it poor fool.[77]

Like Farmborough, Greg was disillusioned with the Russians. She adopts that well-used British metaphor of playing the game to articulate the failure of the soldiers. It is as though they don't understand the decisions they have made and carry responsibility for the consequences of the revolution.

Even Margaret Barber, returning to Moscow in May 1918, found it much changed. She notes that the anniversary of the revolution that year was a public holiday and saw much celebrating in the streets. But beneath the mood of public optimism, were more sinister undertones.

> The people with whom we came in contact or overheard talking in the streets or trams all seemed dissatisfied and grumbling at the hard times in which they were living. People of the upper classes, recognising me as English, often accosted me in the streets, and expressed a wish that the English would come and help bring them bring back the good old times, and the property they had lost.[78]

Like other British women in the city, Barber was under pressure to leave in 1918. However, she determined to continue with her relief work and moved instead to work with Armenian Bolsheviks in Astrakan on the north Caspian coast in August 1918.

The chaos and violence of the cities noted by Greg and Barber was the next challenge to face Florence Farmborough once she had managed to make her way back to Moscow for the final time. It was a new Moscow in a new Russia that greeted her now. It was a city caught in the clutches of winter and famine, as Rendel had noted. Even though she was reunited with the Usov family, it was also becoming dangerous for foreigners. Presumably because she had been in Russia for so long, Farmborough was given a ration permit entitling her to two potatoes or one eighth of a pound of bread per day. A black market for other foodstuffs was well established. The Proletarian State was cracking down aggressively on anyone who may have been influential in the old regime; the wealthy and the educated were particular targets. The family diet was unexpectedly supplemented when an old family servant broke the law and at great personal risk brought them food supplies from their *dacha*.[79] The Bolsheviks also required every Russian to work, often delegating the most menial tasks to the former professional classes. Farmborough notes:

> The Bolshevist regime has now imposed further arbitrary laws. All able-bodied men and women must share the responsibility of the State and participate in the work. So the Red Guards descend on the bourgeoisie, call them out into the streets and allot to each his task.

The better educated the person, the more degrading the task. Women and girls of cultured families are given brooms and made to sweep the streets, sell newspapers, clean out public lavatories; their menfolk are ordered to cart away rubble, act as porters, and run errands for their Bolshevist masters. No protest is recognised; to oppose the Red Guards is to antagonise them and, in due course, be denounced as a counter-revolutionary.[80]

The picture of post-revolutionary Russia that Farmborough paints here may seem familiar to contemporary readers, but must have been very shocking to a conservative young British woman in 1918. None of the other British women considered in this study, with the exception of Mary Britnieva, were so embedded into Russian society that they experienced this level of change from the inside. By 1918, most British women were long gone. Farmborough witnessed the destruction of the society she had known and loved for years. Everyone, herself included, went hungry. She watched the outlawing of religion. 'Sacred images had been pulled down, stamped upon and broken; age-old icons mutilated and slashed, the altars and walls daubed with coloured paint', she noted.[81] And perhaps most shocking of all for her, a new state law relating to the status of women was introduced.

It might have been adopted from some ancient code of primitive savages! This new law decrees that all young women are to be considered the property of the State, and, if unmarried at the age of eighteen, must register at a special Bureau of Surveillance with a view to acquiring a husband! They are then told to choose a man as a legal husband and their union will receive State approbation. All children born to them will automatically become the property of the State.[82]

This attack on women seems almost to be the last straw for Farmborough. Everything about her culture and background cries out against the lack of liberty in the new state. It was time to go home.

On 19th February 1918, the treaty of Brest-Litovsk was signed between Russia and Germany, ending their war. It also ended Farmborough's. As she began to look for a way home, she took stock of her own war records.

I have taken up my diary again. The word 'diary' conjures up the picture of a neat booklet in which daily events are recorded in small clear handwriting. I am afraid that I do not conform to this customary rule. My dairy consists of a conglomeration of scraps of odd paper, any paper which comes to hand. I am going to have trouble in sorting out these fragments, all hastily scribbled notes *in pencil*; on some, no dates have been noted, no pages numbered and often only the key-word can give a clue to the episode I wish to remember. I am writing this in the bedroom at my Russian 'mother's' house in Moscow. My mind is troubled, for in a day or two I shall have to say good-bye and start my homeward journey.[83]

All these literary fragments went with her when she left, waiting to be shaped into the comprehensive narrative that gives a unique picture of Russia at war.

Mary Britnieva avoids all direct discussion of the revolutions in her memoir *One Woman's Story*. The narrative jumps from a chapter recalling the Easter of 1916 when she and her brother, on leave from the British army, visited their mother's country estate, to her marriage in early 1918. The only hint comes in the closing lines of the earlier chapter, 'How wonderful it was, how infinitely beautiful was our country and how little we guessed the dark terrible tragedy that was to befall her in a year's time.'[84] But she does record an incident that gives a clear indication of the danger to foreigners in the early months of the new regime. With a Russian mother and now a Russian husband, Britnieva's citizenship was safe. But her upper-class background put her at odds with the revolutionaries.

> The political outlook was very black, and it was becoming more and more obvious that, contrary to the first expectations of all reasoning people, these new-fangled persons who called themselves Bolsheviks had come to stay for some time in spite of that complete chaos in every single branch of life which was the only visible consequence of their advent to power.
>
> I had, of course, become a Russian subject through marrying a Russian, but the British colony – among whom were my people – were left without any diplomatic representative, although the Consul remained; *his* position was not clear to anyone and least of all to himself.[85]

In the autumn of 1918, as civil war raged in the north, there was a raid on the British embassy. Britnieva's brother and his wife were both detained at gunpoint, her father forced into hiding. Although his wife was soon released, her brother was imprisoned for thirteen weeks. Her mother's house became a centre for safe correspondence and food supplies for all those imprisoned. Notes and money were sent in by way of 'Amieux Frères' sardine tins. 'The tins have a double top', Britnieva recalled, 'and a metal sardine with a pronged tail, which presumably, can be used as a fork, is clamped to the tin itself. These "sardines" can easily be detached and replaced and we used to insert notes and money between the tin itself and the detachable lid.'[86] After his release her brother was ordered to leave the country within forty-eight hours. Her father also left at this time with her youngest sister. Her mother and other sister followed shortly. Mary Britnieva's 'Britishness' had brought her very close to danger even after the revolutions. By 1919 she was the only member of her family remaining in post-war Russia, with no prospect of being reunited for a long time.

Russia's First World War ended before that of the rest of Europe, although, immersed in civil war, the turbulence continued. Elsewhere the battles raged on. But by 1918 the Serbian Front was beginning to move forward again. The final chapter looks at the end of the war in Russia and Serbia, and the legacy of the British women who had proved so important on the Eastern Front.

Notes

1 Sarah Macnaughtan, in Anne Powell (ed.), *Women in the War Zone: Hospital Service in the First World War* (Stroud: History Press, 2009), p. 155.
2 See *ibid.*, p. 296.
3 See Anthony Cross, 'Forgotten British Places in Petrograd/Leningrad', www.russinitalia.it/europa_orientalis/Cross.pdf (accessed 26th November 2012).
4 Macnaughtan, in Powell, *Women in the War Zone*, p. 155.
5 *Ibid.*, p. 156.
6 Muriel Paget, *ibid.*, p. 299.
7 Florence Farmborough, *With the Armies of the Tsar: A Nurse at the Russian Front in War and Revolution, 1914–1918* (New York: Cooper Square Press, 2000 [1974]), p.191.
8 *Ibid.*, p.191.
9 *Ibid.*
10 *Ibid.*, p. 195.
11 *Ibid.*, p. 230.
12 *Ibid.*, p. 220.
13 *Ibid.*, p. 222.
14 *Ibid.*, p. 242.
15 Margaret H. Barber, *A British Nurse in Bolshevik Russia* (London: A. C. Fifield, 1920), pp. 9–10.

16 On the position of Greece in the First World War see Dusan T. Batakovic, 'Serbia and Greece in the First World War: An Overview', *Balkan Studies* 45:1 (2004), 59–80.

17 *Ibid.*, p. 73.

18 Imperial War Museum, London (hereafter IWM), PP/MCR/156, Private papers of Mary McNeil.

19 Mitchell Library, Glasgow (hereafter ML), SWH Archive, Box B, Letter from Elsie Inglis to Muriel Craigie, 22nd July 1916.

20 Katherine Hodges, 'Memoirs', University of Leeds Russian Archive, quoted in Leah Leneman, *In the Service of Life: The Story of Elsie Inglis and the Scottish Women's Hospitals* (Edinburgh: Mercat Press, 1994), p. 77.

21 Dorothy Kennard, in Powell, *Women in the War Zone*, p. 264.

22 *Ibid.*, p. 265.

23 *Ibid.*, p. 267.

24 *Ibid.*

25 Yvonne Fitzroy, *With the Scottish Nurses in Roumania* (London: John Murray, 1918), p. 36.

26 *Ibid.*, p. 37.

27 See Chapter 2.

28 The Turkish name used by the women for the settlement at Ciocarlia, Constanta, in south-eastern Romania.

29 Margaret Fawcett, in Audrey Fawcett Cahill (ed.), *The First World War Papers of Margaret Fawcett* (Pietermaritzburg: Wyllie Desktop Publishing, 1993), p. 71.

30 IWM, 20400, Private papers of Miss F. E. Rendel, 29th October 1916.

31 Fitzroy, *With the Scottish Nurses in Roumania*, p. 65.

32 Quoted *ibid.*, pp. 66–7.

33 For more information on the personal relations in the SWH at this difficult time see Leneman, *In the Service of Life*, pp. 95–100.

34 See the Introduction.

35 Peter Gatrell, *Russia's First World War: A Social and Economic History* (London: Pearson Education, 2005), p. 3.

36 Farmborough, *With the Armies of the Tsar*, p. 233.

37 Grigori Rasputin, Russian Orthodox Christian and mystic, sometimes referred to as the 'Mad Monk'. He was murdered in December 1916.

38 Lionel Kochan and Richard Abraham, *The Making of Modern Russia* (London: Penguin Books, 1990), p. 284.

39 Leon Trotsky, *History of the Russian Revolution*, quoted *ibid.*, p. 285.

40 Fitzroy, *With the Scottish Nurses in Roumania*, p. 125.

41 Rendel, Private papers, 19th March 1917.

42 Farmborough, *With the Armies of the Tsar*, pp. 262–3.

43 Fawcett, *Papers*, p. 44.

44 Fitzroy, *With the Scottish Nurses in Roumania*, pp. 127–8.

45 Barber, *A British Nurse in Bolshevik Russia*, p. 16.

46 *Ibid.*, p. 47.

47 IWM, PP/MCR/409, Private papers of Ysabel Birkbeck, 12th March 1917.

48 *Ibid.*, 13th March 1917.

49 *Ibid.*, 14th March 1917.

50 Alexander Kerensky had established himself as an important figure in the new government by the summer of 1917. His army reforms were intended to reduce the autocratic nature of the service in line with his revolutionary ideas.

51 See Kochan and Abraham, *Modern Russia*, p. 291.

52 Farmborough, *With the Armies of the Tsar*, pp. 266–7.

53 *Ibid.*, p. 282.

54 *Ibid.*, p. 286.

55 Fitzroy, *With the Scottish Nurses in Roumania*, pp. 157–8.

56 Elsie Inglis, quoted in Eva Shaw McLaren, *Elsie Inglis: The Woman with the Torch* (New York: Macmillan, 1920), p. 73.

57 Rendel, Private papers, 5th September 1917.

58 For more information about Inglis' illness, certainly some form of cancer, see Leneman, *In the Service of Life*, pp. 137–40.

59 *Ibid.*, p. 138.

60 E. M. Butler, *Daylight in a Dream* (London: Hogarth Press, 1951), p. 35.

61 Fawcett, *Papers*, p. 56.

62 Farmborough, *With the Armies of the Tsar*, p. 289.

63 *Ibid.*, p. 316.

64 *Ibid.*, p. 330.

65 *Ibid.*, p. 335.

66 *Ibid.*, p. 336.

67 See Paul Fussell, *Abroad: British Literary Travelling between the Wars* (Oxford and New York: Oxford University Press, 1982), p. 206.

68 Farmborough, *With the Armies of the Tsar*, p. 339.

69 *Ibid.*, p. 339.

70 Fussell, *Abroad*, p. 206.

71 Farmborough, *With the Armies of the Tsar*, p. 344.

72 This self-parody is reminiscent of Mary Kingsley. See the discussion in Chapter 1.

73 For further details of the revolution see Kochan and Abraham, *Modern Russia*, ch. 15.

74 Farmborough, *With the Armies of the Tsar*, p. 360.

75 *Ibid.*, p. 364.

76 BBC documentary, directed by Christopher Cook, *Yesterday's Witness: English Nurse with the Tsar's Army*, broadcast 25th September 1974.

77 IWM, 01/17/1, Private papers of Miss E. A. Greg.

78 Barber, *A British Nurse in Bolshevik Russia*, p. 25.
79 The country house belonging to the Usov family. Their *dacha*, like all others, was now the property of the servants who had formally worked on it. But one servant had remained loyal.
80 Farmborough, *With the Armies of the Tsar*, p. 382.
81 *Ibid.*, p. 383.
82 *Ibid.*, p. 384.
83 *Ibid.*, p. 390.
84 Mary Britnieva, *One Woman's Story* (London: Arthur Barker, 1934), p. 64.
85 *Ibid.*, pp. 69–70.
86 *Ibid.*, p. 82.

7

The aftermath and the legacy

> Nevertheless I cannot get tired doing my duty towards you the same
> towards many others of you country girls having done my people so
> deeply obliged to you all personally and to British society too.... Without
> your hard work at Ostrovo and elsewhere behind our lines, the Serbs
> would not be able to execute the splendid work they did. Is a necessity
> for us all (for me personally too) to bow deeply from the old Nish to all
> stoic dear British Ladies having helped Serbs to grow strong enough for
> the to-day's task.[1]

When the war ended in Russia in February 1918, Florence
Farmborough's troubles were far from over. She was an alien in a
foreign land in extreme political turmoil; she had never been more
displaced. Throughout the war her status as an English woman had
been a novelty, but it had never had any impact on the safety of her
position. Now she was no longer welcome in Communist Russia. Like
Mary Britnieva's British family, she needed to leave the country as
soon as possible. But travel remained difficult, particularly for a young
woman alone. After cutting through much red tape, in March 1918
she managed to get a place on the last goods train to leave Moscow,
travelling on the Trans-Siberian Railway to Vladivostok. The journey
took a month and although conditions were not comfortable, it gave
Farmborough the time to reflect on all that she had experienced.

Christine Hallett has suggested that Farmborough, like other
British women in Russia, conveys in her narrative the way in which
'the geographical journey mirrors the journey of the soul. The vast
terrains of the Russian steppes and the mountainous regions and forests of Eastern Europe provide the back drop to the physical horrors of
war and renewal – the flying columns' healing work.'[2] Farmborough
herself wrote, 'I had always hoped that my war experiences would,

despite their misery and bitterness, act as a stimulus to my spiritual life, would heighten my compassion, would "strengthen my soul in all goodness".[3] No doubt her many triumphs over adversity will have gone some way to mending her broken spirit. Her difference, in terms of gender and in terms of nationality, her status as a woman traveller and medical practitioner, enabled her to use these landscapes to develop that spiritual journey. Her account of the Vladivostok train leaves the war behind, focusing instead on the travelogue. These landscapes enable her to come to terms with all she has seen and achieved.

> As we gradually make our way across this mighty land of Siberia so, gradually, do my overwrought feelings find solace. The unusual train, the proximity of compatriots, the familiar mother tongue, the discomforts we are sharing; all these help. And strange though it may sound – Siberia is for me the greatest tonic of all. I begin to love this immense spacious land, with its wealth of weird and rare lineaments. I know that its very name conjures up torment for thousands of Russians but, I tell myself, that misery comes from a harassed people, not from the land; these wide, changeless spaces can bring only comfort and peace.[4]

This surely is symbolic of what Carl Thompson terms the '*epiphanic* insight into the self' that travel writing inspires.[5] The landscape offers a reward and journey comes to an end. For Farmborough, the First World War was a vital part of the journey, but only one part. She was made a Fellow of the Royal Geographical Society upon her return to England and later lectured in English in Valencia. She made English-language broadcasts on Spanish National Radio during the Civil War and was in the Women's Voluntary Service back in Britain during the Second World War. Later she lived in Jamaica and returned to Russia in 1962. In 1974, to accompany the publication of her memoir, she was the subject of a BBC documentary, *Yesterday's Witness: English Nurse with the Tsar's Army*, during which she revisited some of her most pivotal war experiences. She died in 1978 at the age of ninety-one. Her travels *With the Armies of the Tsar* were only the beginning.

Elsie Corbett and her friend Kathleen Dillon had been driven from Serbia in 1916, having spent several months as prisoners of war. But they returned to the Balkans later that year with the SWH determined to play a part in the repatriation of Serbia when the time came. Corbett explains:

> We had last seen our Serbian army starting on the terrible trek that took them across the snowy mountains of Albania, where very many

of them perished. The survivors, nursed back to health in British and French Hospitals, had now been reorganized and shipped back to Salonica to take up positions in the Moglena Mountains about eighty miles west from that town, and just beyond Lake Ostrovo. The Serb Red Cross, very well acquainted with the Scottish Women by this time, had asked them for a hospital and an ambulance column, and we were the response to this request.[6]

Dillon wrote a rather more subjective response in her unpublished record, 'The History of the First Transport Column of the Scottish Women's Hospitals'.

> This interlude of 3½ months in the enemy's hands had naturally made us wildly keen to get back as near as possible to Serbia again for though we had been well treated, the mere fact of being a prisoner is humiliating – even if stopping with your patients instead of retreating has been more or less a matter of your own choice.[7]

Dillon's assertion implies some of the same sense of imperial superiority that inspired the women to remain in Serbia after the 1915 invasion, and illustrates a kind of innate confidence that she has a further part to play in the action in Serbia. Dillon's account, written retrospectively, covers the period from August 1916, when she returned to the Balkans as a driver with the SWH unit led by Mrs Kate Harley, who was killed in a shell burst in 1917. Dillon later took over as the leader of the transport column. Her account details the experiences of the unit throughout the rest of war, including their periods of relative stalemate in the mountains of Macedonia and the gradual move forward into Serbia. It is both a lyrical account and a historical document that gives a clear idea of the kind of life lived by the SWH women over a two-and-half-year period. She takes the time in the narrative to examine the places they stay in and pass through, drawing once again on those powerful influences of travel writing. For example, here she switches to the present tense to better articulate experience of the landscape.

> The midday sun scorches on the sandy plain, and little 'dust devils' rise up here and there, whirling themselves wildly towards the blue sky, and the filthy dust and sickening black flies are over everything; but as evening falls and the sun begins to sink in crimson, the world is a dream of beauty again, and as you hear the Russian regiment singing its evening hymn in one magnificent volume of voices you think that they must have souls after all.[8]

The combination of the present tense and the direct address has the effect of drawing the reader into the landscape. Dillon pulls at all the senses to create as full a picture as she can. We can feel the 'dust devils', the flies and the heat of the sun; we can visualise the colours, the blue sky and black flies, subdued by the crimson sunset; we can hear the harmonies of the soldiers, providing an elegy for the mountains. Although this passage does not advance Dillon's narrative, it does seem central to understanding the way in which she, and other women in the East, processes their experience. Her emphasis on the aesthetic and the sensual has a significant impact on the reader's understanding of the landscapes and environment in which the women lived and worked.

Dillon also devotes much of her account to detailing the day-to-day working life of the drivers, responsible for transporting wounded soldiers along treacherous mountain roads to base and field hospitals. It was not unusual for cars to fall over the cliffs, but they were usually travelling so slowly that the drivers were able to jump out in time. Obtaining petrol was a constant problem. And the cars themselves were constantly breaking down. The women needed to be good mechanics simply to get through each day. Dillon remembers:

> We had two cars that were not running and were very short of spare parts of almost every sort, for our committee at home had been unable to send us anything for a long time, owing to the great difficulties in the way of getting leave to buy Ford parts, and getting them shipped when bought. We had been breaking a lot of axles, hubs and transmission, but the car generally stops; whereas a broken hub or axle means that you lose all control, unless the wheel comes off and the car lets you down.... One car broke nine hubs in a year and became rather unpopular.[9]

Despite the unreliability of the cars, when the Serbian army once more advanced into its homeland in September 1918, the SWH transport unit went with it. 'If anybody had told me before the war that I would drive a car, and cause other people to drive cars, without lights, down a narrow winding road in the dark, a yard from a precipice and with broken carts, dead horses, and all sorts of unexpected obstacles on it I should have thought that they knew me very little', Dillon notes.[10]

A combined force, which Misha Glenny calls 'the Allied Army of the Orient' including representatives from all the allies, opened fire on the Germans and Bulgarians in Macedonia on 14th September 1918.[11] Glenny suggests that this was the real beginning of the end of the war. Although this army included British and French troops, the SWH women seem to have been the most visible British representatives as they made a steady progress towards Belgrade. As the Bulgarian army capitulated before them, the local people everywhere in the Balkans gave them a heroes' welcome. They were particularly interested in the British women, who remained something of an oddity. 'We got to Leskovatz at 1 o'c next day, and were given a great reception; fruit, flowers, bread and cakes were showered upon us, amidst much hugging, and I sympathized with one of our Unit who said it was "hard to be Scotch on these occasions."'[12] Long before the formal Armistice on 11th November, it was very clear that the Serbian army would be victorious.

Writing in 1964, Elsie Corbett does articulate doubts about the role the women played in this final push, but she is clear on one thing: they remained 'beacons of Britishness', with invaluable symbolic significance.

> It is difficult to know, and impossible to explain, what good we thought we were doing on that Advance. For one thing we were obeying orders; but the Serbs were a primitive and mystical people and there was a curious bond between us and their army. We were their sisters, and we were also the might of England fighting on their side. We accepted more than our share of food and shelter, but I hope perhaps, in a curious way, we were worth it.[13]

The bond to which Corbett refers was the same one that had inspired so many British women to voluntarily become prisoners of war in 1915 as they refused to leave their patients. It gave Mabel St Clair Stobart the strength to lead her soldiers over the mountains during the great retreat and gave Flora Sandes a vocation in the Serbian army. It drove Elsie Inglis to accompany her Serbian soldiers to Russia when she already knew she was suffering from cancer, and then to refuse to leave without them as revolution engulfed the state.

After her service in Russia was cut short by revolution, Ellie Rendel was determined to finish the war with the SWH. She arrived in Serbia in October 1918 as the end of the war drew closer. She noted in a letter home:

> It was a very interesting drive [to the Front]. The German and Bulgarian soldiers had passed that way in very rapid flight only a week before. The road was littered with all kinds of strange objects which they had

thrown away in their hurry. Helmets, haversacks, cartridge cases, unexploded bombs, old letters etc., etc., lay about everywhere.[14]

They made their way forward across all the debris of the battlefield. Rendel notes the very human make-up of objects left behind. Some of it is what we might expect, the natural waste of war, but the other very personal items reinforce the sense of the retreating army as individuals. The letters left behind on the road are not so very different from the letter in which Rendel records them. There is much that is familiar here, although the last time Rendel had experienced a retreat, it was as a member of the fleeing army.

In October 1918 the SWH unit that had been working at Lake Ostrovo was moved to Vranya as the Serbian army advanced. This unit was now under the leadership of the young Dr Isabel Emslie. At the end of October, Emslie's hospital was given official responsibility for the health of the British Transport drivers stationed in the region. For the first time the SWH worked directly with the RAMC, that same organisation that had rejected Elsie Inglis' offer of help back in 1914. They were very busy with this undertaking as the Spanish influenza epidemic was beginning to take hold and the British soldiers seemed to be more susceptible than the native Serbians. Despite this occupation, Emslie was very conscious of the landscape surrounding her and of the difficulties faced by the returning Serbian soldiers passing by the hospital. Many had been away for three years and had no idea what they would find of the families they had left behind. In her memoir, *With a Woman's Unit in Serbia, Salonika and Sebastopol* (1928), she recalls the sadness of watching the Serbian soldiers return.

> Many were the tragedies of these home-comings. Men would go home full of hope and find no wife, no children and no house; they had died or been hanged and the house burnt. This is not the time to tell of the Bulgar atrocities, but we heard nightmare tales from men who had come back half demented, and from the women who had remained in Serbia during the war. Many men shot themselves at once on their return and others went completely 'to the devil'.[15]

It is unclear how reliable Emslie's account is; it may be that she was prone to exaggeration. Her accounts of the 'Bolshevists', which I will discuss later, clearly demonstrate the ways in which her political views impact on her representation of events. And like so many of the British women who worked in the East, she became devoted to the Serbian and Russian people.

As they made their way to Belgrade with the armies, Corbett and Dillon followed a road that allowed them to make a long-dreamt-of excursion. Dillon recalls that 'E. C. and I were able to make an expedition from here to Vrnjatchka Banja [*sic*] where our hospital had been in 1915. We had never really expected to see it again, though we had always said that it was our goal.'[16] 'I had never been so happy in my life as I was during our eight months in Vrnjatchka Banja', adds Corbett.[17] The women found the town less changed than they feared and were able to catch up with some old friends, but found the consequence of occupation less terrible than they expected. Unlike Emslie, Dillon and Corbett found more harmony as they journeyed into Serbia. Many of the soldiers with whom they travelled did find their families unharmed. Corbett noted that 'We heard a good many atrocity stories, but none of them actually first-hand, and it was very difficult to make out how much the civilian population had suffered; but we had feared things would have been much worse. This flu' [*sic*] epidemic was the worst disaster there had been, and was nobody's fault.'[18]

It is perhaps rather curious that very few of the women in Serbia seem to record the actual Armistice in their written records. But the success of the Serbian army was clear by October 1918. Peace had been signed with Bulgaria on 29th September and the other invading armies were on the move. Whatever may have happened elsewhere, Serbia was liberated. Writing retrospectively, Isabel Emslie offers another explanation for this reticence.

> On November 11, 1918, we heard it was Armistice day, but nobody seemed happy about it, and we hardly seemed to realize what it meant. We had now got up nearly all our equipment and our hospital was clean. The whole building had been wired up by Rose West and her assistant, and our Lister engine gave us electric light – a circumstance that gave us far more delight than the Armistice.[19]

Just as the women of the retreat had prioritised the domestic three years earlier, so now in newly liberated Serbia, the same practicalities of daily life take precedence over the symbolic victory of the Armistice. Electric light and getting enough food remain more important. These sentiments echo those of Ellie Rendel, one of the few women in Serbia who does note the Armistice. She confirms this ambivalence in a letter home dated 4th December 1918.

> It is a long time since I have written – not since the armistice. We were at Uskub [Skopje] then & no one took any interest in the news except

ourselves. We had two bottles of champagne for dinner to celebrate the event and we gave our patients cigarettes and wine. Shortly afterwards we had orders to close the hospital and go to Sarajevo which we are in the act of doing now.[20]

Perhaps it was because Rendel was newly arrived in the country that she felt more in touch with the events in Western Europe? But Serbia seems to have passed into peace after nearly seven years of war, without much ceremony. In Russia, too, the Armistice was not much marked, not least because she had already left the war and was enveloped in a different one. Sister Helena Hartigan was a member of the QAIMNSR posted to Archangel on the hospital ship *Kalyan* in late 1918 as part of the British support for the Russian 'White' armies who were fighting the Bolsheviks in the ongoing civil war. She recorded:

> The arrival of a mail was a great event – we were sometimes six weeks without one – the mail came by dog sleigh across the White Sea, and the wireless gave us what news we had, including the news of the Armistice. As our troops were still fighting and saw no hope of cessation, there was little enthusiasm for the news of the Armistice reaching us.[21]

The seven years of warfare in Serbia had left a significant mark on the country. The process of rebuilding Serbia, not as an Eastern, but as a Western nation, was going to be a long and difficult one, especially as the war had seen the virtual collapse of the Ottoman Empire, and left a legacy of instability in the Balkans. Some of the women who had dedicated their lives to Serbia in the preceding years were determined to be a part of this process. And inevitably the business of winding down the hospital units and subsequent demobilisation of the staff was a slow one. The transport unit of the SWH was one of the first things to be broken down, as it was clearly no longer needed once the fighting had stopped. Kathleen Dillon and Elsie Corbett took the same route home via Hungary in March 1919 as they had done after being released from captivity in 1916. Dillon recorded:

> It was a sad moment when we saw the old cars put onto a barge and sent down the Danube again to Belgrade, and knew that our work for our friends, the Serbian soldiers, had come to an end. The cars were given by the S.W.H. to the Medical Service of the army to be distributed to different hospitals. Three of our people stayed behind us, two of them to work for the Serb Relief Fund, and one went to the S.W.H. at Vranya with their new cars.[22]

The SRF, which had been one of the first organisations to send hospital units, including that of Mabel St Clair Stobart, continued its work into the 1920s. It was picking up on a well-established tradition of relief work in the East, organised and carried out by British women. For example, the Quaker-run Friends' Mission in Constantinople had been in operation since the 1880s and, under the direction of Ann Mary Burgess, had built an entire self-help/relief industry, enabling Armenian women to manufacture and sell their 'ethnic' arts and crafts across Britain. Burgess' network was reliant on women philanthropists as well as the Friends of Armenia support organisation.[23] Russia saw the first major work of one of the most famous and long-standing relief organisations. Founded in 1921 by Eglantyne Jebb, Save the Children Fund, based in Geneva, carried out important work in the Volga regions of Russia, battling post-war famine, running soup kitchens despite the Bolshevik triumph.[24]

The Serbians, too, actively looked for further aid from the British women. Dr Curcin of the Royal Serbian Legation began the process of rebuilding the cultural and educational foundations of Serbia as early as the autumn of 1918, when he called on Jessie Laurie, treasurer of the SWH, to assist him in restocking the libraries of Belgrade. In his correspondence he makes it very clear that he feels indebted to the work of the British women. Indeed, he had gone on record as early as 1916, making his respect very clear.

> The English nurses saw that the Serbian peasant was willing to do anything she asked if she spoke nicely to him, and he would learn to open the windows of his own home just as he had learnt to use soap and to change his shirt. She realized his readiness to improve himself and his appreciation of progress. Thence came her wish that their acquaintance might ripen into something more and not remain an episode of this great War. Can anything show more clearly the greatness and goodness of a truly cultured people? And is there a greater consolation for the Serbs in the War?[25]

It is not surprising, then, that Curcin should be looking to extend the relationship. Laurie replied to his request on 18th November 1918.

> I am very interested to hear that you are starting a scheme to collect books on a larger scale for the destroyed National Library in Belgrade and other Serbian towns....
>
> It is kind of you to say you feel the victory on the battlefields has been won chiefly through the efforts of the British, and that you hope with the end of the war your relations with the Scottish Women's Hospitals

may not cease. We can hardly grasp the fact that our work is so near an
end after so many years of effort.[26]

As this letter indicates, the SWH committee did not have any clear
plans for involvement in Serbia after the war. Leah Leneman argues
that 'In fact, there was no real vision at all of what future role, if any
the Scottish Women's Hospitals might play. The Committee were
mainly reacting to advice from those in the field, a non-strategy
which had worked well enough during the war but which was far
from satisfactory in its aftermath.'[27] Many of the medical women
'in the field' wished to carry on the work they were doing with the
recovering wounded and the local populations. Isabel Emslie had
made a real success of the hospital at Vranya and was reluctant to
leave it after the Armistice. Her administrator, Mary Green, wrote to
Jessie Laurie in December 1918, 'Dr Emslie has done splendidly. She
looks such a young C. O., but is most capable and has made wonderful
strides to bring order out of colossal chaos. I think the committee may
well be proud of what has been done here by the Scottish Women's
Hospitals.'[28] But the committee, far away in Scotland, although probably proud, was unreceptive. If there was any vision at all, it was for
a long-term memorial to Elsie Inglis in Belgrade, rather than focusing
on where their help was needed most.

At about the same time that Dillon and Corbett were going
home, the SHW committee were planning to move their Girton and
Newnham unit to Belgrade to realise this vision. Dr Ruth Conway, of
that unit, wrote home, saying:

> [W]e are to be the 'Elsie Inglis Memorial Hospital' i.e. are recognized
> as senior of the 3 Balkan units though our name is not the Elsie Inglis
> Unit at the moment. Cheerioh! Just think, it is really colonizing that we
> do, only voluntary units will represent Britain in Serbia as the French
> (*loathed* as they *are*) are to take over this part of Europe alas, & the Serbs
> I believe are dying to have us.[29]

This desire to create a long-term memorial to Inglis went through
a number of manifestations. This one was rather short-lived, but
Conway's reaction to it is interesting in itself. I have argued elsewhere
that the 'colonizing' spirit of Empire had a significant impact on the
way in which these women perceived themselves and their role in the
East. Conway clearly identifies herself as a 'beacon of Britishness' and
relishes the prospect of endorsing that British presence in post-war

Serbia. This is reinforced by the implied colonial rivalry with the French authorities. It is the British women who have earned the love and trust of their Serbian allies and therefore represent desirable colonists.

In practice, the SWH occupation of Serbia from 1919 onwards did not pan out as very colonial. Isabel Emslie's unit moved to Belgrade in October 1919. She was surprised by the significant hospital provision already established in the city under the Serbs. 'All the doctors seemed to be in Belgrade and it was the ambition of every medical man and woman to work there.'[30] The large number of Russian refugees pouring into the country following the revolutions and fleeing the ongoing civil war, also struck her for the first time. A number of hospitals and orphanages were set up, some of which remained operational for a number of years. Dr Katherine MacPhail set up the Anglo-Serbian Children's Hospital in Belgrade, which remained operational until the beginning of the Second World War and then for some years afterwards until the political situation became too difficult for her to remain. Mabel Groutich, the American woman who had first led the hospital unit containing Flora Sandes in 1914, set up an orphanage on the Dalmatian coast which she ran until 1937. Olive Kelso King, an Australian, formerly of the SWH, ran canteens across the country in 1919–20, funded by her father back in Australia. Evelina Haverfield, assisted by Vera Holme, set up an orphanage that she ran until her sudden death from pneumonia in March 1920. So British medical women and relief workers remained in the Balkans for some time in various capacities. Isabel Emslie's hospital was the last SWH to shut down, in March 1920. She recorded:

> Many of them [SHW women] had given up much, perhaps too much, to stay so long in Serbia, but they had done this willingly and cheerfully. Although we had not been quite the first, we were the last of the Scottish women, and their work was now finished. The need for foreign missions was over, and there was no doubt in my mind that the Serbians should now try to cope with the medical situation.[31]

The last thing Emslie did in Serbia was travel around the country erecting marble headstones on the graves of all the Scottish women who had died during the conflict. She then joined Lady Muriel Paget's Child Welfare Scheme and headed for Russia, where civil war still raged.

The fate of the Elsie Inglis memorial in Serbia was precarious. The committee moved on from the initial idea of the Girton and Newnham unit taking up residence there, to pursue an old dream of Inglis': to set up a training school for Serbian nurses. By 1920, they were ready to wind up the SWH and set up a trust to administer the substantial fund for the Elsie Inglis Memorial Scheme. Leneman notes that this stood in the region of £45,000, £34,000 of which had been collected for the SWH.[32] The trust intended to use some of the money to work with the Women Doctors of Belgrade to set up a hospital there that would include the training school. But progress was very slow. A donation of £10,000 was to be given to Belgrade to secure this memorial, subject to the doctors receiving a free site on which to build the hospital. However, channels of communication were clouded and the Serbian women did not share the SWH vision. The SWH secretary, Helen Ferguson, wrote to the Scottish Board of Health in April 1921, outlining the problems.

> Two members of the SWH Committee went to Belgrade last spring with a view to establishing there in memory of Dr Elsie Inglis a Training School for Serbian Nurses, and to give a grant to the women doctors of Serbia for the building of a women's Hospital. They have recently returned and report that they used every effort to have the scheme for training Serbian nurses carried out, but found that it is impossible to do so on a satisfactory basis.
>
> My Committee therefore has decided to abandon the first part of their scheme, but intend to give the money raised in Scotland for the Elsie Inglis Memorial in Serbia to the building fund of the proposed Women's Hospital in Belgrade.[33]

Inglis would no doubt have still been very happy with this scheme. Prior to her involvement in the SWH she had always specialised in women's medicine and would surely have returned to it. Problems remained, however, when the Mayor of Belgrade refused to donate land to the scheme in perpetuity. The SWH would not contribute their £10,000 without guarantees that the hospital would be built, so they then had to wait while the women doctors set about raising the rest of the money they needed for the work to proceed. It was a long-winded process. As Leneman notes, 'The first stone of the women doctors' hospital was in fact laid in 1923, and they got their money, but it was not opened until October 1929.'[34] It included an 'Elsie Inglis Pavilion' devoted to gynaecology. Lady Isabel Hutton, formerly Dr Emslie, visited Belgrade in 1956 and confirmed that this hospital had been absorbed in the General Hospital, but she was confident that the treatment of women remained a focus even if the Inglis name was gone.[35] A longer-lasting memorial was established in Edinburgh in the form of the Elsie Inglis Memorial Hospital, which opened in 1925 and was part-funded by the SWH trust fund. This hospital closed in 1988. An Elsie Inglis Nursing Home on the same site closed in 2011.

One further initiative emerged from the wartime work of British women in Serbia, the Society for the Training of Serbian Women. This was publicised in the *Common Cause*, the organ of the National Union of Societies for Equal Citizenship (formerly the NUWSS). This organisation picked up on the theme of addressing the plight of Serbian women and children that remained popular in the early post-war years. Like all such causes, it was represented as worthy.

> The Society for Training Serbian Women (a registered war charity) is a society of women for women. It was founded by English and Serbian women together, for it was felt the salvation of Serbia lies in the hands of her women. At the lowest computation, half her male population has perished, so it is to her women she must look for the continuation of her life and civilization. To her the education of women is no new thing, for she has had women doctors for many years, but now all her means of education lie in the dust, her University and School buildings are wrecked and shattered, every book in her libraries and private houses has been deliberately burned, and her printing presses ruthlessly destroyed. In her present devastated condition, the Serbian Government cannot turn its attention to the intellectual needs of the country. It is for us therefore to supply those needs, for on them rest the future advancement and progress of Serbia.[36]

This article betrays both the social class and feminist background of the British women who continued to concern themselves with Serbia following the Armistice. The devastation of Serbia was indeed great, and would ultimately lead to the complete reshaping of the Balkans, yet British women, who had long campaigned for their own equality, continued to prioritise the educational rights of their Serbian sisters. The society intended to relocate Serbian girls and young women, mostly orphans, with British families, enabling them to access education and ideally, British universities. It is unclear how successful the society proved to be, but with so many other demands on people's lives and pockets in the immediate post-war years, it is difficult to imagine it being a lasting success.

While the British women who had devoted themselves to Serbia during the war were able to continue to work with the country in the aftermath, there was no such route available into Communist Russia. The bitter civil war that followed the 1917 revolutions continued until 1921, leaving much devastation and resulting in Russia closing its doors to the rest of Europe. Indeed Europe had closed its door to Russia by refusing to invite her to the Peace Conference at Versailles in 1919. British troops, which included Helena Hartigan's hospital ship, withdrew from north Russia in 1920. Even Margaret Barber finally left Russia in December 1919, although with some reluctance. Unlike the few remaining British women, Barber had long worked with the Bolsheviks in her relief operation. She notes:

> No animosity, however, was shown to me as a Britisher, I suppose because I was not a capitalist. Besides, feeling is no longer national but international. They firmly believe they are fighting only against capital, and they therefore show no hostility to actual officers and soldiers of the enemy, as they think they are only fighting them out of ignorance.[37]

The British troops fighting with the Russian 'White' armies were surprised to see Barber, not recognising her as a Red Cross nurse because she joined them so unexpectedly from the Bolsheviks. The opulent life-style of the British officers caused Barber some distress after her years of working with the most deprived members of Russian and Armenian society.

But one lone outpost of British women remained, in Sebastopol. Isabel Emslie arrived there in June 1920, intent on caring for sick children. 'While on ship I learnt much about the Bolshevist reign of terror in Russia. My own part of the world had been so engrossing that I had not fully realized the seriousness of the Russian Revolution', she wrote.[38] She began to realise it very quickly.

Emslie remained in the Crimea for six months. She and the other women in Muriel Paget's mission were the only British women. The British army that had been supporting the Russian 'White' army against Bolshevism was in the process of withdrawing when she arrived. The British support of the 'Whites', who still held the region, ensured that Emslie inherited strong anti-Bolshevik sensibilities. The rhetoric that she adopts throughout this part of her memoir makes her political views very clear. By November 1920 Sebastopol was under siege, but the siege was swiftly broken. On Armistice Day the British and all their charges were ordered to leave. Emslie records that

'Admiral Hope had sent word that he would not allow a single British person to remain in Sebastopol and that if there was the slightest protest on my part I was to be brought down in irons.'[39] It appears that even then she did not fully understand the danger of her position, perhaps as a consequence of having seen so much suffering since the outbreak of the War. But it is clear that as they sailed away from the defeated town, this part of the East was finally closing its doors upon the West. Emslie's observations of this retreat are worth quoting at length.

> During this Armistice Day of 1920, two years after the end of the Great War, the last patriots of a Great Empire were leaving their native land for ever. The bay was thick with craft of every kind and people were pouring helter-skelter on to the ships in their flight from the Bolshevists. They knew what a short distance the fiends had to come, and the evacuation was therefore most precipitous and frenzied. Most of the fugitives had had previous experience of the Bolshevists, and had already fled from town to town to escape them. It was not only the intelligentsia who fled, but the poor as well, many of whom had already tasted the horror of impending death at the hands of these monsters. I had always been told that it was the first few days after the coming of the Bolshevists that were the most to be feared; there would be wild slaughter by the mob, many of them degenerates, sadists and cocainists, and they would show no justice or mercy, and would indulge in an orgy of killing and torture.[40]

Even writing eight years after the event, Emslie doesn't curb her language as she describes the dreaded 'Bolshevists'. They are 'fiends', 'monsters', 'degenerates', 'sadists' and 'cocainists', as well as torturers and murderers. None of the accounts of the British women who encountered the 1917 revolutions at first hand are as virulent in their hatred as Emslie's. That she should ally herself with the 'White' Russians is unsurprising and inevitable, but the passion in this extract indicates a level of hatred and perhaps fear that goes beyond the political. No doubt the fear was justified to some extent, but perhaps Emslie had seen enough of war and suffering. It was time for her to go home.

The Russia that she left behind, soon to be the Union of Soviet Socialist Republics or the Soviet Union, swallowed up most records of the part played by British women in the First World War. There were to be no marble headstones here. The Communism that had so frightened Emslie in 1920 grew in strength in the inter-war years under Stalin despite the anxieties of the West. Following the Second World

War it spread to the Eastern Bloc countries of Poland, Czechoslovakia, Hungary, Romania, Bulgaria and East Germany. The other Balkan countries would eventually absorb this political orthodoxy, too. The British women would not have recognised their old haunts.

Following the collapse of the Ottoman and Austro-Hungarian Empires in 1918, the Balkan states began to realise the long-term dream of their educated classes: the formation of the Kingdom of the Serbs, Croats and Slovenes, known colloquially as Yugoslavia, and renamed the Kingdom of Yugoslavia in 1929. It was declared on 1st December 1918. For the delegates at Versailles this new kingdom 'was established without clear borders and with no clear constitutional order'.[41] None of the Great Powers at Versailles had officially recognised this new country, because its borders threatened Italian expansionist ambitions.[42] There was much discussion about how it should be constituted. Glenny goes on to argue that:

> This was no idle debate but a passionate, bitter struggle, which eventually consigned Yugoslavia to ashes. The failure of Yugoslavia's founders, in particular Serbia's monarchists, to work out an equitable solution to the national question ensured the victory of a royal dictatorship over parliamentary democracy within a decade of the country's birth, and the entire state's violent collapse when the European constitutional order buckled under the weight of Nazism in the late 1930s.[43]

It was to this fragile state that another British woman came travelling in 1936: Rebecca West. And in 1941 she published the book of her travels in the East, *Black Lamb and Grey Falcon*.[44] Victoria Glendinning has suggested that 'Rebecca West was one of nature's Balkans as a chronicler as well as in her own person.'[45] Who better qualified, then, to take up the story of the next generation in the inter-war years.

Bonnie Kime Scott suggests that '*Black Lamb* is a book of compound genre – scholarly history, art appreciation, travel guide, anti-imperial tract, mystical meditation, and autobiography.'[46] As such the book envelops many of the writings of the earlier women. West's interest in Yugoslavia was first kindled by a constitutional crisis in 1934. While recovering from an operation in a London nursing home, she heard on the radio the news that King Alexander of Yugoslavia had been assassinated in Marseille. The news shocked West, as she assumed that the international fallout of the assassination would inevitably lead to another war. Although this did not prove to be the case immediately, by the time she completed *Black Lamb* another war was raging, every bit as devastating as the first. As she ponders the assassination and its implications in her Prologue, West begins to set up the principal thesis of her book: that we can read the political turmoil of the 1930s and subsequent war back through the history of Yugoslavia and the Balkans, back to the fateful battle of Kosovo Polje, 28th June 1389, on the 'Field of Blackbirds'.

The grey falcon of West's title relates to the prophet Elijah, taking the form of the bird, to deliver his fateful message to the Serbian prince Tsar Lazar. The Tsar's choice of a heavenly kingdom over an earthly one had, according to Serbian myth, condemned the Serbian people to death for five centuries. The relative gains of the nineteenth century and the First World War, leading to the formation of the Kingdom of Yugoslavia, were all stepping-stones on the way to overcoming Lazar's earthly legacy. The black lamb of the title is altogether more sinister. West and her husband encounter black lambs at various points in their journey, but the symbolic significance does not become clear until they visit Macedonia and witness an ancient ceremony in the Sheep's Field. What they imagine will be an attractive peasant celebration turns out to be a horrific sacrificial fertility rite, betraying the primitive beliefs of the population and conforming to the long-established Balkan reputation for barbarism. When they arrive, the rock at the centre of the Sheep's Field is already bloodstained from a night of ritualistic activity, but they still witness the heart of the ceremony.

> Now the man who was holding the lamb took it to the edge of the rock and drew a knife across its throat. A jet of blood spurted out and fell red and shining on the browner blood that had been shed before. The gipsy had caught some on his fingers, and with this he made a circle on the child's forehead. Then he got down again and went round the rock another three times carrying another black lamb. 'He is doing this,' a bearded Moslem standing by explained, 'because his wife got this child by coming here and giving a lamb, and all children that are got from the rock must be brought back and marked with the sign of the rock.'[47]

West is appalled by what she sees, despite her great admiration for Balkan culture. She finds it difficult to equate the men responsible with the act itself, even though they go to great lengths to explain its symbolic importance.

> The men who told us these things were good animals, with their bright eyes and long limbs and good bones. They were also intelligent. Their

remarks on the stone were based on insufficient information, but were logical enough, and when they talked of matters less mysterious than fertility, such as their experiences in the last war, they showed considerable good sense and powers of observation.[48]

Yet their actions still serve to reduce them to animals in West's eyes, whatever their previous experiences. Empathy is impossible: 'what they were doing at the rock was abominable'.[49]

Later, when West has had time to consider the ritual of the black lamb, she uses it in a different way, working in conjunction with the grey falcon, to interpret her wider impressions of a humanity on the cusp of another war. West equates the choice of Lazar, his sacrifice of his people, to the left-wing, liberal and pacifist thinking of her own generation. West directly equates the actions of Neville Chamberlain at Munich with those of Lazar. 'The difference between Kossovo in 1389 and England in 1939 lay in the time and place and not in the events experienced, which resembled each other in details of which we of the later catastrophe think as peculiar to our nightmare.'[50] As Lazar failed to stand up to the violence of the Turk, so the appeasers of the 1930s were destined to submit to the violence of Nazism, their people to be sacrificed, as black lambs, on the multiple battlefields of another war. 'Again the grey falcon had flown from Jerusalem, and it was to be with the English as it was with the Christian Slavs; the nation was to have its throat cut as if it were a black lamb in the arms of a pagan priest.'[51] Those who sacrifice themselves and others, the martyrs, placed at the very heart of Christianity, must inevitably let down those who depend on them.

> 'Since it is wrong to be the priest and sacrifice the lamb, I will be the lamb and be sacrificed by the priest.' We thereby set up a principle that doom was honourable for innocent things, and conceded that if we spoke of kindliness and recommended peace it was fitting that afterwards the knife should be passed across our own throats. Therefore it happened again and again that when we fought well for a reasonable case and were in sight of victory, we were filled with a sense that we were acting according to the divine protocol, and turned away and sought defeat, thus betraying those who had trusted us to win them kindliness and peace.[52]

It is an indictment of Western left-wing politics, the failure of her own people to learn from the history of Yugoslavia. 'I feel that we Westerners should come here and learn to live. But perhaps we are ignorant about life in the West because we avoid thinking about death.'[53]

In the legend of the grey falcon and in the rituals of the black lamb, it is impossible to avoid thinking about death. However, this Eastern ability to engage with all of life was no more protection from the Nazis than the Western liberal policies of appeasement that allowed the expansion of Hitler's Germany to begin.

Clare Colquitt argues that:

> The image of the man asleep, of a nation asleep, is one of the central motifs of this work, for this image relates both to Yugoslavia's past – to the legend of Prince Lazar and his dream of the grey falcon – and to West's rhetorical purpose, which was not so much to 'justify' her belief in this strangely 'comprehensible' land, a land which by 1941 had already been devastated by Hitler's forces, but rather to persuade her own people through Yugoslavia's example that they must strive to stave off the sleep of death which would both induce and follow Nazi conquest.[54]

As West and her husband travel across Yugoslavia in the company of their guide, Constantine, a Serb and a Jew, a sinister shadow accompanies them. This takes the form of Constantine's German wife, Gerda. While the earlier women of the Eastern Front had literal enemies embedded in the Balkan landscape, West has a symbolic one. She is anxious about meeting Gerda, fearing the worst, but the persona she creates for the German woman is carefully crafted as a metaphoric representation of the ideological and cultural threat of the Nazi regime. Gerda acknowledges only Germanic culture as valuable and manifestly displays disturbing xenophobic tendencies towards all other races, most particularly all Yugoslavs and the Jews. This of course encompasses her poet husband, who finds himself pulled between two opposing forces as the journey continues.

Gerda insists on accompanying the party as they tour Macedonia, despite appearing to dislike her English visitors. Their fragile peace crumbles completely when they visit a German war memorial, which despite the defeat of Germany in the First World War seems to be designed as a statement of German military might, 'a fortress dominating the town'.[55] West and her husband are appalled by the inappropriate design of the memorial, both its forbidding structure and its lack of recognition of the individual dead whom it should commemorate. Gerda interprets their discomfort as an attack on her people, leading to a schism that puts additional strain on the visitors' relationship with their guide. This is further exacerbated by Gerda's attitude to the Serbian people. Colquitt suggests that 'For Gerda, the ranks of the "stupid" are legion. Slavs, gypsies, Marxists, and Jews – all are stupid and therefore worthy of contempt because their values run counter to those of "Hitler's Germany".'[56] Never is Gerda's hatred more poignant than at the French war cemetery at Bitolj. Gerda looks out over the 7,000 graves and remarks, 'Think of all these people dying for a lot of Slavs.'[57] As West's husband, Henry Maxwell Andrews, identifies in a lengthy assessment of Gerda's character, following her final departure from them, she embodies all the negative characteristics most commonly associated with the German nation. He suggests that 'nobody who is not Gerda can believe how bad Gerda is. We did not, at the beginning.... That she invited herself to be our guest and then continuously insulted us is not a proposition acceptable to the mind.'[58] Colquitt argues that:

> West and Andrews agree that Gerda is 'an international phenomenon.' However the couple conclude 'that there may be enough Gerdas concentrated in separate areas to make her in effect a nationalist phenomenon. She probably exists,' Andrews asserts, 'in sufficient numbers in Central Europe to make it an aggressive, and indeed, irresistible power.' Although West and Andrews hold that her empire 'cannot last long ... while it lasts it will be terrible.'[59]

Gerda represents the ultimate threat both to domestic harmony and to international peace. Her characterisation, almost a caricature, works on multiple levels. Constantine, torn apart by love and domestic duty and loyalty, eventually chooses the doomed road that will engulf Yugoslavia by 1942, resulting in an inevitable estrangement from his British friends, with whom he seems to have far more in common. The journey through Yugoslavia, which so inspires West in cultural and humanistic terms, takes place under the shadow of a pointless sacrifice and the menace of an expanding 'Gerda's empire.

Like British women in the First World War, West was shaped by the society and culture that produced her, and this significantly influences the way she chooses to write about the East. She was passionate about Yugoslavia and its people, but her passion is laced with fear throughout. She notes that:

> So I resolved to put on paper what a typical Englishwoman felt and thought in the late nineteen-thirties when, already convinced of the inevitability of a second Anglo-German war, she had been able to follow the dark waters of that event back to its source. That committed me to what was in effect some years of retreat spent among fundamentals.

I was obliged to write a long and complicated history, and to swell that with an account of myself and the people who went with me on my travels, since it was my aim to show the past side by side with the present it created. And while I grappled with the mass of my material during several years, it imposed certain ideas on me.[60]

West's great work certainly achieves all these things, and her own personality and opinions are stamped throughout the text. Like her predecessors, she brings her own identity into the alien landscapes and gives voice to the indigenous people along the way. Whether West's is a 'typical' voice is another matter. Janet Montefiore argues that 'Both Rebecca West and her husband Henry Andrews are, indeed, not so much typical products of English culture as its ideal representatives.'[61] But perhaps she means ideal representatives from a twenty-first-century perspective. While West openly acknowledges that she is a product of empire, she is fundamentally critical of what that might mean, noting that empires have a dark side which should not be ignored. She is suspicious of all the empires in history, Ottoman and Austrian for example, that have blighted the Balkans. She is critical of the British Empire: she needs to be to emphasise her warning against the growing German Empire. At the same time, West's trip was funded by the British Council and was formally an engagement of cultural exchange, so she needed to keep hold of her British identity throughout. In some ways she is as much a representative of her country as the earlier women. Montefiore goes on to suggest that 'she is in the last analysis an English patriot. She thus writes both as a woman of her own time and place, and as a kind of everyman or everywoman.'[62] She speaks with the same resonance as the British women of the First World War; she predicts the instabilities of the late twentieth century and she continues to speak in a voice that is authentic and convincing in the modern world.

This authenticity is in part due to the multidimensional nature of the text. This is clearly travel writing, but like Mary Kingsley, West is not looking to colonise. In accordance with tradition, her landscapes are often aestheticised. The people, too, are vividly described, but West uses her travelogue to contribute to her overall political message. 'I find it most natural that the Macedonian peasants should embroider their dresses, that they should dance and sing. For, of course art gives us hope that history may change its spots and man become honourable. What is art? It is not decoration. It is the re-living of experience.'[63] Rather than colonise, West draws out the aesthetics of the people and landscapes to enable her to argue for the regeneration of humanity. The indigenous population of Macedonia and the rest of the Balkans use their culture to celebrate life, to present optimism about a future that can incorporate the past without violence. The colourful costumes are a cultural constant; they act as beacons to guide civilisation through the current catastrophe of Nazi oppression. Thus the travelogue becomes political in an alternative sense.

Black Lamb and Grey Falcon is also life writing. It represents a collated experience of three trips to Yugoslavia that West made in 1936, in 1937 with her husband and in 1938 as Europe accelerated towards another war. The narrative of the book suggests that it is a record of single journey, the 1937 trip, and is based to some degree on the journal West kept during this period. Montefiore points out that West's book corresponds well with Paul Fussell's notion of the travel book as a 'sub-species of memoir'.[64] But she also argues that *Black Lamb* may be read as a work of fiction as well as a political tract that has a feminist agenda underlying the wider issues of the 1930s, dominated by the Nazi pursuit of empire. For all these reasons, Victoria Glendinning suggests, 'It turned out to be the central book of her life: a two volume, 500,000-word work not only of history, archaeology, politics, conversation, folklore, prophecy and the evocation of landscape, but the work in which Rebecca West formulated her views on religion, ethics, art, myth and gender.'[65] The multi-layering of experience combined to present one journey; the lengthy political dialogues between West and her husband are designed to illustrate debate rather than recreate the authentic moment together with the many anecdotal stories of individuals that are interlaced through the text. All these things help to build a complex and sophisticated book that operates on multiple levels. It is these stories that convince Janet Montefiore of West's feminism despite earlier criticisms. Contemporary commentator Mary Ellmann accused West of prioritising the polarisation of men and women and of deferring to her husband all too frequently.[66] But Montefiore suggests that West's feminism is subtler and more powerful as a consequence. 'For *Black Lamb and Grey Falcon* is, among other things, a strongly feminist text. Rebecca West's feminism is everywhere apparent in her interest in the unwritten lives of the female relatives of great men.'[67] She is also preoccupied throughout the book with the lives of ordinary women, both educated and intellectual, but also those of the peasant women of all ethnic backgrounds that she encounters on her travels. In this way her record and her feminism echo those of the earlier women, whose writings so often digress to examine the lives of their Eastern sisters.

But West does more with her language, illustrating her literary background and Modernist influences. She borrows other literary techniques to inject her book with startling imagery, much of which brings to mind the innovations of Imagism twenty years earlier. 'He was lovelier because he was smiling and the smile of an Albanian is cool and refreshing as a bite out of a watermelon.'[68] This curious juxtaposition conveys both the appearance and the idea of the man, perhaps more effectively than a more conventional image.

David G. Farley argues that *Black Lamb and Grey Falcon* is a distinctly Modernist work. He suggests that:

> [B]y employing strategies that she had utilized throughout her career, both in her novels and in her essays, West manages to create a work unique in its ability to harness tradition and experimentation for the purpose of recording the history and culture of a country about which many in England had little knowledge, while at the same time making manifest the crisis facing the West of the prospect of another war.[69]

It is an epic journey that does resemble some other Modernist works in its structure, and West does deploy many narrative strategies, including imagery, extensive dialogue and multiple voices, mythology and allegory such as that developed through Gerda, all of which locate the work in a Modernist tradition.

Colquitt argues that:

> West sees her own mission as a grey falcon as both elegiac and hortatory; for as she celebrates the Slavs who in World War II 'never capitulated' although they were 'destroyed' (1147), West seeks to rally her own people to follow the heroic example of the Yugoslavian army – to resist the combined forces of 'Gerda's Empire' even if resistance means death.[70]

And the British people respond. West sees an equivalent heroism in the way her own people react to the horrors of the blitz.

> Now, though their knees knocked together, though their eyes were glassy with horror, they joked from sunset, when the sirens unfurled their long flag of sound, till dawn, when the light showed them the annihilation of dear and familiar things. But they were not merely stoical. They worked, they fought like soldiers, but without the least intoxication that comes of joy in killing, for they could only defend themselves, they could not in any way attack their assailants. In this sobriety, men and women went

out and dug among the ruins for the injured while bombs were still falling, and they turned on fire, which it is our nature to flee, and fought it
at close range, night after night, week after week, month after month.
There have been heroes on the plains of Troy, on the Elizabethan seas,
on the fields of Flanders, in the Albanian mountains that go down to the
sea, but none of them was more heroic than these.[71]

Some of those helping to sort through the rubble of bombed England
had a history of a previous war in the Balkans or Russia: women of
the Eastern Front on the home front of another war.

It is this heroism, patriotism, and acute sense of national identity
that really connects the Serbs to the many British women who passed
through during the First World War and after. For many of those facing difficult situations, flight, captivity, the trauma of warfare, it was
their 'Britishness' that helped them through, whether as representatives of absent allies or women of Empire. Even Rebecca West, whose
political thinking was much more radical than that of most of the
wartime women, represented Britain and brought with her a profound
sense of who she was. This solid sense of national identity found a parallel among the Serbian people. Despite the upheavals of 500 years of
conquest, the myths and the legends of medieval Serbia, of the Dusane
dynasty and of the tragic Tsar Lazar had grown powerful enough to
fuel the nationalist movements of the nineteenth century and carried a
strong resonance throughout the twentieth. West notes that Yugoslavs
recited 'The Downfall of the Serbian Empire' as they awaited the arrival
of the Nazis in 1941, invoking the tragedy of Lazar's decision to offer
them hope beyond the present.[72] And the ghost of Lazar remained present in the troubled years of the later century.

Tim Judah notes the strategic usage, not just of the Lazar legend,
but also of his body, in the 1980s as Serbian nationalism seemed
to take a much more sinister turn in the eyes of the world. Judah
notes the distinct similarity between a speech delivered by Slobodan
Milosevic at Kosovo Polje in 1987, and one historically attributed to
Lazar in 1389, on the eve of his own tragic battle. He argues that:

> In all of European history it is impossible to find any comparison with
> the effect of Kosovo on the Serbian national psyche. The battle changed
> the course of Serbian history, but its immediate strategic impact was far
> less than many subsequently came to believe. Its real lasting legacy lay
> in the myths and legends which came to be woven around it, enabling it
> to shape the nation's historical and national consciousness.[73]

Lazar's preserved body, which had been used to symbolise Serbian national identity countless times in the intervening centuries, was used again in the approach to the six hundredth anniversary of his choice. On the back of Milosevic's words in 1987 he began a new journey around the country from monastery to monastery, drawing enormous crowds to pray before him for the success of Serbia. Judah suggests that 'These were the beginnings of the years of euphoria which were to be followed so quickly by the war, the short-lived new Serbian Empire and its disastrous demise.'[74]

The Balkan wars of the 1990s destroyed the second Yugoslavia and tainted the reputation of Serbia in the eyes of the world following the harrowing stories of genocide and the mass upheavals of whole populations. It is difficult now to remember that Serbia was once so loved and respected by her foreign visitors. Despite valiant efforts, she was a great loser of the early part of the century. Judah reminds us that 'During the Balkan Wars Serbia lost some 30,000 men. The First World War cost it 275,000 men and wartime diseases another 800,000 civilians. These losses amounted to a quarter of the population and two-thirds of its male population between the ages of fifteen and fifty-five.'[75] It is a tragedy rarely thought of in the twenty-first century, shadowed as it has been by later events, just as the Russian experience has spent so many decades locked behind the doors of Communism that it is often overlooked in First World War histories. It is here that the British women of Serbia and Russia can play another important role a century after they bestowed medical care and humanitarian aid on the Eastern Front. They can remind us all of what has been forgotten, and give voice to those who have been silent for too long.

> As I now read over the apparently incoherent jumble of words, everything comes back to me vividly, so that not only do I see, but I also smell and hear in retrospect, and long to be able to transmit something of it all to others.[76]

Notes

1 Letter to Ishobel Ross (SWH) from Captain Mikail L. Dimitrivich of the Serbian army, dated 10th October 1918 (before the official Armistice), in Ishobel Ross, *Little Grey Partridge: First World War Diary of Ishobel Ross Who Served with the Scottish Women's Hospitals Unit in Serbia*, ed. Jess Dixon (Aberdeen: Aberdeen University Press, 1988), pp. 92–3.

2 Christine E. Hallett, 'Russian Romances: Emotionalism and Spirituality in the Writings of "Eastern Front" Nurses, 1914–1918', *Nursing History Review* 17:1 (2009), p. 113.

3 Florence Farmborough, *With the Armies of the Tsar: A Nurse at the Russian Front in War and Revolution, 1914–1918* (New York: Cooper Square Press, 2000 [1974]), p. 330.

4 *Ibid.*, p. 396.

5 Carl Thompson, *Travel Writing* (London and New York: Routledge, 2011), p. 115.

6 Elsie Corbett, *Red Cross in Serbia 1915–1919* (Banbury: Cheney & Sons, 1964), p. 65.

7 Mitchell Library, Glasgow (hereafter ML), SWH Archive, Tin 11, Kathleen N. Dillon, 'The History of the First Transport Column of the Scottish Women's Hospitals', undated, pp. 1–2.

8 *Ibid.*, pp. 25–6.

9 *Ibid.*, p. 91.

10 *Ibid.*, p. 110.

11 Misha Glenny, *The Balkans 1804–1999: Nationalism, War and the Great Powers* (London: Granta, 2000), p. 353.

12 Dillon, 'History of the First Transport Column', p. 135.

13 Corbett, *Red Cross in Serbia*, p. 139.

14 Imperial War Museum, London (hereafter IWM), 20400, Private papers of Miss F. E. Rendel, 18th October 1918.

15 Isabel Emslie Hutton, *With a Woman's Unit in Serbia, Salonika and Sebastopol* (London: Williams and Norgate, 1928), p. 162.

16 Dillon, 'History of the First Transport Column', p. 146.

17 Corbett, *Red Cross in Serbia*, p. 168.

18 *Ibid.*, p. 169.

19 Hutton, *With a Woman's Unit*, p. 164.

20 Rendel, Private papers, 4th December 1918.

21 Helena Hartigan, 'To North Russia on the Hospital Ship "Kaylan", 1918–1919', www.scarletfinders.co.uk/159.html, p. 3 (accessed 9th November 2015).

22 Dillon, 'History of the First Transport Column', p. 157.

23 For more information on this see Michelle Tusan, 'The Business of Relief Work: A Victorian Quaker in Constantinople and Her Circle', *Victorian Studies* 51:4 (Summer 2009), 633–61.

24 See Jill Liddington, 'Britain in the Balkans', in Ingrid Sharpe and Matthew Stibbe (eds), *Aftermaths of War: Women's Movements and Female Activists, 1918–1923* (Leiden: Brill, 2011), p. 407.

25 Dr M. Curcin, *British Women in Serbia and the War* (London: n.p.), p. 12; repr. from *The Englishwoman*, September 1916.

26 ML, SWH Archive, Tin 13, Letter from Mrs Jessie Laurie to Dr M. Curcin, 18th November 1918.

27 Leah Leneman, *In the Service of Life* (Edinburgh: Mercat Press, 1994), p. 190.
28 ML, SWH Archive, Tin 8, Letter from Mrs Mary Green, administrator SHW, Vranja, to Mrs Jessie Laurie, 27th December 1918.
29 Ruth Verney, Letter to 'Everyone', 27th December 1918, Liddle Collection, University of Leeds Library. Quoted in Leneman, *In the Service of Life*, p. 191.
30 Hutton, *With a Woman's Unit*, p. 217.
31 *Ibid.*, p. 228.
32 Leneman, *In the Service of Life*, p. 205.
33 ML, SWH Archive, Tin 48, Letter from Helen Ferguson to the Secretary of the Scottish Board of Health, 4th April 1921.
34 Leneman, *In the Service of Life*, p. 207.
35 *Ibid.*, p. 215.
36 *The Common Cause* 11:530 (6th June 1919), p. 90 (author unknown).
37 Margaret H. Barber, *A British Nurse in Bolshevik Russia* (London: A. C. Fifield, 1920), p. 53.
38 Hutton, *With a Woman's Unit*, p. 234.
39 *Ibid.*, p. 266.
40 *Ibid.*
41 Glenny, *The Balkans*, p. 366.
42 For a full discussion of the role of Italy in the defining of Yugoslavia in 1919 see *ibid.*, pp. 366–77.
43 *Ibid.*, p. 366.
44 Rebecca West, *Black Lamb and Grey Falcon: A Journey through Yugoslavia* (Edinburgh: Canongate, 2006 [1942]).
45 Victoria Glendinning, *Rebecca West* (London: Macmillan, 1988), p. 168. As 'one of nature's Balkans', West was an outsider, difficult to categorise as a writer.
46 Bonnie Kime Scott, *Refiguring Modernism: Postmodern Feminist Readings of Woolf, West, and Barnes* (Bloomingdale and Indianapolis: Indiana University Press, 1995), pp. 149–50.
47 West, *Black Lamb*, p. 824.
48 *Ibid.*, p. 825.
49 *Ibid.*
50 *Ibid.*, pp. 1118–19.
51 *Ibid.*, p. 1121.
52 *Ibid.*, pp. 914–15.
53 *Ibid.*, p. 917.
54 Clare Colquitt, 'A Call to Arms: Rebecca West's Assault on the Limits of "Gerda's Empire" in *Black Lamb and Grey Falcon*', *South Atlantic Review* 51:2 (May 1986), p. 78.
55 West, *Black Lamb*, p. 763.
56 Colquitt, 'A Call to Arms', p. 80.

57 West, *Black Lamb*, p. 766.

58 *Ibid.*, p. 800. Andrews' assessment of Gerda's character is lengthy, pp. 799–806.

59 Colquitt, 'A Call to Arms', p. 85.

60 West, *Black Lamb*, p. 1089.

61 Janet Montefiore, *Men and Women Writers of the 1930s: The Dangerous Flood of History* (London and New York: Routledge, 1996), p. 179.

62 *Ibid.*, p. 180.

63 West, *Black Lamb*, p. 1127.

64 Montefiore, *Men and Women Writers*, p. 182.

65 Glendinning, *Rebecca West*, p. 154.

66 Cited *ibid.*, p. 167.

67 Montefiore, *Men and Women Writers*, p. 187.

68 West, *Black Lamb*, p. 915. For a more detailed discussion of Imagism in West's fiction see Angela K. Smith, *The Second Battlefield: Women, Modernism and the First World War* (Manchester: Manchester University Press, 2000), ch. 6.

69 David G. Farley, *Modernist Travel Writing: Intellectuals Abroad* (Columbia: University of Missouri Press, 2010), p. 47.

70 Colquitt, 'A Call to Arms', p. 86.

71 West, *Black Lamb*, p. 1130.

72 *Ibid.*, p. 1145.

73 Tim Judah, *The Serbs: History, Myth and the Destruction of Yugoslavia* (New Haven and London: Yale University Press, 1997), p. 30.

74 *Ibid.*, p. 39.

75 *Ibid.*, p. 101.

76 Hutton, *With a Woman's Unit*, p. 14.

Select bibliography

Memoirs and letters at the Department of Documents, Imperial War Museum

Miss M. Barclay (attributed), Anonymous report written in Scutari, 7th December 1915, 4320

Miss E. Bertram, 'Experiences in Serbia', First World War Papers

Ysabel Birkbeck, Private papers, PP/MCR/409

Miss E. A. Greg, Private papers, Letter dated July 14th 1915, 01/17/1

Mary McNeil, Private papers, PP/MCR/156

Lady L. Paget, *With Our Serbian Allies: Second Report*, Printed for private circulation, 1916, 34602, 9

Sir Ralph Paget, 'Report on the Retreat of Part of the British Hospital Units from Serbia, October – December 1915', 8761

Miss F. E. Rendel, Private papers, 20400

Miss K. E. Royds, of the Scottish Women's Hospitals, letter to her mother, 30th November 1915, 12811

Miss Flora Scott, Matron of the Sixth Reserve Military Hospital, Skoplje, 6977

Mabel St Clair Stobart, Unpublished diary, EN1/3/COR/015

Memoirs and letters at the Mitchell Library, Glasgow

Dr Adeline Campbell

Kathleen N. Dillon, 'The History of the First Transport Column of the Scottish Women's Hospitals', typescript

Helen Ferguson

Mrs Mary Green

Dr Elsie Inglis

J. H. Kemp

Mrs Jessie Laurie

Dr Katherine MacPhail

Gertrude Pares

Dr Eleanor Soltau

Primary sources

Abraham, James Johnston, extracts from his autobiography, *A Surgeon's Journey*, available at www.vlib.us/medical/serbia.htm (accessed 9th November 2015)

Aldridge, Olive, *The Retreat from Serbia through Montenegro and Albania* (London: Minerva, 1916)

Barber, Margaret H., *A British Nurse in Bolshevik Russia* (London: A. C. Fifield, 1920)

Barbusse, Henri, *Under Fire* (London: Everyman, 1988 [1917])

Berry, James, *The Story of a Red Cross Unit in Serbia* (London: J. & A. Churchill, 1916.

Borden, Mary, *The Forbidden Zone* (London: William Heinemann, 1929; repr. London: Hesperus Press, 2008)

Britnieva, Mary, *One Woman's Story* (London: Arthur Barker, 1934)

Butler, E. M., *Daylight in a Dream* (London: Hogarth Press, 1951)

Corbett, Elsie, *Red Cross in Serbia 1915–1919* (Banbury: Cheney & Sons, 1964)

Curcin, Dr M., *British Women in Serbia and the War* (London: n.p.), reprinted from *The Englishwoman*, September 1916

Davies, Ellen Chivers, *A Farmer in Serbia* (London: Methuen & Co., 1916)

Dearmer, Mabel, *Letter from a Field Hospital* (London: Macmillan and Co., 1916)

Farmborough, Florence, *Russian Album 1908–1918* (Salisbury: Michael Russell, 1979)

Farmborough, Florence, *With the Armies of the Tsar: A Nurse at the Russian Front in War and Revolution, 1914–1918* (New York: Cooper Square Press, 2000 [1974])

Fawcett Cahill, Audrey (ed.), *The First World War Papers of Margaret Fawcett* (Pietermaritzburg: Wyllie Desktop Publishing, 1993)

Fitzroy, Yvonne, *With the Scottish Nurses in Roumania* (London: John Murray, 1918)

Hartigan, Helena, 'To North Russia on the Hospital Ship "Kaylan", 1918–1919', www.scarletfinders.co.uk/159.html (accessed 9th November 2015)

Hutton, Isabel Emslie, *With a Woman's Unit in Serbia, Salonika and Sebastopol* (London: Williams and Northgate, 1928)

Inglis, Elsie, 'The Tragedy of Serbia', *The Englishwoman* 30 (1916)

Kingsley, Mary H., *Travels in West Africa: Congo Français, Corisco and Cameroons* (London: Macmillan, 1897)

Matthews, Caroline Twigge, *Experiences of a Woman Doctor in Serbia* (London: Mills & Boon, 1916)

Pares, Gertrude, 'With the Serbian Retreat', *The Englishwoman* 29 (1916)

Powell, Anne (ed.), *Women in the War Zone: Hospital Service in the First World War* (Stroud: History Press, 2009)

Remarque, Erich Maria, *All Quiet on the Western Front* (London: Picador, 1991 [1929])

Ross, Ishobel, *Little Grey Partridge: First World War Diary of Ishobel Ross Who Served with the Scottish Women's Hospitals Unit in Serbia*, ed. Jess Dixon (Aberdeen: Aberdeen University Press, 1988)

Sandes, Flora, *An English Woman-Sergeant in the Serbian Army* (London, New York and Toronto: Hodder and Stoughton, 1916.

Sandes, Flora, *The Autobiography of a Woman Soldier: A Brief Record of Adventures with the Serbian Army 1916–1919* (London: H. F. & G. Witherby, 1927)

Stobart, Mabel St Clair, *War and Women: Form Experience in the Balkans and Elsewhere* (London: G. Bell & Sons, 1913)

Stobart, Mabel St Clair, *The Flaming word in Serbia and Elsewhere* (London: Hodder and Stoughton, 1917)

Stobart, Mabel St Clair, *Miracles and Adventures* (London: Rider & Co, 1935)

Thurstan, Violetta, *Field Hospital and Flying Column: Being the Journal of an English Nursing Sister in Belgium and Russia* (New York: G. P. Putnam's Sons, 1915)

The Times, 28th January 1915, issue 40763, p. 11, col. B

The Times, 13th April 1915, issue 40827, p. 10, col. D

West, Rebecca, *Black Lamb and Grey Falcon: A Journey through Yugoslavia* (Edinburgh: Canongate, 2006 [1942])

Secondary sources

Anderson, Linda, *Autobiography* (London: Routledge, 2001)

Batakovic, Dusan T., 'Serbia and Greece in the First World War: An Overview', *Balkan Studies* 45:1 (2004), 59–80

BBC, *Yesterday's Witness: English Nurse with the Tsar's Army*, directed by Christopher Cook, broadcast 25th September 1974

Benstock, Shari (ed.), *The Private Self: Theory and Practice of Women's Autobiographical Writings* (Chapel Hill and London: University of North Carolina Press, 1988)

Bhabha, H. K. (ed.), *Nation and Narration* (London: Routledge, 1990)

Blanton, Casey, *Travel Writing: The Self and the World* (London and New York: Routledge, 2002)

Bourke, Joanna, *Dismembering the Male: Men's Bodies, Britain and the Great War* (London: Reaktion Books, 1996)

British Nursing Journal, 9th October 1915

Broughton, Trev Lynn and Linda Anderson (eds), *Women's Lives/Women's Times: New Essays in Auto/Biography* (Albany: State University of New York Press, 1997)

Bunkers, Suzanne L. and Cynthia A. Huff (eds), *Inscribing the Daily: Critical Essays on Women's Diaries* (Amherst: University of Massachusetts Press, 1996)

Bush, Julia, *Edwardian Ladies and Imperial Power* (London: University of Leicester Press, 2000)

Buzard, James, *The Beaten Track: European Tourism, Literature, and the Ways to Culture 1800–1918* (Oxford: Clarendon Press, 1993)

Colquitt, Clare, 'A Call to Arms: Rebecca West's Assault on the Limits of "Gerda's Empire" in *Black Lamb and Grey Falcon*', *South Atlantic Review* 51:2 (May 1986), 77–91

Cooper, Helen Margaret, Adrienne Munich and Susan Merrill Squier (eds), *Arms and the Woman: War, Gender and Literary Representation* (Chapel Hill and London: University of North Carolina Press, 1989)

Cross, Anthony, 'Forgotten British Places in Petrograd/Leningrad', www.russinitalia.it/europa_orientalis/Cross.pdf (accessed 26th November 2012)

Dadrian, Vahakn N., 'The Armenian Question and the Wartime Fate of the Armenians as Documented by the Officials of the Ottoman Empire's World War I Allies: Germany and Austria Hungary', *International Journal of Middle East Studies* 34:1 (2002), 59–85

Das, Santanu, *Touch and Intimacy in First World War Literature* (Cambridge: Cambridge University Press, 2005)

Farley, David G., *Modernist Travel Writing: Intellectuals Abroad* (Columbia: University of Missouri Press, 2010)

Freud, Sigmund, 'Our Attitude towards Death', in *Civilisation, Society and Religion* (London: Penguin Books, 1985)

Fussell, Paul, *The Great War and Modern Memory* (Oxford: Oxford University Press, 1977)

Fussell, Paul, *Abroad: British Literary Travelling between the Wars* (Oxford and New York: Oxford University Press, 1982)

Gatrell, Peter, *Russia's First World War: A Social and Economic History* (London: Pearson Education, 2005)

Gilbert, Sandra M., 'Soldier's Heart: Literary Men, Literary Women, and the Great War', *Signs* 8:3, Women and Violence (Spring 1983), 422–50

Glendinning, Victoria, *Rebecca West* (London: Macmillan, 1988)

Glenny, Misha, *The Balkans 1804–1999: Nationalism, War and the Great Powers* (London: Granta, 2000)

Goldsworthy, Vesna, 'Black Lamb and Grey Falcon: Rebecca West's Journey through the Balkans', *Women: A Cultural Review* 8:1 (1997), 1–11

Grayzel, Susan R., '"The Outward and Visible Sign of Her Patriotism": Women: Uniforms, and National Service during the First World War', *Twentieth Century British History* 8:2 (1997), 145–64

Grayzel, Susan R., *Women's Identities at War: Gender, Motherhood and Politics in Britain and France during the First World War* (Chapel Hill and London: University of North Carolina Press, 1999)

Grba, Milan, 'British Medical Units and Serbia in the First World War, *South Slav Journal* 16:3/4 (1995), 27–37

Gullace, Nicoletta, *The Blood of Our Sons: Men, Women and the Regeneration of British Citizenship during the Great War* (Basingstoke: Palgrave Macmillan, 2002)

Hall, Richard C., *The Balkan Wars 1912–13: Prelude to the First World War* (London and New York: Routledge, 2000)

Hallett, Christine E., *Containing Trauma: Nursing Work in the First World War* (Manchester and New York: Manchester University Press, 2009)

Hallett, Christine E., 'Russian Romances: Emotionalism and Spirituality in the Writings of "Eastern Front" Nurses, 1914–1918', *Nursing History Review* 17:1 (2009), 101–28

Hallett, Christine E., *Veiled Warriors: Allied Nurses of the First World War* (Oxford: Oxford University Press, 2014)

Heilmann, Ann (ed.), *Feminist Forerunners: New Womanism and Feminism in the Early Twentieth Century* (London: Pandora, 2003)

Hogan, Rebecca, 'Engendered Autobiographies: The Diary as a Feminine Form', *Prose Studies* 14:2 (September 1991), 95–107

Howell, Jessica, Anne Marie Rafferty and Anna Snaith, '(Author)ity Abroad: The Life Writing of Colonial Nurses', *International Journal of Nursing Studies* 48:9 (September 2011), 1155–62

Jenkins, Ruth Y., 'The Gaze of the Victorian Woman Traveller: Spectacles and Phenomena', in Kristi Siegel (ed.), *Gender, Genre and Identity in Women's Travel Writing* (Oxford and New York: Peter Lang, 2004), pp. 15–30

Jones, Heather, *Violence against Prisoners of War in the First World War* (Cambridge: Cambridge University Press, 2011)

Judah, Tim, *The Serbs: History, Myth and the Destruction of Yugoslavia* (New Haven and London: Yale University Press, 1997)

Keegan, John, *The First World War* (London: Hutchinson, 1998)

Kochan, Lionel and Richard Abraham (eds), *The Making of Modern Russia* (London: Penguin Books, 1990)

Kramer, Alan R., 'Prisoners in the First World War', in Sibylle Scheipers (ed.), *Prisoners in War* (Oxford: Oxford University Press, 2010), pp. 75–90

Krippner, Monica, *The Quality of Mercy: Women at War, Serbia 1915–18* (London and Newton Abbot: David & Charles, 1980)

Larabee, Mark D., 'Baedekers as Casualty', *Journal of the History of Ideas* 71:3 (July 2010), 3–13

Lee, Janet, 'Sisterhood at the Front: Friendship, Comradeship, and the Feminine Appropriation of Military Heroism among World War I First Aid Nursing Yeomanry (FANY)', *Women's Studies International Forum* 31:1 (January–February 2008), 16–29

Leneman, Leah, *In the Service of Life: The Story of Elsie Inglis and the Scottish Women's Hospitals* (Edinburgh: Mercat Press, 1994)

Leneman, Leah, *Elsie Inglis* (Edinburgh: NMS Publishing, 1998)

Lieven, D. C. B., *Russia and the Origins of the First World War* (London: Macmillan, 1983)

McLaren, Eva Shaw, *The History of the Scottish Women's Hospitals* (London: Hodder and Stoughton, 1919)

McLaren, Eva Shaw, *Elsie Inglis: The Woman with the Torch* (New York: Macmillan, 1920)

McMeekin, Sean, *The Russian Origins of the First World War* (Cambridge, MA and London: The Belknap Press of Harvard University Press, 2011)

Marshall, Catherine, 'Women and War', in Margaret Kamester and Jo Vellacott (eds), *Militarism versus Feminism: Writings on Women and War by Catherine Marshall, C. K. Ogden and Mary Sargant Florence* (London: Virago, 1987)

Mazower, Mark, *The Balkans: From the End of Byzantium to the Present Day* (London: Phoenix Press, 2001)

Miller, Louise, *A Fine Brother: The Life of Captain Flora Sandes* (London: Alma Books, 2012)

Mills, Sarah, *Gender and Colonial Space* (Manchester and New York: Manchester University Press, 2005)

Montefiore, Janet, *Men and Women Writers of the 1930s: The Dangerous Flood of History* (London and New York: Routledge, 1996)

Morris, Mary (ed.), with Larry O'Connor, *The Virago Book of Women Travellers* (London: Virago, 1996)

Neiberg, Michael S. (ed.), *The World War I Reader* (New York and London: New York University Press, 2007)

Nietzsche, Friedrich, *The Gay Science* (London: Vintage, 1974)

Noakes, Lucy, *Women in the British Army: War and the Gentle Sex, 1907–1948* (London and New York: Routledge, 2006)

Ouditt, Sharon, *Fighting Forces, Writing Women* (London: Routledge, 1994)

Petrovic, Ilija, 'Foreign Medical Help in Serbian Liberation Wars from 1912 until 1918', *Archive of Oncology* 18:4 (December 2010), 143–8, www.onk.ns.ac.rs/Archive (accessed 9th November 2015)

Potter, Jane, *Boys in Khaki, Girls in Print: Women's Literary Responses to the Great War 1914–1918* (Oxford: Clarendon Press, 2005)

Pratt, Mary Louise, *Imperial Eyes: Travel Writing and Transculture* (London and New York: Routledge, 1992)

Purvis, June, *Emmeline Pankhurst: A Biography* (London: Routledge, 2002)

Rivkin, Julie and Michael Ryan (eds), *Literary Theory: An Anthology* (Oxford: Blackwell, 2004)

Robinson, Jane, *Wayward Women: A Guide to Women Travellers* (Oxford: Oxford University Press, 1990)

Robinson, Jane (ed.), *Unsuitable for Ladies: An Anthology of Women Travellers* (Oxford and New York: Oxford University Press, 1994)

Said, Edward W., *Orientalism* (London: Penguin Books, 2003)

Salih, Sara (ed.), with Judith Butler, *The Judith Butler Reader* (Oxford: Blackwell, 2005)

Scheipers, Sibylle (ed.), *Prisoners in War* (Oxford: Oxford University Press, 2010)

Schweizer, Bernard, 'Rebecca West and the Meaning of Exile', *Journal of Literature and the History of Ideas* 8:2 (June 2010), 1–8

Service, Robert, *A History of Modern Russia: From Tsarism to the Twenty-First Century* (Cambridge, MA: Harvard University Press, 2009)

Sharpe, Ingrid and Matthew Stibbe (eds), *Aftermaths of War: Women's Movements and Female Activists, 1918–1923* (Leiden: Brill, 2011)

Siegel, Kristi (ed.), *Gender, Genre and Identity in Women's Travel Writing* (Oxford and New York: Peter Lang, 2004)

Smith, Angela K., *The Second Battlefield: Women, Modernism and the First World War* (Manchester: Manchester University Press, 2000)

Smith, Angela K. (ed.), *Women's Writing of the First World War: An Anthology* (Manchester: Manchester University Press, 2000)

Smith, Angela K., *Suffrage Discourse in Britain during the First World War* (Aldershot: Ashgate, 2005)

Smith, Angela K., 'The Mists Which Shroud these Questions: Mabel St Clair Stobart, the First World War and Faith', *Literature and History*, 3rd series, 20:2 (Autumn 2011), 1–15

Stanley, Liz, *The Autobiographical I: The Theory and Practice of Feminist Auto/Biography* (Manchester: Manchester University Press, 1992)

Strachen, Huw, *The First World War* (London: Simon & Schuster, 2006)

Summers, Anne, *Angels and Citizens: British Women as Military Nurses 1854–1914* (London and New York: Routledge & Kegan Paul, 1988)

Thompson, Carl, *Travel Writing* (London and New York: Routledge, 2011)

Todorova, Maria, *Imagining the Balkans* (Oxford: Oxford University Press, 2009)

Tusan, Michelle, 'The Business of Relief Work: A Victorian Quaker in Constantinople and Her Circle', *Victorian Studies* 51:4 (Summer 2009), 633–61

War 1914: Punishing the Serbs (London: The Stationery Office, 1999)

Wheelwright, Julie, *Amazons and Military Maids* (London: Pandora, 1989)

Wolff, Larry, *Inventing Eastern Europe: The Map of Civilization on the Mind of the Enlightenment* (Stanford, CA: Stanford University Press, 1994)

Woolf, Virginia, *Orlando* (London: Hogarth Press, 1928)

Woolf, Virginia, 'Women and Fiction', in *Collected Essays*, vol. 2 (London: Hogarth Press, 1966), pp. 141–8

Index